Alternative Ideas from 10 (Almost) Forgotten Economists

"*Alternative Ideas from 10 (Almost) Forgotten Economists* brings alive for our time the most fundamental insights that economics has to offer, enabling readers to both better understand the world and empowering them to change it for the better. Irene van Staveren's writing is a rare combination: clear, accessible, scholarly, passionate, and entertaining all at once."
—Robert Pollin, *Distinguished University Professor of Economics and Co-Director, Political Economy Research Institute (PERI), University of Massachusetts-Amherst*

"Irene's book '*Alternative Ideas from 10 (Almost) Forgotten Economists*' makes it very clear that there is a rich diversity of ideas and theories.
 A book you would want to read if you have limited time but want to know what is going on in the world of new, non-standard economic visions.
 Written with passion, it inspires to read more about economists that you might have heard about for the very first time."
—Peter Blom, *CEO of Triodos Bank Group and co-founder and co-chair of the Sustainable Finance Lab*

Irene van Staveren

Alternative Ideas from 10 (Almost) Forgotten Economists

Irene van Staveren
Erasmus University Rotterdam
The Hague, The Netherlands

ISBN 978-3-030-57608-0   ISBN 978-3-030-57609-7 (eBook)
https://doi.org/10.1007/978-3-030-57609-7

© The Editor(s) (if applicable) and The Author(s), under exclusive licence to Springer Nature Switzerland AG 2015, 2021
This work is subject to copyright. All rights are solely and exclusively licensed by the Publisher, whether the whole or part of the material is concerned, specifically the rights of translation, reprinting, reuse of illustrations, recitation, broadcasting, reproduction on microfilms or in any other physical way, and transmission or information storage and retrieval, electronic adaptation, computer software, or by similar or dissimilar methodology now known or hereafter developed.
The use of general descriptive names, registered names, trademarks, service marks, etc. in this publication does not imply, even in the absence of a specific statement, that such names are exempt from the relevant protective laws and regulations and therefore free for general use.
The publisher, the authors and the editors are safe to assume that the advice and information in this book are believed to be true and accurate at the date of publication. Neither the publisher nor the authors or the editors give a warranty, expressed or implied, with respect to the material contained herein or for any errors or omissions that may have been made. The publisher remains neutral with regard to jurisdictional claims in published maps and institutional affiliations.

This Palgrave Macmillan imprint is published by the registered company Springer Nature Switzerland AG.
The registered company address is: Gewerbestrasse 11, 6330 Cham, Switzerland

Contents

Introduction		1
Chapter 1:	Karl Marx on Capitalism	9
Chapter 2:	Hyman Minsky on Financial Crises	31
Chapter 3:	John Maynard Keynes on Debt and Demand	49
Chapter 4:	Frank Knight on Risk and Uncertainty	65
Chapter 5:	Barbara Bergmann on Gender Biases	79
Chapter 6:	Thorstein Veblen on Inequality	97
Chapter 7:	Amartya Sen on Financial Capabilities	117
Chapter 8:	Gunnar Myrdal on Social Vulnerability	137
Chapter 9:	Adam Smith on the Abuse of Markets	157
Chapter 10:	Joan Robinson on Economic Pluralism	177
Conclusion: Economics for a Postcapitalist Economy		197
Index		205

About the Author

Irene van Staveren is Professor of Pluralist Development Economics at the International Institute of Social Studies of Erasmus University Rotterdam. She is the author of various books, including a textbook: Irene van Staveren, *An Introduction to Economics from a Pluralist and Global Perspective* (2015). This book has been transformed into a mooc (massive open online course) on Coursera under the title Introduction to Economic Theories. Van Staveren is a member of the Dutch think tank Sustainable Finance Lab and advisory board member of Rethinking Economics NL. She is a columnist for *Trouw*, a Dutch daily newspaper, on economics and social and ecological sustainability. She has been awarded the Gunnar Myrdal Prize for her book *The Values of Economics—An Aristotelian Perspective* (2001). She is also the 2014 receiver of the Thomas Divine Lifetime Achievement Award by the Association of Social Economics.

LIST OF FIGURES

Chapter 1: Karl Marx on Capitalism

Fig. 1 The Dow Jones index of the New York Stock Exchange, February 2008–June 2020. (Source: https://www.macrotrends.net/1319/dow-jones-100-year-historical-chart, accessed on June 18, 2020)   13

Fig. 2 Market exchange versus capitalist accumulation. (Note: c = commodity; m = money. Source: author)   17

Chapter 2: Hyman Minsky on Financial Crises

Fig. 1 Fed official interest rate (%) 1955–2019. (Source: author, based on data from the Federal Reserve Bank, https://www.federalreserve.gov/datadownload/Download.aspx?rel=H15&series=c7ca9f58d350a500bb83e230e208cf9b&lastObs=100&from=&to=&filetype=spreadsheetml&label=include&layout=seriescolumn, accessed on June 18, 2020)   32

Fig. 2 Exchange through financialization. (Note: m = money. Source: author)   36

Fig. 3 The financial and economic cycles in the US 1970–2011. (Source: author, based on Matthias Drehmann, Claudio Borio and Kostas Tsatsaronis, 'Characterizing the Financial Cycle: don't lose the sight of the medium term!,' BIS Working Papers, no. 380 (Basel: Bank for International Settlements, 2012))   39

Fig. 4 Development of home prices, costs and population in the US 1890–2018. (Note: Left axis: index numbers for real building price index and real home price index; long term interest rate. Right axis: millions for US population. Source: author's calculations based on data provided by Robert Schiller, http://www.econ.yale.edu/~shiller/data.htm, accessed on June 18, 2020)   42

Chapter 3: John Maynard Keynes on Debt and Demand

Fig. 1 Development of S&P-500 NYSE stock prices and earnings 1871–2015. (Source: author's calculations based on data provided by Robert Schiller, http://www.econ.yale.edu/~shiller/data.htm Accessed on June 18, 2020. Note: Left axis: real price. Right axis: real earnings) 50

Fig. 2 Private debt as percentage of GDP, 2017. (Source: Calculated by author based on IMF, "New Data on Debt", 2 January 2019, https://blogs-imf-org.eur.idm.oclc.org/2019/01/02/new-data-on-global-debt/ Accessed on June 19, 2020) 52

Fig. 3 Average house prices in the UK and London 2005–2019. (Source: Calculated by author based on data from UK House Price Index, Office for National Statistics, https://www.ons.gov.uk/economy/inflationandpriceindices/bulletins/housepriceindex/september2019 Accessed on June 19, 2020) 53

Chapter 4: Frank Knight on Risk and Uncertainty

Fig. 1 The random walk of asset prices according to the EMH-theory. (Source: Author) 68

Fig. 2 The random walk of asset prices in EMH-theory with an exogenous shock. (Source: Author) 70

Fig. 3 Fat tail distribution with high risk of extreme values. (Source: Author) 71

Chapter 5: Barbara Bergmann on Gender Biases

Fig. 1 Bergmann's crowding theory of wage inequality. (Source: Author) 87

Chapter 6: Thorstein Veblen on Inequality

Fig. 1 Decline of the global labour share of income (% of GDP), 1980–2019. (Source: United Nations Global Policy Model and World Economy Database. Graph made by Jeronim Capaldo (UNCTAD)) 98

Fig. 2 Income inequality and globalization in developing countries, 1992–2012. (Source: Rolph van de Hoeven, 'Income inequality in developing countries, past and present', M. Nassanke and J. Ocampo (eds.) *The Palgrave Handbook of Development Economics*. Cham: Palgrave Macmillan, 2019: 335–376. Data based on SWIID and Globalization Index) 99

Fig. 3 Change (%) in US household income (1979–2012). (Source: Author, based on Andrew Sayer, *Why We Can't Afford the Rich* (Bristol: Policy Press, 2015)) 100

Fig. 4 The relationship between equality and growth. (Source: Author) 107

Chapter 8: Gunnar Myrdal on Social Vulnerability

Fig. 1 Cumulative causation. (Source: author) 143

Chapter 9: Adam Smith on the Abuse of Markets

Fig. 1 CO_2 concentration 1990–2020 (parts per million). Note: CO_2 concentration is subject to seasonal variation, which explains the pattern along the trendline. (Source: author, based on publicly available data from NOAA: www.esrl.noaa.gov/gmd/ccgg/trends/, Accessed on 22 July 2020)   158

Fig. 2   Price per ton CO_2 in the ETS since the financial crisis (euro). (Source: Author, based on data from EMBER: https://ember-climate.org/carbon-price-viewer/, Accessed 29 June 2020)   161

Chapter 10: Joan Robinson on Economic Pluralism

Fig. 1   Debate in the top-five economic journals 1920–2013. Note: The graph shows the number of articles in the big five economic journals that contain 'comment', 'reply' or 'rejoinder' in a title as percentage of all articles published in that year. The big five at the *American Economic Review*, *Econometrica*, the *Journal of Economic Literature*, the *Journal of Political Economy*, and the *Quarterly Journal of Economics*. (Source: Joe Francis, 'The Rise and Fall of Debate in Economics,' 2014. https://www.joefrancis.info/economics-debate/, Accessed on June 8, 2020)   182

LIST OF TABLES

Chapter 5: Barbara Bergmann on Gender Biases

| Table 1 | Top 16 competencies, which top leaders exemplify most | 85 |

Chapter 6: Thorstein Veblen on Inequality

| Table 1 | Tax relief policy in the US, 2011 | 101 |

Chapter 7: Amartya Sen on Financial Capabilities

| Table 1 | Banker's moral compass | 121 |
| Table 2 | Bankers' space to use their moral compass | 121 |

Introduction

The 2008 financial crisis offered an opportunity to change economics—critical economists like myself were optimistic about this. In June 2009, The British newsmagazine *The Economist* welcomed a long-awaited revision of economics programmes in colleges and universities, with a cover showing a melting textbook. But hardly anything changed in economics departments over the past decade. For about 40 years, it has been dominated by the neoclassical paradigm assuming self-interested and utility-maximizing agents expressing their exogenous and purely subjective preferences through demand and supply in free markets, constrained only by their resources.[1] A revealing overview article of the discipline argues that it is far more inward-looking, homogeneous and obsessed with rankings than any other social sciences discipline.[2] This has its impact on the real-world economy through its policy advice favouring market-based solutions and its general distrust of government.[3] Hence, the dominant economic paradigm goes beyond theory and method. It includes a worldview, institutional framework, and set of policies—often referred to as neoliberalism or market fundamentalism. A telling example is how up to 2008 financial models used by individual traders helped to collectively shape financial markets towards the image of an average low-risk scene in which high tail-risk, systemic risk and rising uncertainty were made invisible and unimaginable.[4]

Today, with a financial sector that has remained large and vulnerable, an economy generating rising inequality and rapid climate change, and which has shown to be very vulnerable to a pandemic, the world deserves even more urgently economic change as well as a change in economics that would help such a change materialize. But whereas most economists continue doing their highly specialized modelling and have adopted context-free randomized controlled trials as the golden standard for policy research, some even defend the current economic system—capitalism—as the best imaginable. They do so by arguing that the alternative is either North Korean style communism or anarchy.[5] But they forget that these two are more political systems than economic ones. The deeper problem is that they confuse capitalism with markets. Capitalism is only three centuries old. Markets are around much longer and have existed for centuries without capitalism. There are feasible alternatives for capitalism, but they all involve a role for markets. In the first half of the previous century, economic anthropologist Karl Polanyi compared various economic systems and discovered that they all consist of three domains of economic interaction: markets, a state (in whatever form, from nation state to tribal hierarchy), and the self-regulated community economy of mutual care, cooperation and commons.[6]

The challenge is to change but not to abolish markets—that would be foolish. Try to think of it. No labour market but some central planning agency that tells you which job to take or working for your own account but not being able to sell your goods or services to anyone. No product markets—but how can you consume the basic necessities if you do not have the resources and skills to grow and manufacture them by yourself, or with your local community without any form of exchange to get resources from outside your community? And, indeed, no international trade at all. And no form of financial markets for savings, credit and investment. Not even a highly regulated one or one run entirely by state banks allocating demand and supply of finance between households and firms. And try to imagine a state without any tax income. It would only function by brute force, demanding forced labour instead of taxes and going back to feudalism. An economy consisting of only a state and a community economy will function at a very low level of wellbeing—no resources for decent health care, public schools or scientific research, for example. Moreover, an economy without trade will punish those living in countries with limited natural resources and favour those who are lucky enough to be close to abundant fresh water, fertile soil and minerals. It may sound romantic, a world without markets, but to me it seems a nightmare in which the lucky and the powerful are likely to get what they want, either through the state run by elites due to a lack of a tax base, or by ignoring the state, which sounds equally undesirable. It will be a nasty world, just like a world without a state, as Thomas Hobbes argued almost four centuries ago. Just as nasty as a world without communities with their unpaid work in families, mutual caring and voluntary work in and between households, and their collective action around community resources. The challenge for a better economy is to abolish *capitalist* markets and to craft a new balance between the state, the market and a thriving community economy—indeed, a postcapitalist economy.

Fortunately, there are some economists who believe that this is possible. The best known perhaps is Kate Raworth, who imagines an economy that operates within the boundaries of social inclusion and environmental sustainability in her book *Donut Economics*.[7] The book has drawn much criticism from some economists, while other economists have simply ignored it. But outside economics, *Donut Economics* has attracted wide interest, from students, policy makers and business leaders alike. And rightly so, because its message is important and hopeful, although not new. The metaphor is wonderful and helps to get the message across that scholars critical of the dominant paradigm have advocated for decades. From the Club of Rome's *Limits to Growth* published in 1972 to the UN's *Human Development Report 2013* called *Humanity Divided*, Thomas Piketty's *Capital in the 21st Century* of 2014 and Tim Jackson's *Prosperity Without Growth* of 2017.[8] The donut metaphor entails a normative message about the upper and lower boundaries of a new economy for all. The donut provides an appealing normative framework for an alternative economy, like other recent publications have done focussing on a decent society or an inclusive society.[9] Such normative views give an economy a purpose and that is much-needed to reorient the world economy as well as our local economies towards the boundaries of the Paris Climate Agreement on the one hand and to make it respond to global poverty, inequality and social exclusion, as referred to in the Sustainable Development Goals, on the other hand. I am in favour of a donut economy, a decent economy and an inclusive society. But we can only achieve it when we also develop the economics for it. A normative framework on its own won't get us there.

Many others have advocated economic change as well as a transformation of economics. Indeed, the same economists who call for an alternative economy tend to be the ones criticizing neoclassical economics. But we need to go beyond criticism and normative frameworks. We need to imagine how a better economy can be brought about with an economic science that addresses the key issues. We need concepts, theories, models, indicators and methods that broaden our understanding of markets, economic behaviour and economic institutions. Just like the dominant economic paradigm shapes our current capitalist economy, we urgently need different economic thinking to contribute to the emergence of a postcapitalist economy, even if this will be tentative and open-ended. But there is an enormous lack of imagination among economists. My colleagues all around the world seem to be paralysed by the mistaken view of TINAC: There Is No Alternative for Capitalism. Or, and that is particularly the case for the younger economists and students, they simply have no clue how other economic theories, methods and policies look like or that they even exist. Because over the past four decades they have only been taught the tools of the mainstream filled with utility maximization equations and market equilibrium ideals coupled with mathematical models which are supposed to follow the format of propositions and theorems that need to be proven not in the real economy but in theory only.[10] No wonder that a global student movement has emerged after the financial crisis calling for pluralism in economic curricula.[11] And no wonder that several critical economists have set up networks in which they share their real-world-based studies of economic change.[12]

But we do not need to reinvent the wheel—economists of the past have developed, adapted and elaborated various alternative economic theories that often go back a long time. Some of the economists in this book even received a Nobel Memorial Prize for their contributions but are now almost forgotten. They have demonstrated that there are alternative ways of organizing production, finance, consumption, trade and wellbeing. They have studied and contributed to the economics we need for change. My selection of ten economists is based on the usefulness of their ideas for addressing today's challenges in economics to address the wicked problems we face today. Of course, there are others who did not make it to this book but whom I could have chosen. I decided to include ten—one per chapter. This number is large enough to show the variety of economic ideas in the history of economic thought, while it is small enough to do justice to each of them, their ideas, and the practices of their ideas in economic reality. The economists are, in chronological sequence, Adam Smith, Karl Marx, Thorstein Veblen, Frank Knight, John Maynard Keynes, Joan Robinson, Hyman Minsky, Gunnar Myrdal, Amartya Sen, and Barbara Bergmann. Each chapter has the same structure. I will first discuss the problem that is being addressed, introducing a particular problem related to the unsustainability and vulnerability of our current economy since the 2008 financial crisis and its link to current economics. This is followed by the insight provided by the economist and its theoretical basis. Then follows a short description of the economists and their life,[13] while each chapter ends with two examples of how the idea has been translated in practical alternatives that are feasible and, indeed, put into practice today despite of, as well as challenging, the capitalist economy.

I hope that this approach will inspire readers to reflect on alternatives for economic analysis on behalf of an economy that will be ready for the challenges ahead. Above all, I hope that this book sparks your imagination to contribute to an economics that serves an inclusive and climate neutral economy. You could even do this if you are neither an economist, nor planning to become one. There are many ways to contribute to a more relevant and meaningful economics. If you are a policy maker, you can support pluralism in economic education at all levels and commission economic policy advice from different economists rather than only the mainstream view. If you are a politician, you can decide to shift funding for economic research and teaching towards pluralist programmes and approaches. If you are a businessperson, you can hire economists with a much broader scope than the mainstream and express your demand for such economists. If you are an activist, you can team up with pluralist economists to work on feasible alternatives based on the ideas of unorthodox economists. If you are an interested citizen, you can challenge the TINAC view that is ubiquitous in newspapers, radio and TV shows, social media and political party programmes. Whatever you do with this book, I sincerely hope that it helps you to be inspired and to inspire others with your own reflections and contributions to the diversity of ideas about a postcapitalist economy.

Finally, my own inspiration for writing this book came from the economists themselves, two of them I was privileged to meet several times, and from the various heterodox economics associations that I am member of. It is thanks to all those courageous, creative and competent economists that I never gave up my research and teaching in pluralist economics and that I even wrote a pluralist introductory textbook.[14] In particular, I want to thank Geoffrey Harcourt for believing in this book, the Rector of my institute, Inge Hutter, for supporting me writing it while I was on partial sick leave, and my husband, Eric Brinkhorst, for reminding me that I should take my time for this book and take as much care of myself as I do of the ideas of the almost forgotten economists.[15]

NOTES

1. Critiques of this paradigm emerged as early as 1899 with Thorstein Veblen's *Theory of the Leisure Class*, criticizing the hedonistic assumption of economic rationality as a lightning calculator of pleasure and pains: Thorstein Veblen, *Theory of the Leisure Class. An Economic Study of Institutions*, edited by B.W. Huebsch (New York: Viking, 1931 [1899]). Since then, numerous nonorthodox economists have followed suit, and the criticisms have multiplied since the 2008 financial crisis. This time with wide support from outside academia, including *The Economist*. But also from students, for example with a manifesto: Joe Earle, Cahal Moran and Zach Ward Perkins, *The Econocracy – the Perils of Leaving Economics to the Experts* (Manchester: Manchester University Press, 2016). Chapter 11 of this book will discuss criticism as well as the state of the debate in economics.
2. Marion Fourcade, Etienne Ollion and Yann Algan, "The Superiority of Economists," *Journal of Economic Perspectives* 29, 1 (2015): 89–114.
3. See, for example, four recent critiques of the dominant economic paradigm's theory and practice: Ha-Joon Chang, *Economics: The User's Guide* (London: Penguin, 2014); Steven Payson, *How Economics Professors Can Stop Failing Us* (Lanham: Lexington, 2017); Mariana Mazzucato, *The Value of Everything, Making and Taking in the Global Economy* (London: Penguin, 2018); David Colander and Craig Freedman, *Where Economics Went Wrong: Chicago's Abandonment of Classical Liberalism* (Princeton: Princeton University Press, 2018).
4. For an insightful reflection on this, see David Colander, Michael Goldberg, Armin Haas, Katarina Juselius, Alan Kurman, Thomas Lux, and Brigitte Sloth. "The Financial Crisis and the Systemic Failure of the Economics Profession," *Critical Review – A Journal of Politics and Society* 21, 2–3 (2009): 249–267.
5. Examples of such apologies for capitalism: Deirdre McCloskey, *Bourgeois Virtues: Ethics for an Age of Commerce* (Chicago: University of Chicago Press, 2006); Giacomo Corneo, *Is Capitalism Obsolete? A Journey through Alternative Economic Systems* (Cambridge (MA): Harvard University Press, 2017); Joseph Stiglitz, *People, Power, and Profits. Progressive Capitalism for an Age of Discontent* (New York: W.W. Norton, 2019).
6. Karl Polanyi, *The Great Transformation* (New York: Farrar & Rinehart, 1944). I was so impressed by this view that I did my PhD research on the topic, tracing the three economic domains back to Adam Smith and Albert Hirschman, who each in their own way confirmed Polanyi's view that a well-functioning economy consists of three value domains: freedom in markets, justice in the state and care in the community economy. Irene van Staveren, *The Values of Economics – an Aristotelian Perspective* (London: Routledge, 2001). A recent analysis of market fundamentalism based on the work of Polanyi can be found here: Fred

Block and Margaret Summers, *The Power of Market Fundamentalism. Karl Polanyi's Critique* (Cambridge (MA): Harvard University Press, 2016).
7. Kate Raworth, *Donut Economics. Seven Ways to Think Like a 21st-Century Economist* (New York: Random House, 2017).
8. Donella Meadows, Dennis Meadows, and Jørgen Randers William W. Behrens III, *The Limits to Growth* (Washington D.C.: Potomac Associates, 1972); UNDP, *Humanity Divided. Confronting Inequality in Developing Countries* (New York: United Nations Development Program, 2013); Thomas Piketty, *Capital in the 21st Century* (Cambridge (MA): Harvard University Press, 2014); Tim Jackson, *Prosperity without Growth – Foundations for the Economy of Tomorrow* (London: Routledge, 2017).
9. Pamela Abbott, Claire Wallace, and Roger Sapsford, *The Decent Society – Planning for Social Quality* (London: Routledge, 2016); IPSP, *Rethinking Society for the 21st Century* (Cambridge: Cambridge University Press, 2018).
10. William Thomson, "The Young Person's Guide to Writing Economic Theory," *Journal of Economic Literature* 37, 1 (1999): 157–183.
11. Rethinking Economics is an international student movement active in 15 countries: http://www.rethinkeconomics.org/. Accessed on July 15, 2020.
12. These networks include Promoting Economic Pluralism: https://economicpluralism.org/. Accessed on July 15, 2020. Economics for Inclusive Prosperity: https://econfip.org/. Accessed on July 15, 2020. Next to these new initiatives, there is a wide variety of long-standing heterodox economics associations, from social economics to feminist economics and from institutional economics to interdisciplinary themes, for example the capability approach and the self-management of commons by communities.
13. The short biographies in each chapter are compiled from various sources, including: Harry Landreth and David Colander, *History of Economic Thought*, 4th edition (Boston: Houghton Mifflin, 2001). Steven Pressman, *Fifty Major Economists*, 3rd edition (London: Routledge, 2013).
14. Irene van Staveren, *Economics after the Crisis – a Global and Pluralist Perspective* (London: Routledge, 2015).
15. This book is a translation and revision of Irene van Staveren, *Wat wij kunnen leren van economen die (bijna) niemand meer leest* (Amsterdam: Boom, 2016).

Bibliography

Abbott, Pamela, Claire Wallace, and Roger Sapsford. *The Decent Society – Planning for Social Quality*. London: Routledge, 2016.
Block, Fred, and Margaret Summers. *The Power of Market Fundamentalism. Karl Polanyi's Critique*. Cambridge (MA): Harvard University Press, 2016.
Chang, Ha-Joon. *Economics: The User's Guide*. London: Penguin, 2014.
Colander, David, and Craig Freedman. *Where Economics Went Wrong: Chicago's Abandonment of Classical Liberalism*. Princeton: Princeton University Press, 2018.
Colander, David, Michael Goldberg, Armin Haas, Katarina Juselius, Alan Kurman, Thomas Lux, and Brigitte Sloth. "The Financial Crisis and the Systemic Failure of the Economics Profession." *Critical Review – A Journal of Politics and Society* 21, 2–3 (2009): 249–267.

Colander, David, and Harry Landreth. *History of Economic Thought*, 4th edition. Boston: Houghton Mifflin, 2001.
Corneo, Giacomo. *Is Capitalism Obsolete? A Journey through Alternative Economic Systems*. Cambridge (MA): Harvard University Press, 2017.
Earle, Joe, Cahal Moran, and Zach Ward Perkins. *The Econocracy – the Perils of Leaving Economics to the Experts*. Manchester: Manchester University Press, 2016.
Fourcade, Marion, Etienne Ollion, and Yann Algan. "The Superiority of Economists." *Journal of Economic Perspectives* 29, 1 (2015): 89–114.
IPSP. *Rethinking Society for the 21st Century*. Cambridge: Cambridge University Press, 2018.
Jackson, Tim. *Prosperity without Growth – Foundations for the Economy of Tomorrow*. London: Routledge, 2017.
Mazzucato, Mariana. *The Value of Everything, Making and Taking in the Global Economy*. London: Penguin, 2018.
McCloskey, Deirdre. *Bourgeois Virtues: Ethics for an Age of Commerce*. Chicago: University of Chicago Press, 2006.
Meadows, Donella, Dennis Meadows, and Jørgen Randers William W. Behrens III. *The Limits to Growth*. Washington D.C.: Potomac Associates, 1972.
Payson, Steven. *How Economics Professors Can Stop Failing Us*. Lanham: Lexington, 2017.
Piketty, Thomas. *Capital in the 21st Century*. Cambridge (MA): Harvard University Press, 2014.
Polanyi, Karl. *The Great Transformation*. New York: Farrar & Rinehart, 1944.
Pressman, Steven. *Fifty Major Economists*, 3rd edition. London: Routledge, 2013.
Raworth, Kate. *Donut Economics. Seven Ways to Think Like a 21st-Century Economist*. New York: Random House, 2017.
Staveren, Irene van. *The Values of Economics – an Aristotelian Perspective*. London: Routledge, 2001.
——— *Economics after the Crisis – a Global and Pluralist Perspective*. London: Routledge, 2015.
——— *Wat wij kunnen leren van economen die (bijna) niemand meer leest*. Amsterdam: Boom, 2016.
Stiglitz, Joseph. *People, Power, and Profits. Progressive Capitalism for an Age of Discontent*. New York: W.W. Norton, 2019.
Thomson, William. "The Young Person's Guide to Writing Economic Theory." *Journal of Economic Literature* 37, 1 (1999): 157–183.
UNDP. *Humanity Divided. Confronting Inequality in Developing Countries*. New York: United Nations Development Program, 2013.
Veblen, Thorstein. *The Theory of the Leisure Class. An Economic Study of Institutions*, edited by B.W. Huebsch. New York: Viking, 1931 [1899].

Chapter 1: Karl Marx on Capitalism

THE PROBLEM

Our current economy is unsustainable in a variety of ways. We face climate change, resource depletion and loss of biodiversity as a consequence of relentless economic growth driven by material consumption. This is paralleled with social exclusion of millions of people in the global south and increasing income inequality in countries in both the global north and the global south. In addition, we regularly suffer from severe financial crises with an ever wider and deeper impact on a global scale. In this chapter, I will focus on the near implosion of capitalism during the 2008 financial crisis.

The fall of Lehman Brothers in September 2008 triggered a deep crisis in the global north, with important side-effects for the global south. Banks collapsed, citizens collected their savings in long lines at money machines, firms could no longer obtain credit, the prices of houses plummeted, economic growth turned into decline and unemployment increased as fast as it did after the oil crises in the 1980s. Stock exchanges went down as well and traders and consumers alike lost trust in the financial sector. The 2008 financial crisis and the long economic recession that it caused were in some ways more serious than the 1929 Wall Street Crash and the ensuing Great Depression, and certainly having a much wider impact beyond the US and Western Europe.

What started as the subprime crisis in the US in 2007 soon led to the euro crisis in Europe in 2009. The sudden end to the bubbles of stock prices, houses and two-digit profit rates of banks revealed the weaknesses of the eurozone. Some economists joked about the PIGS-countries (Portugal, Ireland, Greece and Spain) as if the euro crisis had nothing to do with the northern members of the eurozone. And while the crisis in Greece was prolonged by the Troika demanding inhuman and ineffective austerity measures, the chair of the Troika, Dutch Minister of Finance Jeroen Dijsselbloem, solved the crisis in Cyprus by forcing a haircut on the Russian and European bankers and investors on the island.[1] They had to accept losses, which reduced the burden on tax payers and reinforced the fact that with taking risk, investors have to accept the downside of it as well. But Greece received virtually no debt relief at all.

Tragedy in Greece

For Greece, the policies forced by the European Union (EU) and International Monetary Fund (IMF) were relentless and kept the country much longer in recession than was the case for other countries. Greek GDP declined by 45% between 2008 and 2016, and increased since then but in 2018 it was still 40% below the pre-crisis level.[2] Although the public deficit was relatively high and public debt had accumulated beyond what was allowed by the Maastricht criteria for stability of the euro (government deficit of maximum 3% of GDP and public debt of maximum 60% of GDP), the biggest problem leading up to the crisis in Greece was unsustainable private debt. But the private debt was even higher in the northern eurozone, in particular by banks. Banks' total debt was highest in Ireland and the Netherlands, over ten times GDP, but less than three times on average in Greece, Spain, Portugal and Italy.[3]

It is precisely this high indebtedness of northern European banks, which explains the harsh austerity demands by the Troika on Greece, because part of the assets of these banks were invested in Greek government bonds and shares of Greek banks. An interesting independent overview study from the European School of Management and Technology describes the rescue operation and shows that it was not the Greek government nor the Greek population but the commercial banks in the northern eurozone countries that were in fact saved by the first two emergency loans provided to the Greek government.[4] Ninety-five per cent of the 216 billion US dollar rescue loans disbursed between 2010 and 2015 were used to pay off debt and interest to IMF and the EU, which helped northern Eurozone banks to get rid of their Greek assets without having to take the downside risk of these investments. The study shows 'that less than 5% of the overall funds went to the Greek fiscal budget, with the overwhelming rest going to existing creditors in the form of debt repayments and interest payments'.[5] In the meantime, the Greek taxpayers have been paying back the loans for already a decade now, and are still suffering from the worst decline in income in the eurozone.[6] On top of this, the economy hardly recovers, as is signalled by an unemployment rate of 19%—the highest rate in the EU.[7] Moreover, it was among the hardest hit economies during the lockdown as a consequence of the COVID-19 pandemic due to a large dependence on tourism.

Under Water in the Netherlands

Although the social consequences of the crisis were hardest in Greece, followed by other southern countries of the eurozone, the Netherlands was hit particularly fiercely because of the size of the banking rescue operation. Two of the four large Dutch banks were nationalized (ABN AMRO and SNS Reaal), while ING and insurance companies received massive state support. In total the state provided support of around 45 billion euro over the period 2008–2013, which was 7% of average GNP over that period.[8] This has led, in turn, to high public debt and enormous cutbacks on public spending, in particular in education and health care. And the emergency support during the COVID-19 crisis is even higher.

The housing market was more heavily affected than elsewhere in Europe, due to very generous Dutch mortgage policies. These included a loan-to-value ratio (ltv) of 110% and a generous fiscal benefit for mortgage interest paid, which homeowners were allowed to deduct fully from their income tax statement. As a consequence, the Dutch housing market experiences stronger cycles than elsewhere, with a decline of 20% in house values up to 2013, compared to the euro-area average of 5%.[9] This was followed by a steep rise in prices and a significant increase of large private investors housing market, driving up rental prices too. In 2018, prices of houses sold increased 13% as compared to the previous year.[10] Hence, today, both buying and renting are very expensive in the Netherlands.

Moreover, 85% of Dutch houses are under mortgage debt. At the depth of the housing crisis, 1.5 million households had higher debts than the market value of their homes—resulting in underwater mortgages, as the Dutch say referring with some irony to our permanent struggle with the sea level. The disbalance between mortgage debt and house values caused a standstill to the market for residential real estate for five years.[11] Unemployment rose to 7.4% in 2014 and only reached the same level as before the crisis in 2019, with 3.3%.[12]

The Crisis: A Surprise?

Back to the origin of the crisis in the US. It started as a subprime crisis and quickly spread across the whole economy in the US and the EU and resulted in a global recession. What is striking about this crisis, as compared to crises over the past few decades, such as the debt crisis of the 1980s in Latin America and the Asian financial crisis at the end of the 1990s, is that it struck at the heart of capitalism. Many academic economists and economic policy makers simply said that nobody could see it coming. The general public, parliamentarians, people who lost their jobs, and students in every field of the social sciences were shocked and outraged by this excuse. Capitalism almost imploded, and there was not a single economist who had predicted it, noticed any signs, or had given a warning?

Her Majesty Queen Elizabeth asked, at a visit to the London School of Economics, why economists had not given any warning. The response was defensive, the standard textbook explanation of any crisis, namely an external shock to the economic system. In other words, the explanation of the crisis was that it was not caused within the economy but from outside. A matter of bad luck, very bad luck. This was the explanation provided by all well-known and influential economists. For example, an American professor of financial economics, Frederic Mishkin, had been very well paid for his advisory report to the government of Iceland in 2006, in which he claimed that the country had a strong economy—less than two years before its collapse.[13] Another financial economist, Nobel Memorial Prize winner Eugene Fama, continues to defend the external shock theory of the financial crisis. In his view, the economic system itself is always tending towards equilibrium, just as his financial models do. What is interesting is that he shared the prize with two other economists (Robert Shiller and Lars Peter Hansen) who do not believe in his financial market equilibrium theory. The fact that Fama was awarded the prize is perhaps more telling about the Swedish Central Bank, which awards and funds the Nobel Memorial Prize in economics, than about the value of Fama's theory. The family of Alfred Nobel has even distanced itself from the Nobel Memorial Prize and only supports the original Nobel Prizes, awarded by the Swedish Academy of Sciences.

Instead of being reassuring, the answer of the top economists that the crisis was just a matter of bad luck, their response resulted in bewilderment. If this could happen just like that, it could happen again, isn't it? And, again, without any warning. Why would we have well-paid and influential economists if they ignore the colossal elephant in the middle of financial markets? And if they did perhaps sense something, why haven't they asked themselves who was feeding the animal and with what?

Crises Are Part and Parcel of Capitalism

A few economists, even some bankers and financial sector supervisors, did feel or smell the elephant in the room. They figured out that the beast was fed with toxic derivatives by banks, traders and brokers, resulting in an enormous pile of dung consisting of debt. They did worry and did sound alarm bells. But nobody listened. The whistleblowers in the financial sector were ignored, taunted or sidelined. The same was true for the group of academic economists who did not believe in the equilibrium dogma of neoclassical economic theory and who were united in various heterodox economics associations in which they discussed the risk of increasing debt for the stability of the financial system. But their warnings were ignored too—both by the overwhelming majority of academic economists and by the authorities responsible for the supervision of the financial sector. In 2010, one of the heterodox associations, the World Economics Association, awarded a prize to the economist who had predicted the crisis most accurately. The winner was the Australian economist Steve Keen, with his regular warnings of a bursting bubble on the US housing market. Since then, he has been a celebrated speaker all around the world, explaining his debt model of financial instability based on the work of Hyman Minsky—whom we will meet in the next chapter.

The Dutch thinktank the Sustainable Finance Lab, of which I am a member, had invited Steve Keen to a give a seminar at the University of Amsterdam for an audience of senior finance specialists. Two years after the nationalization of ABN AMRO, the audience was still confounded by what had happened and what was unfolding in the euro crisis. Many of them were open to a different economic explanation. I had met Keen before and wanted to hear more about the predictive power of his model. At that time, I was secretly pleased by the thought that, as a PhD student back in 1997, I had put my name under a petition against the introduction of the euro under the weak conditions that it was, indeed, introduced five years later.[14] A small group of heterodox economists had predicted the problems. We just didn't know when a euro crisis would strike. Foreseeing a crisis is one thing, predicting the timing is quite another. Steve Keen appeared to be very close.

Financial crises do not arise from external shocks. They are part and parcel of capitalism. This insight was first expressed by Karl Marx, followed by John Maynard Keynes and Hyman Minsky. Financial crises are an inherent part of the dynamics of capitalist economies. The economic cycle of boom and bust is not just a side effect of capitalism but is its key dynamic force. Cycles are generally measured by the movements of GDP, while the stock exchange provides a good early signal of this movement, next to price movements in various asset markets. Figure 1 shows the development of the Dow Jones stock index over the past 13 years (end of month values)—from the top before the financial crisis (October 2007) to the COVID-19 lockdown in the first half of 2020. It shows how deep the crisis was in 2008 but also how steep the rise of the index has been since then.

Fig. 1 The Dow Jones index of the New York Stock Exchange, February 2008–June 2020. (Source: https://www.macrotrends.net/1319/dow-jones-100-year-historical-chart, accessed on June 18, 2020)

The figure also shows small changes along the trend line—these are random and caused by various small differences in supply and demand. But what matters for understanding crises are the ups and downs in the trend.

After the crisis hit, it took firms six years to get back to the market value of October 2007. But not only firms and their shareholders suffered. Many workers lost their jobs, their pension investments and their homes. While the retired suffered from a reduction in their pension income and those dependent on welfare payments suffered income losses due to the austerity policies that followed the bailout of banks. In a capitalist economy, a stock market crash hits everyone—directly or indirectly.

Since the recovery in 2013, the Dow Jones has gained 10,000 points, the same number as was lost in the crisis. And the trend is still up, apart from a short but steep decline due to the COVID-19 lockdown. This upward trend of share values is worrysome, because GDP is not increasing so fast, and neither are real incomes of workers. In fact, the trend on stock exchanges worldwide signals that, again, a bubble is building up. Marx has offered a sharp analysis of the underlying mechanisms of such capital accumulation. He provides us with the insight of this chapter. The two other economists that I mentioned focus on crisis recovery (Keynes) and financial markets as the origin of the bubbles (Minsky) and their work will be discussed in the subsequent chapters.

THE INSIGHT

Just like the financial crisis of 1929, which resulted in the Great Depression, and the financial crises of the 1870s followed by the Long Depression, the 2008 financial crisis marked the end of an asset bubble generated by the driving forces of capitalism itself—not from an outside shock from politics, war or an epidemic. This may sound as a communist critique of capitalism, going back to Karl Marx' and Friedrich Engels' pamphlet *The Communist Manifesto*.[15] However, the critique was well argued and spelled out at length by Marx in his book *Das Kapital*, which appeared 20 years later, as his reaction to the failed labour revolutions around the mid-nineteenth century.[16] He wrote *Capital* in order to understand capitalism and to see how it may be changed from the inside rather than through revolution. Hence, the book became the first thorough analysis of the workings of capitalism and is appreciated by many economists, heterodox and orthodox, as a lucid critique of capitalism. Right after the 2008 crisis hit, many economists from left to right who had ever taken the effort to read the 1000 page long book (or, I suspect, a summary of it) admitted that Marx' sharp analysis of the weaknesses of capitalism, in particular through its cycles of boom and bust, is still valid today.

Marx developed an understanding of the cycles of capital accumulation and destruction, paralleled with rising employment and wages during a boom and rising unemployment and declining wages after the bust. He himself came from an entrepreneurial family, which had converted from Jewish to Protestant when in Germany, after a brief period of liberalism, Jews were again restricted in their choice of professions. Due to his middle-class background, Marx was able to see the driving forces of capitalism from the inside, but also how these forces led to instability and inequality. He criticized the exploitation of workers in dirty, loud and dangerous factories. He labelled this industrial employment alienation: workers had become mere extensions of machines. The capitalist class not only benefitted in terms of accumulating profits, but also repressed any form of autonomy of workers and benefitted from the large labour potential arising from landless farmers. From the end of the eighteenth century onwards, mechanization of agriculture, enclosure of the commons, and population growth in cities had resulted in a fast growing labour supply of the proletariat—of men, women and children. Marx noted sharply that industrialization exploited this abundant supply of workers, hiring them at very low wages under gloomy working conditions.

He observed a dramatic increase in inequality between the two classes and in *Capital* he provided the data to support his analysis. He showed detailed figures of wages, costs of living, and mothers and children dying from preventable diseases in cities in England, but also referring to data from elsewhere in Europe. He predicted that the rising inequality was sowing the seeds of capitalism's demise, because, he argued, inequalities cannot grow forever and profits cannot accumulate uninterruptedly. His great insight was that only economic crises were able to make a temporary end to the accumulation process—ruthless and without sparing either workers or capitalists. This insight was confirmed again in 2008. Since the mid-1980s, income inequality had risen worldwide, with capital income growing much faster than labour income. Also, the power of financial markets, where most of the capital had accumulated, had increased correspondingly. This dimension of the 2008 financial crisis was also predicted by Marx. It was Marx who used the term *haute finance* in *Capital* and used it to refer to the aristocracy aligning with bankers in what he labelled as *bankocracy*.[17] The fall of Lehman Brothers illustrated that, again, the growth of profits, capital and income inequality could not continue forever and was halted—temporarily—by a financial crisis.

The State as Saviour of Capitalism

The implosion of capitalism was prevented by a concerted action of governments who bailed out banks and insurance companies with emergency loans and nationalization. Capitalism did not fail because Marx was wrong. Ironically, it was the state which prevented that capitalism collapsed. That was something Marx would never have imagined. The alliance between the aristocracy and bankers in his days had evolved to include the state as well 150 years later.

In 2009, when bankruptcies had been prevented by nationalizations, and billions of financial support had been extended to large private financial institutions, nobody talked about Marx anymore. Capitalism was saved by the state so that communism—with full nationalization of all private businesses and personal property was again precluded as a feasible option. As before the crisis,

Marx became identified again with USSR-type communism and the authoritarian societies of North Korea, Cuba and China. This association, however, is misleading. Marxism emerged from the *Communist Manifesto* that Marx published together with Friedrich Engels in the revolution year 1848, hoping for a peaceful social revolution. When the revolution was violently suppressed by states all over Europe, Marx decided to analyse capitalism, which led to the publication of *Capital* 20 years later. By then, he had distanced himself from parts of the socialist movement in France. Whereas they called themselves Marxists, he wrote in a letter to his son-in-law, Paul Lafargue, that if there is anything certain, it was that he himself was not a Marxist.[18] Marx remains the first critic of capitalism and not the naïve ideologist of communism, even though communist regimes have claimed not only Marxism but also Marx himself to be their source of inspiration. When he was still a journalist in 1842, he famously claimed in an article in the Rhein Newspaper that when the goal turns the means holy, the goal is unholy.[19] And, also in his journalist days, he was a strong supporter of press freedom. He would never have supported the brute state force and censorship of the communist systems that were erected in his name.

At the same time, Marx was aware that the capitalist class had the political influence to secure its interests, with a combination of ideology and power, which would allow a revival of capital accumulation after each crisis of capitalism. And here, Marx again appeared to be right in 2008. After the banks had been saved and the economy started to grow again a few years later, it was business as usual, from labour markets to financial markets and from consumer markets to exports. Capitalism was back on its throne and had not made room for alternative forms of markets, apart from some non-capitalist innovations such as crowdfunding and bottom-up peer-to-peer platforms. But in 2008 there was no alternative in the face of bankruns and a systemic crisis affecting the whole economy. Not saving the temples of capitalism was simply not an option because banks had grown too big to fail and too much entangled through their mutual short-term funding with toxic financial assets. And the banks knew this very well. The crucial role of competitive markets in a capitalist system to weed out unprofitable firms and to encourage innovative businesses was stopped short by the bailouts. Nevertheless, many economists and policy makers believed that markets would take back their role soon and that with proper state supervision—such as stricter bank regulation—capitalism would be tamed. But Marx knew better. And so should we if we would take his analysis in *Capital* more seriously.

The First Capitalist Principle

Whereas Marxism is often credited with the principle of rejecting private property, in *Capital* Marx analysed the driving forces of capitalism as a system in which capital hires labour and not the other way around. The purpose as well as the means of this system is capital accumulation. Let me discuss the accumulation principle first as it forms the primary motive of capitalism, according to Karl Marx.

Accumulation of capital arose already before the Industrial Revolution, when markets expanded beyond consumer goods and labour power to asset markets for land, real estate, machines, factories, bonds and shares. But accumulation gained pace with the Industrial Revolution, when commodification increased rapidly. Accumulation marks the transformation of market exchange from goods to goods, in which money performs the role of means of exchange, to exchange from money to money, in which goods perform the role of means for this exchange. This is illustrated in Fig. 2, which depicts two sequences of exchange. Sequence A describes general market exchange whereas sequence B portrays capitalist market exchange. In the chains of exchange, C stands for commodity and M for money. After every exchange a prime is added to mark a new good (C′, C″, etc.) or capital accumulated through profits (M′, M″, etc.). Sequence A starts with a good that a producer does not need for own consumption, C. Think of apples from an orchard. These are sold in exchange for money, M. This money is used by the owner of the orchard to purchase a good that she does not produce herself, C′, for example bread. Then the baker receives money, M′ and buys meat from the butcher, C″ a week later. In short, sequence A describes markets in which money has the role of means of exchange and store of value, which became increasingly important only after the middle ages.

Sequence B looks similar but is fundamentally different. It starts with money, M, in the form of capital. This may be inherited, accumulated as rents or profits, acquired through a loan, or from selling shares. This money enters the exchange as an investment in the production, or simply trading, of good C. However, good C is not what the capitalist is interested in. The purpose is to trade C for more money in order to increase M to M′ with a profit. This may be done as an entrepreneur buying raw material and labour power, which are transformed into a product for which the market value is more that the amount invested. After that exchange, M′ is invested in another round of C′, resulting in another profitable trade, the result of which is M″. In short, sequence B portrays capital accumulation. Every time, more capital can be invested in more profitable activities, so that the stock of M grows. But sequence A shows that the same cannot happen with C, because commodities are unique units that do not accumulate in transactions, unless they are a form of money or investment goods, such as gold or real estate. Moreover, sequence B allows for increased risk-taking as well as diversification, chasing more profitable activities with part

Fig. 2 Market exchange versus capitalist accumulation. (Note: c = commodity; m = money. Source: author)

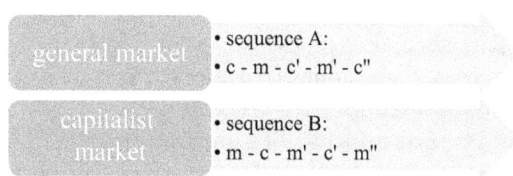

of the capital performing the role of buffer. That is the basis of capitalist entrepreneurship: transforming capital in more capital through any profitable activity. Its most developed form is the limited liability company, with publicly traded shares on a stock exchange. This form of capital acquisition was first used by the Dutch East India Company (VOC) in 1602, which led to the Amsterdam Stock Exchange as the world's first stock market. It was precisely for this reason that Marx wrote: 'Holland was the head capitalistic nation of the seventeenth century.'[20]

Accumulation not only furthers the growth of a firm, but it also enables economic power through acquiring competitor firms, which increases the ability of accumulation through market power. This has happened widely in the banking sector in the decades before the financial crisis, while afterwards this process of consolidation continued, leading to a few megabanks dominating the market, particularly in Europe. Marx already foresaw that this feature of accumulation undermined competition and eventually would lead to monopolies. Moreover, more capital accumulation in less hands also fuels political power, through donations to political parties and lobbying for reduced regulation and taxation. Entrepreneurial risk is part and parcel of both exchange chains A and B, but in chain B it is increasingly shifted away from the owners of capital to consumers, workers and taxpayers. In chain B, accumulation is the driving force in which capital is the start and end point of exchange and in which firms, goods, labour, society and nature have become means to the end of accumulation of capital that becomes more and more concentrated at the top. Apples, bread and meat will rot when not consumed, but capital can be acquired, combined, spread, invested, and traded for the sake of further accumulation.

Marx saw that for the capitalist class accumulation was an end in itself not merely because capitalists would be greedy people or immoral persons, but because it is the logic of the capitalist system which forces them to accumulate in order to remain competitive. Firms can only remain competitive, Marx recognized, when they exploit cost advantages, which can only be done by increasing the scale of production. But this requires more sales, which will only happen with lower prices, which, in turn, requires an increase in productivity so that more can be produced and sold with less capital and/or labour per unit of production. Moreover, it does not matter in which activity the money is invested, as long as it is the most profitable one around. And this latter consequence of capital accumulation has led to the fact that the length of keeping shares and other financial assets has reduced every decade. The bottom line in exchange chain B is the question which shares deliver the highest returns in the shortest period of time. At that point, the type of good, C, to which capital is related becomes almost irrelevant. In fact, many investors have no idea in which activities their money is invested. Do you know where your savings are invested in by your bank and pension fund?

The first principle of capitalism that Karl Marx unearthed is the principle of capital accumulation: making money with money for which commodities are a means and by which risk is increasingly shifted towards other stakeholders through market power.

The Second Capitalist Principle

As already indicated above, the second capitalist principle is the fact that capital hires labour and not the other way around. This principle, often referred to as private property by Marxists, reflects an inherent asymmetry in capitalist markets. But the key problem is not private property but its distribution between the classes. As long as some only have their labour power whereas others have capital—whether in the form of money, land or other assets—production will inevitably occur through investments by the owners of capital in productive activities complemented by the hiring of labour to make these investments profitable. This asymmetry between the production factors K (capital) and L (labour) eventually turns into income inequality because the bargaining power between capital and labour is unequal. A single owner, or manager who has been delegated the task to hire labour, can hire hundreds or thousands of men and women, who each will try to negotiate their wage. Unless labour is scarce (during the short boom stage of the economic cycle) capital selects workers and not the other way around, which produces a downward pressure on the market wage rate. Unemployed workers compete with each other for scarce vacancies, bidding the wage rate down. This inequality in bargaining power leads to an increase in the capital share of total income at cost of the labour share.

Labour law provides a limit to the level of exploitation enabled by the second capitalist principle through minimum wages and various forms of labour protection. Indeed, many of the demands of Marx and Engels for the protection of labour have been met, for the formal economy at least, in the 150 years that have passed since the publication of their manifesto. But unemployment and the threat of unemployment in the face of technological development and globalization, remains a key factor supporting the unequal bargaining position of labour versus capital. Labour unions provide necessary counterweight with their threat of strikes. But since the failure in the Western world of the mass strikes of the 1970s and 1980s to keep unprofitable coal mines and textile factories open, labour unions have lost membership and influence. Moreover, the flexibilization of labour markets that followed in the 1980s has resulted in a decline in the share of workers on fixed contracts and an increase in self-employed and flexible workers with temporary contracts. For the Netherlands, the Central Bank has calculated that over the period 1996–2015, for every percentage point increase in the flexible labour force share, the labour share of income has declined by 0.23 percentage points.[21]

The two capitalist principles uncovered by Karl Marx mutually reinforce each other and thereby speed up inequality. The larger the accumulation, the more capital is available for new technologies that increase productivity and displace labour, which will further undermine the bargaining power of workers over wages, contracts and working conditions. And this is not only happening during recessions, when unemployment is high. It is also the case when economies are experiencing a boom phase of the economic cycle, for example between the recovery from the financial crisis until the Great Lockdown in 2020. Unemployment rates were low, profits were high, but wages did hardly increase. So even in periods that wages should benefit from relative job scarcity, in particular wages at the bottom of the wage ladder tend to remain low in today's stage of global capitalism.[22]

In his influential study, *Capital in the 21st Century*, the French economist Thomas Piketty has confirmed the trend of increasing inequality in a variety of economies across the world.[23] Interestingly, he has demonstrated that inequality has increased steadily since the times of Marx, with a correction between the First World War and the 1970s. The reasons for the temporary decline in inequality are, according to Piketty, the 1929 financial crisis and the destruction of much of the stock of physical capital during the two world wars. But after the 1970s we are back to the standard capitalist dynamics that Marx observed. Since the 1980s, capital income has increased faster than GDP, and hence, faster than labour income. Piketty warns that this results in a rentier-economy in which the rich enjoy more and more rents and dividends from accumulated capital with less and less incentive to work or to invest in entrepreneurial activities in the real economy (i.e. the economy of tangible goods and services). In such an economy, those who only depend on their labour power to earn an income will inevitably receive a decreasing share of national income. The way out, according to Piketty, is higher wealth taxes (like we had in the 1970s) and a GDP growth rate above the rate of interest. However, this second point—a higher GDP than the interest rate—is actually happening in many economies but without any impact on inequality. And the problem with higher economic growth is that it tends to result in the exploitation of nature—something which Marx already mentioned in *Capital*. So, an increase in wealth tax seems to be the only feasible option available—apart from a shift to a post-capitalist economy.

The insight from Marx is that capitalism has an in-built dynamic of expansion and inequality. This is reflected by a continuous expansion of markets at the cost of the role of the state (for regulation and redistribution) and the space for the community economy (for caring and sharing). Today, we can see even more clearly than in Marx' days that capitalism has taken advantage of markets to the extent that they no longer function for everyone and not at all for vulnerable groups and the planet. But markets have shown to be able to function very well without the asymmetries of capital hiring labour and capital accumulation at cost of labour income. An important lesson from Marx is that markets do not need capitalism. State-owned companies can function just as efficiently as privately owned ones, when properly guided by benchmarks set by the government and controlled by parliament and independent market authorities. For example, four years after its nationalization, ABN AMRO became a profitable bank again and has remained profitable since, even though today the majority of shares are still owned by the Dutch state. Aramco, the Saudi-Arabian state-owned oil company is estimated to be the most profitable company in the world—more profitable than Apple and Shell.[24] Hence, markets can function very well without private ownership of firms. Innovation, cost savings, efficiency, client-orientation, re-investment of profits and long-term strategy can all thrive in markets with state-owned companies, workers' cooperatives and community-based non-profit firms, in which the asymmetries between capital and labour and the accumulation of capital extracted from business operations are constrained or completely absent. But as long as the economy at large remains capitalist it will be accumulation-oriented and therefore also growth-oriented. We can tame rising inequality with higher taxes but we cannot at the same time tame accumulation and the exploitation of our planet in capitalist markets. The analysis in *Capital* indicates that it is impossible to fix capitalism to deliver wellbeing for all with more equality and within our planetary boundaries.

THE ECONOMIST

(Karl Marx, 1818 Trier–1883 London)

Karl Marx was born in a Jewish middle-class family in Germany. As a student, he spent more than his allowance and once was caught by the police for being drunk. He studied first in Bonn, then in Berlin, and later received his PhD from the University of Jena. One of his teachers was the philosopher Hegel and his theory of dialectics—the historical development from thesis and antithesis to synthesis—influenced Marx' thinking about capitalism. Marx married with Jenny von Westphalen and the couple had seven children, but only three survived to adulthood. After his death, his daughter Laura translated Marx' work and spread his ideas in France together with her husband, Paul Lafargue. Marx tried to make a living in journalism but the family was often dependent on financial support from family and friends. He was socially engaged and criticized the dismal working conditions in factories that paralleled the quickly expanding industrialization throughout Europe. Due to his criticism in the newspapers for which he worked, he had to leave first Germany, then Paris and then Brussels. The family eventually settled down in exile in London.

He regularly visited the Netherlands, where his mother was born, partly hoping to receive financial support from his uncle Philips, the grandfather of the founders of the electronics multinational. But his uncle stopped the support for the family, even when Marx sent his wife to ask for it, out of dissatisfaction with Marx' socialist projects. Marx' sharp observations of the social costs of capitalism and his thorough knowledge of the economic literature from David Ricardo to Adam Smith and the major French economists, eventually resulted in his magnum opus in which Hegel's dialectics is reflected in the idea of class struggle. He used this class theory to study the dynamics of capitalism in terms of power of the bourgeoisie over the labour class. He explained that profits arose from the extraction of surplus value from labour above the market value of the wages paid to labour. With ever more mechanization, labour productivity increased and with it the extraction of surplus value, Marx observed by visiting factories and discussing with his friend Friedrich Engels. Engels was in fact a capitalist—he managed the textile factory of his father in Manchester—but he shared Marx' socialist ideals.

His close observations of both the role of labourers and of capitalists helped Marx to understand capitalism not as a business strategy or management style but as a system in which both classes were inescapably tied to their roles—profit making for the one and wage earning for the other. His analysis made clear that the surplus above and beyond the normal business profit to compensate for the costs and risks attached to investment was the key problem of capitalist production. Later, economists would refer to shareholders as residual claimants—those who take all that remains of a firm's returns after wages and inputs have been paid their market value. In other words, Marx discovered that the only ones who did not earn according to market value but generally well above it (except during crises), were the capitalists.

Without labour rights and alternative sources of income, the relationship between the two classes turned more and more unequal, Marx observed. This resulted in a rentier-economy with ever more risky investments in an expanding financial sector, which inevitably resulted in financial crises—which, indeed, were frequent in the times that Marx worked on *Capital* and in particular when he wrote the second volume, dealing with the circulation of capital. Hence, the instability of capitalism, according to Marx, is a consequence of the unequal relationship between labour and capital.

The first volume of *Capital* appeared in 1867, and the second volume appeared almost 20 years later, in 1885. Marx died when working on the third volume (and was still revising parts of the second volume) and left it to Engels to write it from the notes that he had left behind. But since this last volume is so speculative of what Marx would have written himself, *Capital* is commonly published as containing only volumes I and II. One of the reasons that the book took him so long was Marx's bad health, which, in turn, was probably due to the poor living conditions in London. Understanding and criticizing capitalism was Marx' intellectual legacy, but his political legacy is undoubtedly the *Communist Manifesto* of 1848 and the international socialist movement. In recognition of this second legacy, many years after his death the final phrase of the manifesto, 'Working Men of all Lands, Unite,' was added to his tombstone at Highgate Cemetery in London.

Reading Marx
Karl Marx, *Capital – A critical Analysis of Capitalist Production*, Vol. I & II (Hertfordshire: Wordsworth, 2013 [1867]).

Friedrich Engels and Karl Marx, *The Communist Manifesto* (London: Penguin Classics, 2015 [1848]).

Reading About Marx
David McLellan, *Karl Marx: A Biography* (London: Palgrave Macmillan, 2006).

Practising Marx

Is it possible to have non-capitalist economic alternatives without succumbing to the ideology of Marxism that Marx himself rejected or to the authoritarian communist systems that he would have detested? Yes, this is very well possible, I think. There are feasible alternative forms of non-capitalist market activity within, but resisting and challenging, a capitalist context. Weeding out false alternatives, such as the much-celebrated platform economy of Airbnb and Uber, from genuine non-capitalist firms requires us to check promises of alternatives against the two principles of capitalist production, which Marx has given us. First, a non-capitalist market activity should be concerned with goods and services as such and with money in the role of means of exchange—or even without money. This prevents capital accumulation for the sake of accumulation itself. Instead, an alternative market initiative regards a good or service as valuable in itself, just like the workers who produce them, the social connections in the neighbourhood and the natural environment. In a non-capitalist market, the exchange should have the form of sequence A of Fig. 2. Second, profits should not go to external shareholders but remain in the company for the sake of all stakeholders—its workers, investors, clients, communities and nature. Market production can occur without the asymmetry of capital hiring labour and running away with profit. The profit belongs to the company and can be reinvested for the sake of the long-term survival of the company in such a way that it respects all stakeholders, generating a common interest in the long-term prospect of the firm. Obviously, the activities should be commercially viable—we are concerned with a non-capitalist market alternative, not with the public sector or voluntary activities. But the commercial viability, which includes a normal business profit, as Marx recognized too, should function as a precondition for the long-term survival of a company, not as an end in itself. This implies a modest profit for the company as a whole, for the sake of R&D, investment, training of workers, social responsibility, and for delivering value added to the economy and society.

Below I will mention two alternatives that meet Marx' two criteria. An alternative for a capitalist firm and another alternative for capitalist exchange. Both can function in a capitalist as well as a non-capitalist market economy—this simply depends on the number and size of the alternatives. The more the alternatives outnumber capitalist activities and forms of exchange, the more the whole market system will be shifting towards a postcapitalist market economy. Of course, state-owned companies are another alternative to the capitalist firm. But what I like to do is give examples of viable alternatives in the private sector—to spark our imagination of an alternative market economy that is both an alternative to capitalism and to state-run communism.

Cooperative Firms

A cooperative firm is not owned by external shareholders, as is the case with a publicly listed firm, and also not owned by individuals, such as an owner-director or a family. Instead, it is owned by itself and not by any stakeholder in particular (e.g. Rabobank, a large Dutch bank) or owned by its workers (e.g. the large conglomerate Mondragon Society in Spain) or owned by its suppliers (e.g. the Dutch diary firm Friesland Campina, the largest cooperative firm in Europe) or owned by its clients (as in the case of households who collectively own a wind turbine or solar panels for their own use). Even the most capitalist economy of the world, the US, has large and successful cooperative firms, mostly in agriculture and supermarkets but also including credit unions, health care centres and electricity coops.[25] Well-known US-based coops operating internationally are, for example, Associated Press and Carpet One. Outside the US we can find large coops such as Crédit Agricole Group in France, a credit union, ReWe supermarkets in Germany and Arla Foods, a dairy company in Denmark.[26]

Cooperatives tend to promote equality and labour rights and provide an estimated 280 million jobs worldwide, according to the International Labour Organization (ILO).[27] But due to the various types of coops they vary in the extent to which workers and clients really have decision-making power and the extent to which they operate really differently than other firms in their market. Rabobank, for example, operates in 38 countries, serves 8 million customers worldwide and employs 40,000 workers.[28] But its governance structure is just as hierarchical as in publicly listed and privately owned banks, with its member council having only an advisory role on local issues. When I showed my interest in becoming member of the council of one of the hundred local Rabobank offices, the managing team informed me that I should not expect to be able to influence the strategy, the products offered, or funding issues. And when I met with two employees from the treasury department at the Headquarters in Utrecht and asked if the plan of issuing a convertible bond to raise capital right after the financial crisis came from the member council, they laughed at the very idea of it. No, both these financial experts and the management team of the local Rabobank explained to me that the membership council discussed minor matters such as the location of a new money machine or grants to a local art gallery. Neither the employees have any more influence over the bank's strategy than their colleagues at ABN AMRO or ING, for example. Hence, Rabobank operates largely the same as any non-cooperative bank, which is illustrated by its involvement in the manipulation of Libor by its' trading office and the generous bonuses paid to board members.[29]

What the case of Rabobank teaches us is that a cooperative structure without clearly defined ownership or decision-making rights for workers or clients is not necessarily operating differently from a capitalist firm, except for the fact that there is no pressure from shareholders to pay out dividend and to raise the returns on investment on their behalf. Of course, this is an important benefit of a cooperative structure and provides the board of directors with a longer time horizon and room for manoeuvre for the sake of sustainability. But there is much more to be gained from coops if they are really jointly owned and democratically governed. Mondragon Society in northern Spain is the tenth-largest Spanish company with 67,000 employees in Spain, and it is genuinely governed by its workers. It includes a bank, factories and shops, and it comes closer to the utilization of all potential benefits of coops than the Rabobank. In Mondragon, all workers are members and it is the general assembly which has the ultimate decision-making power, while its capital is explicitly ranked subordinate to labour.[30]

Circular and Community Economy

Alternatives to capital accumulation through exchange—sequence B of Fig. 2—should put goods in the centre of exchange again, with money not in its role of means of accumulation but as means of exchange. As Marx said, commodities should be exchanged for their use-value and not for their exchange-value. There are various ways in which this re-centring of use-value is possible. Some are small-scale such as crowdfunding, e-bay trades of second-hand stuff, peer-to-peer lending platforms and community currencies connected to local exchange networks. The common feature of all these non-capitalist market initiatives is that the money involved can hardly be accumulated in any way close to capitalist exchange. For example, in the case of crowdfunding, customers take simultaneously the role of investors and thereby pre-pay for the product with a risk of a failed production activity. In this way, musicians can, for example, pay for the recording of a new album, paying back the funders not in money terms but with a number of CDs, vinyl records or concert tickets. And local exchange networks with their own currencies simply create money in proportion to the size of the local market. These networks often have strict rules against holding cash to prevent hoarding and accumulation, for example, through a time-dependent devaluation of digital currencies not used for purchases.

But all these exchange initiatives are not necessarily genuine alternatives to capitalist markets. A major reason is that they are complementary and not feasible alternatives for the replacement of capitalist exchange. In fact, some alternatives have been captured by capitalist firms who use them as yet another way to make profits from resources that they regard as under-used productive capital. So, whereas couch-surfing is a free and direct peer-to-peer service, Airbnb is a large multinational company with investors interested in returns on investments comparable to other businesses in the hospitality industry. The company declines any responsibility for damage to rooms, quality control, maintenance and customer services for clients, because it portrays itself as a platform bringing supply and demand together, for which it charges a fee up to 20% of the room rate. In the meantime, Airbnb has become so popular that complete cities suffer from invasions of trolly-pulling tourists, for example San Francisco and Amsterdam. Moreover, the capitalist idea of making money out of underused sources of productive capital turns more and more ordinary people into owners of additional apartments to rent them out through Airbnb, thereby reducing the stock of affordable houses for fulltime living and driving up the prices of small apartments. For this reason, the city of Amsterdam has limited the number of days for renting out rooms to 30 days per year.[31] Airbnb is very different from the Amsterdam nonprofit community initiative *Vooruit* which mediates between students and care homes for the elderly. Project *Vooruit* places students in homes for the elderly and in exchange for their cheap rooms the students provide 10 hours a week caring services for the elderly, ranging from walking with them in the park to cooking and eating together.[32] So, whereas Airbnb is a capitalist firm turning ordinary home-owners into capitalists and profiting from a substantial risk-free fee, *Vooruit* is a nonprofit intermediary that creates a win-win situation (which is a key characteristic of markets) for students looking for affordable housing and for lonely elderly people keen on some company.

At macro level, an alternative to capitalist exchange is an exchange not of property but of use-value linked to a recyclable good. This type of alternative is the focus of the circular economy, in which the income-earning incentives for material good production are reversed. Traditionally, the more washing machines sold, the more profit made. But with payment for every single laundry service in a leased machine that remains owned by the manufacturer, the longer the lifetime of the machine, the more laundry services sold per unit of capital. That is a form of material efficiency instead of extractive efficiency in traditional capitalist production. This circular activity requires a long-term view, which is exactly the case, for example, with family wealth investors and pension funds. There are various pilot projects of circular economy products, for example Bundles, through which households can have a Miele recyclable washing machine for which they only pay 40 euro cents per laundry. All maintenance, repair and replacements costs are born by the manufacturer, whose interest it is to produce washing machines with a long lifetime and low repair and recycle costs.[33]

There are seven principles of a circular business model, through which sustainability and customer services are united.[34] First is a sustainable product design leading to a product that is fully recyclable or biodegradable and produced with low energy needs and zero waste. Second comes usage by the customer that should be long-lived, requiring little or no power, and, third, including free maintenance and repair by the supplier/manufacturer. Fourth is a secondhand market, and fifth is cheap refurbishment and easy disassembly in modules and the possibility of upgrading the parts. Sixth is online sales of the product-as-a-service and seventh is recycling at the end of the product lifetime into elements that can be safely re-used at the same quality level or through down-cycling to a lower quality product. In a circular chain of exchange, negative externalities are minimized and personal relationships and commitment become an asset. But it can only compete with the extractive efficiency of capitalist firms when also those firms have to pay for the externalities they cause, in terms of the environment, human rights violations (e.g. using child labour), and rising inequality, by paying their fair share of taxes.

Notes

1. The Troika was the name used for the three institutions responsible for managing the euro crisis with emergency loans, austerity packages, and other policy measures forced upon the southern Eurozone countries in trouble. The Troika consisted of the European Commission, the European Central Bank (ECB) and the International Monetary Fund (IMF).
2. GDP measured in USD: https://data.worldbank.org/country/greece. Accessed on July 7, 2019.
3. Servaas Storm and C.W.M. Naastepad, "Myths, Mix-ups and Mishandlings – Understanding the Eurozone Crisis." *International Journal of Political Economy* 45, 1 (2016): 46–71, Table 2.
4. Jörg Rocholl and Axel Stahmer, "Where did the Greek Bailout Money go?" ESMT White Paper (Berlin: European School of Management and Technology, 2016).
5. Rocholl and Stamer, "Where did the Greek Bailout Money go?"
6. Rocholl and Stamer, "Where did the Greek Bailout Money go?"
7. Eurostat, unemployment by sex and age, annual average: https://ec.europa.eu/eurostat/web/lfs/data/database.
8. https://nos.nl/artikel/607005-staatssteun-spekt-de-staatskas.html. Accessed on July 14, 2019.
9. CBS, "Nederland langs de Europese meetlat" (Den Haag: Centraal Bureau voor de Statistiek, 2019). https://www.cbs.nl/nl-nl/publicatie/2019/20/nederland-langs-de-europese-meetlat-2019. Accessed on July 15, 2020. ECB, "The State of the Housing Market in the Euro Area." Economic Bulletin no. 7. 2018 (Frankfurt: European Central Bank, 2018). https://www.ecb.europa.eu/pub/economic-bulletin/articles/2018/html/ecb.ebart201807_02.en.html#toc1. Accessed on July 11, 2019.
10. CBS, "Nederland langs de Europese meetlat."
11. My own house was for sale for four years in this period and I had to reduce the offer price twice before I could finally sell it—luckily without a loss because I had lived there long enough to pay off half the mortgage debt.
12. CBS Statline: https://opendata.cbs.nl/statline. Accessed on July 9, 2019.
13. Frederic Mishkin and Tryggvi Herbertsson, 'Financial Stability in Iceland' (Rykjavík: Iceland Chamber of Commerce, 2006).
14. The pamphlet was published on February 13th, 1997, by a major Dutch newspaper, *De Volkskrant* and signed by 70 Dutch economists, including myself. The title appeared to be an accurate prediction twelve years later: "With this EMU, Europe is on the wrong path". https://www.volkskrant.nl/economie/met-deze-emu-kiest-europa-verkeerde-weg~bf1ca466/. Accessed on July 22, 2019.
15. They wrote this manifest quite hastily in the revolutionary year 1848, hoping that it would provide the guideline for building a new society after the revolutions that spread throughout Europe at the time. But the uprisings of the labour movement were halted by armed forces in France, Germany, Belgium and other

countries. The manifesto was first published in German. For the English translation, see: https://www.marxists.org/archive/marx/works/download/pdf/Manifesto.pdf. Accessed on July 22, 2019.
16. Karl Marx, *Capital – A critical analysis of capitalist production*, Vol. I & II (Hertfordshire: Wordsworth, 2013 [1867]).
17. "Besides, the new landed aristocracy was the natural ally of the new bankocracy, of the newly-hatched *haute finance*, and of the large manufacturers, then depending on protective duties" (Marx, *Capital*, 508).
18. "Ce qu'il y a de certain, c'est que moi je ne suis pas marxist" (Friedrich Engels, "Lettre à E. Bernstein," 2 novembre 1882. https://www.marxists.org/francais/engels/works/1882/11/fe18821102.htm. Accessed on July 15, 2020. Marx wrote this, probably in 1880, because he disagreed with the revolutionaries who denied any reforms in favour of labour rights within the current system.
19. Karl Marx, *Rheinische Zeitung* 135, 15 May 1842.
20. He added that this also led to VOC's role as "one of the most extraordinary relations of treachery, bribery, massacre, and meanness." (Marx, *Capital*, 526).
21. De Nederlandsche Bank, "Labour Market Flexibilisation linked to Fall in Labour Income Share" Amsterdam: DNBulletin, 1 February 2018. https://www.dnb.nl/en/news/news-and-archive/DNBulletin2018/dnb372062.jsp. Accessed on July 24, 2019.
22. See, a recent analysis of this with US data: Jared Bernstein and Keith Bentele, "The Increasing Benefits and Diminished Costs of Running a High-Pressure Labour Market" (Washington D.C.: Center on Budget and Policy Priorities, 2019). https://www.cbpp.org/sites/default/files/atoms/files/5-15-19fe.pdf. Accessed on July 24, 2019.
23. Thomas Piketty, *Capital in the Twenty-First Century* (Cambridge (MA): Harvard University Press, 2014).
24. This was reported by the *New York Times*, 1st April, 2019. https://www.nytimes.com/2019/04/01/business/saudi-aramco-profit.html. Accessed on July 24, 2019.
25. See for example the annual list of the top-100 cooperatives in the US, published by National Cooperative Bank which was set up by Congress to provide funding to cooperatives: NCB. "The 2018 NCB Coop Top 100." New York: National Cooperative Bank, 2018. https://impact.ncb.coop/hubfs/assets/resources/NCB_Co-op_100_2018_WEB.pdf. Accessed on August 30, 2019.
26. https://www.thenews.coop/49090/sector/view-top-300-co-operatives-around-world/. Accessed on August 28, 2019.
27. https://www.ilo.org/global/topics/cooperatives/lang%2D%2Den/index.htm. Accessed on August 30, 2019.
28. https://www.rabobank.com/en/about-rabobank/results-and-reports/index.html. Accessed on June 18, 2020.
29. Rabobank was fined one billion US dollar for its involvement in the manipulation of LIBOR (London Inter Bank Offered rate): https://www.reuters.com/article/us-rabobank-libor-idUSBRE99S0L520131029. Accessed on August 30, 2019.
30. https://www.mondragon-corporation.com/en/co-operative-experience/our-principles/. Accessed on August 30, 2019.

31. https://www.amsterdam.nl/en/housing/holiday-rentals/. Accessed on June 18, 2020. In addition, Amsterdam has prohibited buying newly built houses for rent: buyers are obliged to live in the house themselves: https://www.amsterdam.nl/bestuur-organisatie/college/wethouder/laurens-ivens/persberichten/amsterdam-beschermt-koopmarkt-duur/. Accessed on June 18, 2020.
32. https://vooruitproject.nl/. Accessed on August 30, 2019.
33. https://bundles.nl/en/miele-washing-machine-subscriptions/. Accessed on August 30, 2019.
34. See, for example, the Circular Economy Toolkit developed by the University of Cambridge: http://circulareconomytoolkit.org/Assessmenttool.html. Accessed July 15, 2020. See also a guideline by the Ellen MacArthur Foundation, "Towards a circular economy: business rationale for an accelerated transition." https://www.ellenmacarthurfoundation.org/assets/downloads/TCE_Ellen-MacArthur-Foundation-9-Dec-2015.pdf. Accessed on August 30, 2019.

Bibliography

Bernstein, Jared, and Keith Bentele. "The Increasing Benefits and Diminished Costs of Running a High-Pressure Labour Market." Washington D.C.: Center on Budget and Policy Priorities, 15 May, 2019. https://www.cbpp.org/sites/default/files/atoms/files/5-15-19fe.pdf. Accessed on July 15, 2020.

CBS. "Nederland langs de Europese meetlat." Den Haag: Centraal Bureau voor de Statistiek, 2019. https://www.cbs.nl/nl-nl/publicatie/2019/20/nederland-langs-de-europese-meetlat-2019. Accessed on July 15, 2020.

De Nederlandsche Bank. "Labour Market Flexibilisation linked to Fall in Labour Income Share." Amsterdam: DNBulletin, 1 February 2018. https://www.dnb.nl/en/news/news-and-archive/DNBulletin2018/dnb372062.jsp. Accessed on July 15, 2020.

ECB. "The State of the Housing Market in the Euro Area." Economic Bulletin no. 7. 2018. Frankfurt: European Central Bank, 2018. https://www.ecb.europa.eu/pub/economic-bulletin/articles/2018/html/ecb.ebart201807_02.en.html#toc1. Accessed on July 15, 2020.

Engels, Friedrich. "Lettre à E. Bernstein. 2 novembre 1882." Marxists Internet Archive (Marxists.org), 2010. https://www.marxists.org/francais/engels/works/1882/11/fe18821102.htm. Accessed on July 15, 2020.

Marx, Karl. *Rheinische Zeitung* 135, 15 May 1842.

———. *Capital – A critical analysis of capitalist production* Vol. I & II. Hertfordshire: Wordsworth, 2013 [1867].

Marx, Karl, and Friedrich Engels. "Manifesto of the Communist Party." Marxists Internet Archive (Marxists.org), 2010. English translation: 1888. https://www.marxists.org/archive/marx/works/download/pdf/Manifesto.pdf. Accessed on July 15, 2020.

Mishkin, Frederic, and Tryggvi Herbertsson. "Financial Stability in Iceland." Rykjavík: Iceland Chamber of Commerce, 2006.

Piketty, Thomas. *Capital in the Twenty-First Century*. Cambridge (MA): Harvard University Press, 2014.

Rocholl, Jörg, and Axel Stahmer. "Where did the Greek Bailout Money go?" ESMT White Paper. Berlin: European School of Management and Technology, 2016.

Storm, Servaas, and C.W.M. Naastepad. "Myths, Mix-ups and Mishandlings – Understanding the Eurozone Crisis." *International Journal of Political Economy* 45, 1 (2016): 46–71.

"With this EMU, Europe is on the wrong path." *Volkskrant*, 13 February 1997. https://www.volkskrant.nl/economie/met-deze-emu-kiest-europa-verkeerde-weg~bf1ca466/. Accessed on July 15, 2020.

Chapter 2: Hyman Minsky on Financial Crises

THE PROBLEM

The bankruptcy of the investment bank Lehman Brothers made the world economy tremble. Not because the bank was so crucial for industries investing in new technologies or expanding export markets. To the contrary, investment banks, as Lehman and its brothers and sisters are cheerfully labelled, hardly invested in the real economy in the years leading up to the crisis. They financed primarily the growth of the financial sector itself, and today, again, returns from investments in financial assets are a major focus of their business.

In the 1990s and 2000s, retail banks joined this shift from the real economy to the financial sector, attracted by spectacular profits. In the Netherlands it was ABN AMRO bank that engaged at full speed with asset trading, together with some of the banks that were involved in its unfortunate and short-lived takeover: Fortis, Royal Bank of Scotland and Banco Santander. Another large Dutch bank, SNS bank, was deeply involved in real estate speculation abroad. How then, was it possible that the collapse of banks that were not crucial for the real economy were able to pull the whole world economy down in their collapse? How can we explain that the failure of a few banks resulted in a chain reaction of bankruns, a worldwide credit crunch, a large fall of world trade, a serious drop in GDP and a sudden increase in unemployment? The explanation of all this has a supply side and a demand side.

The Origin of the Problem

The demand side of the problem was led by a historically low interest rate since 2000. In the 1980s, the official rate at which banks could borrow from central banks in the US and Europe was close to 20%. Over the period 1955–2000 the average interest rate was 5%, and it has never been below 2% (the lowest was between 1955 and 1961). But from the new millennium onwards, the Federal

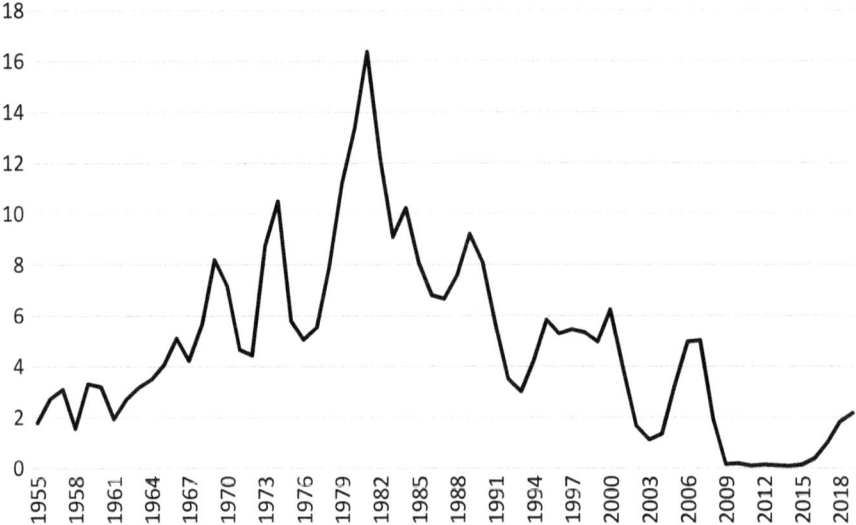

Fig. 1 Fed official interest rate (%) 1955–2019. (Source: author, based on data from the Federal Reserve Bank, https://www.federalreserve.gov/datadownload/Download. aspx?rel=H15&series=c7ca9f58d350a500bb83e230e208cf9b&lastObs=100&from=&to=&filetype=spreadsheetml&label=include&layout=seriescolumn, accessed on June 18, 2020)

Reserve (Fed) kept the interest rate in the US around 1%. See Fig. 1 for the annual average US official interest rate. And since the crisis, it has remained low. After the crisis hit, the extremely low interest rate was the key policy instrument to stimulate the economy in the US and Europe. The ECB's rate has even become negative in 2019. But before 2008 the economy was running full steam. So why then was the interest rate kept so low before the crisis whereas it was not necessary at all to stimulate the supply side of the economy?

Normally, when the economy is booming, interest rates are increased by the Central Bank in order to prevent overheating of the economy and increasing inflation as a consequence. But in the new millennium, many economists and economic policymakers believed that this would not happen anymore. Instead, it was believed that a low interest rate would help poorer citizens of the US to buy a house and to sell it at a profit a few years later. So, banks borrowed at low rates from the Fed, and offered mortgages at higher—but still reasonably low—interest rates to an increasing number of poor households. Millions of poor American households were suddenly given the opportunity to buy their own homes. And they did. First families, then single parents, and eventually whole communities of low-wage Latino's and black Americans who were dependent upon casual jobs and pay-day lenders to pay their bills. Banks, middlemen and a wide variety of mortgage lenders were eager to sell the so-called subprime mortgages because the loans for poorer households were guaranteed by two agencies, known under their comics-type of names, Freddie Mac and Fannie Mae.[1]

The prospects looked safe for everyone involved: the banks were backed-up by the state-provided guarantees, the middlemen earned commissions, and the home buyers obtained low-interest mortgages. The widespread belief was that even if a homeowner would be unable to pay off the loan, the house could be sold with a profit so that the loan could be paid off. In this way, the monetary policy became an escape route for the government for addressing income inequality. Since the 1980s, income inequality had risen steadily in the US. Not only the poorest households but even the middle class had not experienced any improvement of their real incomes. Many even experienced a net decline, while the richest Americans saw their incomes grow even faster than before. So, both for politicians and many ordinary households, the low interest rate provided a solution in an era that income redistribution through fiscal policy had become politically unpopular. Taxation for the rich declined rather than increased, with wide political support from both Republicans and Democrats. Households benefitted from the low interest rates because the mortgages and consumer loans they obtained did not only provide the funds for buying a home but also for keeping up purchasing power. Many households used part of the loans to pay for the rising costs of education of their children and their health care bills. Indeed, more than half of the loans taken by lower income households were obtained against the overvalue of their homes and were used to pay the bills.[2]

It went wrong when an increasing number of households were unable to repay their mortgages or even the interest on it. They were allured by teaser rates but these increased after one or two years (as was written in the small print of the mortgage contracts). However, many borrowers were not informed about this clause because they themselves and the mortgage lenders believed that just before the end of the teaser rate period, they could substitute their loan for a new one, again with a teaser rate. This indeed was possible in the beginning, but not anymore when house prices stopped rising. Mortgage lenders were no longer willing to provide new loans. And worse, the new homeowners found themselves increasingly unable to sell their house—let alone at a profit. When the housing bubble burst, the subprime crisis was born and homeowners got stuck with an unaffordable mortgage and an increasing debt relative to the value of their house. The only escape was to hand in the keys at the bank and walk away. In various other countries in which the housing market collapsed, however, banks did not accept such a walk away from debt. The homeowners were condemned to stay in their unaffordable house and saw their debts—as the difference between the declining value of the house and the fixed value of their mortgage debt—increase year on year. The next in the chain of debt were the banks, which were either left with houses that could not be sold, even at low prices, or faced failing loans from homeowners and soon also from businesses that began to suffer from the economic decline. This brings us to the second cause of the crisis.

On the supply side, the problem was that almost every bank in the US, Europe and emerging economies had bought mortgage-backed securities (MBS). These were US mortgages, many of them subprime, that were cut in pieces and reassembled in packages (called derivatives) that had been sold to them as low-risk assets. Due to this seemingly secure risk-spreading characteristic of MBS, the trade in these derivatives had flourished, in particular because many were sold not through official security exchanges but over the counter, outside the control of the US Securities and Exchange Committee. MBS were not only filling the balance sheets of investment banks but even those of retail banks and performing the role of risk insurance against price changes such as increases in interest rate. But with the failure of a growing number of households to repay their loans and unexpected declines in interest rates instead of increases, holders of MBS lost enormous amounts of money. Retail banks, insurance companies, investment firms and even small cooperative German banks had their balance sheets filled with these toxic assets—they were even found in China, Mexico and Nigeria. In the Netherlands, the top-four banks all had bought billions worth of derivatives and even non-financial institutions had bought them, ranging from city governments to social housing associations. The supply side problem started to show when financial traders in investment banks became suspicious about the extent to which the derivatives consisted of subprime mortgages, when it became known that an increasing number of households were turning in their keys. The scepticism of a few traders quickly led to widespread pessimism in the derivatives markets. This resulted in an unstoppable fall in the market value of derivatives. Everybody wanted to sell them, and nobody knew which loans were packaged in which derivatives and for which share. The presumably safe value of MBS appeared to be built on sand. Lehman Brothers went bankrupt simply because one day, the value of its assets was lower than the value of its liabilities and the bank's equity was too low to make up for the difference. With other banks suffering from the same problem, no financial institution was willing or able to provide the necessary support for Lehman.

In the case of some retail banks, this unfavourable situation led to bankruns by worried consumers afraid that their savings would be lost. After the bankruptcy of Lehman Brothers, other banks filed for bankruptcy, while yet others were nationalized or received billions of state support, ranging from Merryll Lynch in the US, to RBS and Northern Rock in the UK, and from Landsbanki in Iceland, to UBS in Switzerland and Hypo in Germany.

Financialization

How is it possible that a substantial part of bank balance sheets consists of financial assets that are no more than compounds of credits? Isn't the main role of banks to bring in savings and lend this out to households and firms? The answer to these questions is that there is no brake on the growth of financial assets and transactions as long as both sides of the market trust the quality of the assets and are optimistic about their future value. There are no laws or regulations to limit the growth of bank balance sheets. Banks can simply add to their assets and liabilities as long as both sides match. And since the Central Bank sets no limits, there is also no legal limit to the amount of money that banks create. So, by extending credit, banks bring more money into circulation and simply put the amount lent out on both sides of their balance sheets: on the asset side as a loan that will be paid back and on which they earn interest and on the liability side as the amount of credit put on the bank account of a customer. Neither have central banks, or governments, required a meaningful minimum amount of equity capital as a buffer against risky assets. In fact, it was the historically low interest rate set by central banks across the US, the UK and the EU, which encouraged banks to lend out more and more money. No wonder that the banking sector and all other parts of the financial sector had grown so enormously in the two decades before the crisis—in some countries they even grew bigger than the rest of the economy.

Banks, hence, can lend out much more money that they own. And with their very low level of equity capital, their leverage ratio is around 4 to 5. That means that for every euro or dollar that a bank owns in terms of core capital (mainly shareholder equity), it lends it out 20 to 25 times. Their basic earnings model is the difference between the interest paid to savers and the interest received from borrowers, which is called the spread. This model was the only one allowed for retail banks in the US when the Glass-Steagall-Act was in place. This Act was introduced in 1933 in the aftermath of the previous big crisis, the one of 1929. For decades it prohibited retail banks to trade in financial assets, while investment banks were not allowed to take in savings from households. In fact, the law required a strict separation between investment banking (which was taking higher risks) and retail banking (which provided savers with a deposit guarantee in case of a bank failure). During the 66 years that the Glass-Steagall-Act was in place, the US had not experienced a serious financial crisis.

But in 1999 the law was repealed thanks to fierce lobby from the banks, and the wall between the two types of banks disappeared. As a consequence, retails banks were now allowed to lend out more than they took in as savings by filling the gap with trading in financial assets and earning from the margins on this trade. And because these margins were so attractive, banks started to lend out more and filled the increasing funding gap with financial asset trading.

In Europe the financial sector remained relatively stable throughout this period, because traditionally, European banks were savings and loan banks and did not engage much in risky investment activities. When, for example, a large European firm wanted to take over another large firm, or become publicly listed on a European stock exchange, they often hired the services of American investment banks to manage this. But from the end of the 1990s European banks started to chase the same profit margins as American banks and began to set up financial trading departments in London. Within a decade, the largest European banks had turned into universal banks—combining retail banking with investment (e.g. in real estate) and trading in securities.

The new earnings model turned out to be very profitable. Banks bought massive amounts of derivatives, including MBS, and because of the booming market they were able to sell them with juicy profits to both financial and non-financial organizations. Banks' balance sheets increased in parallel, employment in the financial industry rose steadily and profits were well above 10–15%. The credit rating agencies valued the derivatives as solid triple A assets and equally benefitted from the booming market—being paid for their ratings by the same banks that assembled them. There was not a single government agency that was involved in assessing the quality of these toxic financial products or supervising the rating agencies' quality standards. Hence, the trade in derivatives could flourish without any effective control by the state. And central banks—from the Fed to the Bank of England and the European Central Bank—were empty-handed because of the several rounds of deregulation of the financial sector led by a strong banking lobby.

The financial sector was able to grow so fast because it made money with money. This is illustrated in Fig. 2, with sequence C of exchange, which is following the next stage of capitalist exchange from sequence A (pre-capitalism) and sequence B (commodity-based capitalism) presented in the previous chapter, in Fig. 2.

Whereas in the capitalist system of the nineteenth and twentieth century, as Marx had analysed it, investors made money by reducing commodities to means for accumulation, financial capitalism did not need commodities anymore. Money now made money. And not in the conventional way through the spreads earned between paid and received interest, but more often through the trade in derivatives and securitization (trading futures to hedge against price changes). Money became both means and end. Whereas the growth of the real economy—of goods and services—is constrained by the purchasing power of consumers, the financial sector does not face such a constraint. As long as everyone in the sector remains optimistic about the value of the assets traded and expects a continuous increase in the market. What is worrisome, is that today, the joint assets of the largest 25 banks in the world is even higher than it was just before the crisis.[3] Financial capitalism is on a course of fast growth and destabilization again.

From the new millennium onwards, the financial sector grew faster than the real economy and grew into a waterhead on top of the real economy. And although it looked as if the sector was cut loose from the real economy, it appeared to be linked firmly to it with invisible connections. A major connection was the pollution of balance sheets of nonfinancial private companies, public sector agencies and even non-profit organizations, with toxic assets. The

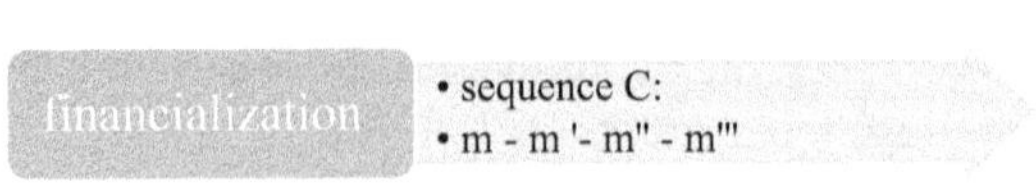

financialization	• sequence C: • m - m'- m" - m'''

Fig. 2 Exchange through financialization. (Note: m = money. Source: author)

boards of these organizations often had no idea what they had bought and believed these were securities that helped them to reduce risks, such as currency risks and rising interest rates. The phenomenon that nonfinancial sectors of the economy are more and more affected by financial products and financial transactions is referred to as financialization. For example, before the crisis, car manufacturer General Motors made more profit with its financial activities, including car loans, than with selling cars. After the crash the company was saved by the federal government. Not only because it suffered from declining sales of automobiles but also because it suffered losses on its financial activities.

The Waterhead of the Dutch Banking Sector

The Netherlands is not a very well-known financial centre, like, for example, Luxembourg or Switzerland, but its banking sector is four times GDP. With this large size relative to the real economy, the Dutch banking sector beats almost every other country in the world. For example, in the US, the top-ten banks together have a joint asset value below 50% of GDP.[4] Worldwide, the number of banks has declined steadily since the 1980s due to mergers and takeovers. The problem in the Netherlands is twofold: the banking sector is both very large and it is highly concentrated, so that there is very little competition. In fact, the crisis has illustrated that three of the four large banks are too big to fail. The Dutch should count themselves lucky that Rabobank did not need state support and that SNS bank failed a few years later than ABN AMRO. The savings operations of ABN AMRO, SNS, ING, and insurance company Aegon, did cost 45 billion euro of taxpayers' money (around 7% of GDP). A direct consequence of this government support was severe cuts in the government budget, in particular in health care and education.

The too big to fail problem is not exclusively the responsibility of the banks themselves. Part of the problem is that both clients and shareholders know very well that the government will support the banks when they fail—a typical moral hazard problem. The deposit guarantee system ensures current account and savings deposits up to 100,000 euro per bank. So, by spreading out one's savings over various banks, customers can be sure that at least up to half a million euro is safe during a crisis. That is not an incentive for bank customers to be critical of bank's risk positions or to change between banks. Customers even received their savings back after the collapse of the Icelandic internet bank Icesave. Hence, if one's savings are so generously guaranteed, many customers simply go for the highest interest rates at home or abroad. Most consumers tend to be much more cautious when they book a holiday or buy a car.

Shareholders of banks too went for the highest returns, being aware that a higher return on investments often implies higher risk. But shareholders also trusted that when banks would fail they would be saved by the state. And in order to attract investors, banks took increasingly more risk, chasing unrealistically high returns for their shareholders. As a consequence of the self-reinforcing dynamics between banks' risk strategies, customers' uncritical willingness to put their savings on any bank deposit, and shareholders' eagerness to benefit from high returns on investment, the benefits of competition had been lost in the Netherlands. It simply did not matter in which of the big four banks one would put one's money. Every ordinary firm that would take excessive risk would lose investors and eventually also customers and may go bankrupt. That is the normal state of affairs in a market economy with sufficient competition and sufficient information about the risk. Today, examples of strong competition and regular bankruptcies abound among clothing shops, electronics sellers and department stores in the Netherlands, but not for large banks. The irony of this is that making money with money has become less risky for customers and investors than making money with selling ordinary commodities for daily needs.

Ten years later, not much has changed. The Dutch banking sector has reduced to 3.5 times GDP. The European Central Bank has implemented stress-tests for banks in the Eurozone, but with too optimistic scenarios. The ECB has started with a European-level banking fund so that in the future bail-outs at the expense of national taxpayers could be prevented. But it takes many years if not decades before the fund will be big enough to be able to save, during a crisis, banks like Deutsche Bank, ING, and BNP Paribas. Most likely, national governments would still step in to save 'their' banks. International regulation of banks has become a bit stricter. But the strong banking lobby in the US, UK and Europe has watered-down the regulation and has managed to claim so many exceptions to the rules that the new regulation packages are very difficult to enforce. To illustrate, the Glass-Steagall-Act of 1933 consisted of 37 pages. The current reform-law in the US, called the Dodd-Frank-Act, has over 30,000 pages. That also explains why the piecemeal implementation is both slow and rather ineffective. This is also the case for the EU and its member states. In the Netherlands, the new regulation by the Dutch Central Bank and the Financial Market Authority is also affected by watering-down effects of the banking lobby. On top of this, banks have set-up extensive compliance departments. Partly to prevent fines but also as a disciplining measure for their own employees. But compliance with extensive micro-regulation is not the same as reducing risk in the banking sector as a whole.

The equity capital of the Dutch banks that were saved was between 3 and 4% at the time they received state support (ING and AEGON) or were nationalized (ABN AMRO and SNS). Today this percentage is between 4 and 5. This is still very low. Up to the 1980s, banks' own capital was at least 10%. Nonfinancial companies generally have 10–20% equity capital. The banking lobby appears to be too strong for parliaments to enforce a higher threshold. Hence, banks continue to operate with small buffers while at the same time financial markets have become less stable and more intertwined with the real economy. We are, therefore, vulnerable to another deep financial crisis as we experienced in 2008.

The Insight

The Post-Keynesian economist Hyman Minsky studied the growth and instability of the financial sector. His explanation for financial instability was that the financial economy is much more fragile than the real economy. Cows give milk and barbers cut hair and there is not too much variation in such activities over the years. If business is not going so well, it is generally not due to poisoned milk or an exploding coiffure, but because consumer preferences change or purchasing power is low. Or due to alternatives on the market, for example, soya drinks or male buns. Or unemployment causing people to cut their hair themselves and eat less cheese. The movement up and down in financial markets is faster and steeper than in the real economy. Keynes already discovered that financial markets are not ordinary markets, when he studied the 1929 crisis. Figure 3 shows that today, this is even more the case than it was in his days and when Minsky published his research a few decades later. The diagram shows how in the US the financial cycle has become much less stable than the business cycle—a basic insight provided by Hyman Minsky.

Instability

Financial markets have an inherent tendency for growth and instability. Growth because they construct their own assets that only partially depend on physical

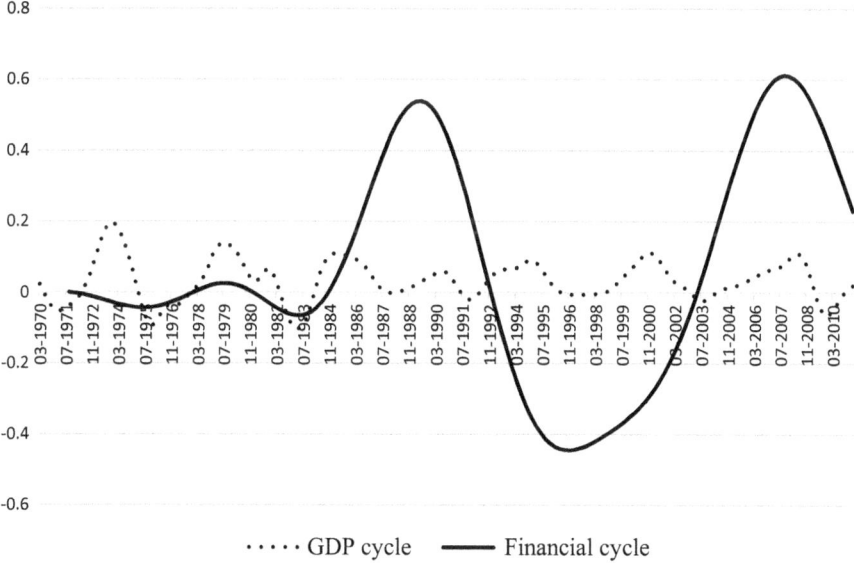

Fig. 3 The financial and economic cycles in the US 1970–2011. (Source: author, based on Matthias Drehmann, Claudio Borio and Kostas Tsatsaronis, 'Characterizing the Financial Cycle: don't lose the sight of the medium term!,' BIS Working Papers, no. 380 (Basel: Bank for International Settlements, 2012))

production. The input is immaterial: the intuitive knowledge of potential financial value and the creativity to turn it into tradable assets. Individual mortgages are difficult to sell at a profit. Why would bank B pay more for it than it is booked on the balance of bank A? And if A want to sell it for less, this is a signal for B that there is something wrong with it—there may be payback problems expected. But a new financial product that consists of parts of mortgages with different risk levels and maturity dates, assembled across different neighbourhoods, is a very different financial asset. Such a derivative has the promise of diversified risk—much lower than the risk associated with a single mortgage. Just like an investment fund or a stock exchange tracking fund are generally safer than investment in a single stock.

The second element of financial instability that Minsky detected, next to inherent growth of the financial sector, was instability, which he referred to as fragility. Minsky's explanation is based on the fact that financial values are largely subjective values. For example, the value of a share of a nonfinancial company: this reflects not only the current market value of a firm but also its expected future cash flow. And that is uncertain. It depends on the perception of traders and investors of general market developments, the opportunities of market expansion of the particular sector and the growth potential of the firm. But the stock value also depends on factors such as a potential take-over by another company, a possible merger with a profitable competitor, the pace of innovation by its competitors, and the likeliness of a profitable new product launch. Moreover, share prices include expectations about intangible factors, such as the company's reputation and status of its brand, the personality of the CEO and the potential successor of the CEO. The price of a share, as registered in the stock exchange, simply cannot have a one-to-one relationship with the real value of a company at any time.

The same holds for government bonds. The price of Greek bonds and their interest rates have shown a multitude of peaks and troughs since the euro crisis. But this does not reflect sudden increases or declines in the value and prospects of the Greek economy, with its labour force, capital stock, land and raw materials. After all, the Greek economy consists largely of the same companies, employees, resources and products during the turbulence of bond prices over time. The volatility of these prices and the interest rate of newly issued bonds is largely due to the optimistic or pessimistic expectations of investors about a wide variety of indicators—GDP growth in particular. During the euro crisis there was another instability factor for Greek bonds. That was the likeliness that Greece would leave the Eurozone and would go back to the Drachma. Hence, the value of government bonds is largely dependent on subjective judgments of traders and investors, just as the value of shares and other financial assets. A well-known illustration of this was when Mario Draghi, the president of the European Central Bank during the euro-crisis, firmly stated in July 2012 that he would do 'whatever it takes' to save the euro. Immediately following his speech, the value of the bonds of south-European countries shoot up.[5]

Shares and bonds are simple financial assets that have at least some relationship to the real economy of firms and countries. But derivatives and securities have much less to do with the reality of workers, resources and technology. Hence, an important lesson from Minsky is that such assets are even more fragile. But the bad news that Minsky delivered is not over yet. He also explained that nothing can be done about it when the financial sector is left by itself. When this is the case, we find ourselves in a state of 'money manager capitalism' according to Minsky. It is an accurate expression for what keeps the exchange sequence C of capitalism going. A stage of capitalism that Marx already foresaw when he used the term *bankocracy*, and which refers to the fact that the driving forces of our economy are no longer factories, land, services, workers, and material innovations such as vaccines or efficient electric cars, but the trade in financial assets by an increasing number of traders, speculators, and fund managers. Moreover, the widespread distribution of dubious financial assets throughout the financial sector results in systemic risk: the distribution of the same high-risk assets across the whole system. Hence, what before 2007 initially looked like risk spreading, appeared to be a widespread saturation of balance sheets with high-risk assets throughout the US, Europe and emerging markets. Chapter 4 will go deeper into the phenomenon of systemic risk, when the work of the economist Frank Knight will be discussed.

The FIRE-Sector

In order to better understand the role of the financial sector vis-à-vis the real economy, Minsky added it to standard economic models. Surprisingly, that had not been done yet and even today, the macroeconomic models used by institutions as the World Bank or national governments do not include the financial sector, or only in a limited sense. The reason for this omission is that in mainstream economic theory, this sector is considered merely as a means channelling money through the economy—like blood vessels transport blood through a body—and not as a sector that has any influence as such on the economy. But just like cardiovascular diseases are the primary cause of death in many countries, the financial sector is the key driver of economic crises. Minsky understood this. He distinguished between the real economy that produces goods and services on the one hand and the monetary economy of finance, insurance and real estate—the FIRE-sector—on the other hand.

The monetary economy provides credit to the real economy, whereas the real economy supplies savings to the monetary economy. The credit obtained needs to be paid back in future with interest. But there are more connections—directly and indirectly. Stocks and bonds are bought by households and firms but also by pension funds that need to pay-out a retirement income for households in the long run. With an economic model that distinguishes between the financial sector and the real economy, Minsky was able to demonstrate that money is more than a lubricant for the real economy and that credit is more than the fuel of economic growth. Minsky's so-called stock-flow model of the economy was able to show the negative role of household debt for the economy and the relationship between debt and capacity to pay-off debt. The FIRE-sector appears to be crucial in the role of debt for the economy. If such macroeconomic models had been developed by economic policy advisors and banking supervisors, the signals of unsustainable debt and systemic risk would probably have been picked up at an earlier stage, well before the crisis broke out.

Minsky's theory about the FIRE-sector and its growth and instability had alerted some economists to the emerging instability well before the bubble burst in 2008. There were indeed a few economists who, inspired by Minsky, were worried and did look at the dark side of the FIRE-sector: the trace of debts and the spread of risky securities it generated throughout the financial and real economy. For economists willing to look at the statistics, the bubbles growing in the FIRE-sector became apparent. Housing prices in the US at the time increased faster than could be expected on the basis of trends in building costs, the interest rate and population growth. This is shown in Fig. 4.

Moreover, the stock exchanges were breaking records since the new millennium, after a quick recovery from the internet-bubble, the dot.com crisis. In addition, commodity prices rose fast as well, from wheat to oil. Here, too, speculation appeared to be the driving force. This hit in particular the poor population in developing countries that were net food importers. They saw food prices rise not only because food was used for biofuel but also because staple food became the target of speculative trade on futures markets. A few economists, such as Robert Shiller, Steve Keen, Ann Pettifor, and Nouriel Roubini, pointed between 2004 and 2008 at the untenable bubbles. They

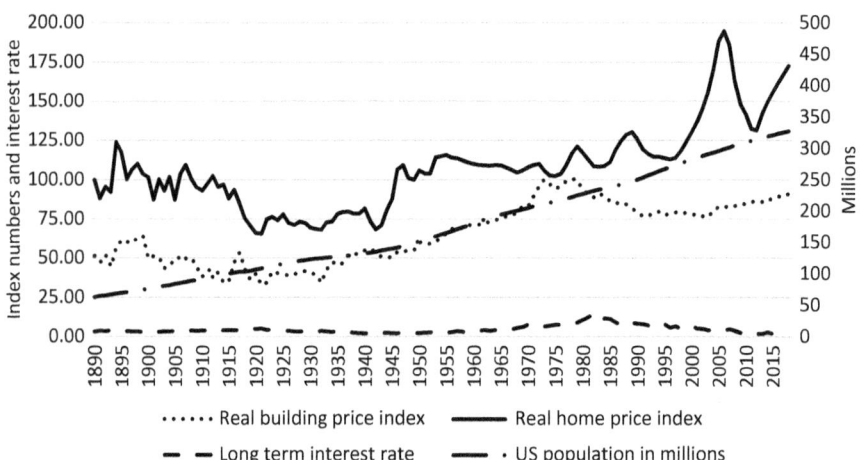

Fig. 4 Development of home prices, costs and population in the US 1890–2018. (Note: Left axis: index numbers for real building price index and real home price index; long term interest rate. Right axis: millions for US population. Source: author's calculations based on data provided by Robert Schiller, http://www.econ.yale.edu/~shiller/data.htm, accessed on June 18, 2020)

warned governments and supervisory agencies, but, as will be explained in the fourth chapter, nobody listened. The large majority of economists was still convinced that the financial sector itself does not create or destroy value but merely functions as a channel for getting money through the real economy. Despite the fact that there was an economist who had explained the entanglement of the financial and the real economy in a good number of academic publications in the 1970s and 1980s.

THE ECONOMIST

Hyman Minsky (1919 Chicago–1999 Rhinebeck)

Hyman Minsky grew up during the Great Depression and was fortunate enough to be able to go to university. He studied mathematics at the University of Chicago and economics at Harvard University. His family had migrated from Belarus, fleeing the chaos around the Russian revolution. His mother was active in the trade union movement, while his father was active in the socialist party in Chicago. Hence, Minsky was raised with socialist principles. The story goes that his parents had met at a gala celebrating the 100th birthday of Karl Marx. His choice for economics was influenced by a guest lecture given by the Polish economist Oskar Lange on the economic theory of socialism. During the Second World War, Minsky served in the American army in the UK, France and Germany. He married and had a son and a daughter. Before his tenure as professor of economics at Washington University in St. Louis, Missouri, he taught at various universities across the US. There, he was also associated with the Mark Twain bank which he considered his laboratory, testing out his ideas on financial market behaviour. After his retirement, he was appointed as distinguished scholar at the Levy Economics Institute (New York).

Minsky shared many ideas with Keynes and even wrote a book about him because he was dissatisfied with the mainstream interpretation of Keynes in the US. Minsky, like Keynes, wanted to understand what had caused the 1929 crisis. He rejected the mainstream theory of market equilibrium and shocks and suspected that the problem was caused not in the real economy but in financial markets. Like Keynes, he realized that the optimism in years of a booming market already carried the seeds of the next crisis. It is the optimism, he found, which turns investors more reckless over time, pushing up risk levels in the market. Until the bubble bursts. He referred to this as a Ponzi-scheme, named after an infamous financial manager in the US who lured investors into a fraudulous system in which old investors were paid out with the investments made by new investors.

But he went further than Keynes in his analysis of financial markets. He discovered a relationship between the growth of financial markets and their instability. The bigger, the more unstable. That is what he termed financial fragility and argued that financial markets move continuously between robust and fragile. This view invalidates the mainstream idea that financial markets are merely pipelines for the transport of money through the economy. That is precisely why he used a different metaphor: in his theory banks are the pumps that push more and more money into the pipelines. The more they pump, the higher their profits. This pump metaphor makes clear that someday the system will burst due to the accumulation of debt at the end of the pipeline. Indeed, Minsky saw private debt building up in three phases. In phase one, households and firms borrow amounts that they pay back without problems, including the interest rate. This spurs optimism leading banks to lend out more. This results in phase two in which borrowers are only able to pay the interest but not the loan itself. Hence, old loans are rolled over into new loans. This is possible as long as the value of the underlying assets increases. This was precisely the assumption behind subprime lending. But eventually, Minsky warned, phase three arrives, in which interest payments become difficult and the value of the collateral goes down, so that banks begin to lose money on their lending activities. This triggers the bursting of the pipeline—the market bubble—an event which Post Keynesian economists refer to as 'The Minsky Moment'.

When the 2008 crisis showed this moment again, economists, policy makers and even some financial traders became interested in the theory behind this concept. Therefore, two of his books were republished in that same year: his book on Keynes and his policy analysis and advise *Stabilizing an Unstable Economy*. Indeed, Minsky gave plenty of policy advise, but ministers of finance and regulators did not listen. Interestingly, in 1993 he published a paper in which he provided comments to Ben Bernanke, who more than a decade later would lead the Fed during the financial crisis.[6] Minsky commented that state support for failing banks plus tax credits for businesses to stimulate investment would not be very effective when the financial system is fragile. He would not have approved of the Fed's policy of pumping millions of dollars into banks without ensuring that these would benefit the real economy. The message throughout his work was that the only helpful policy is to reduce fragility and strengthen robustness of the financial sector.

Reading Minsky
Hyman Minsky, *Can 'It' Happen Again? Essays on Instability and Finance* (London/New York: Routledge, 2016 [1982]).

Reading About Minsky
Dimitri Papadimitriou and Randall Wray, *The Elgar Companion to Hyman Minsky* (Cheltenham: Edward Elgar, 2010).

Watching Minsky's Legacy
Boom Bust Boom, a documentary film about Minsky's legacy in lay-language, produced by the Minskian economist Theo Kocken and Monty Python actor Terry Jones, 2016.

PRACTISING MINSKY

Keeping the Growth of the FIRE-Sector in Check

A first sensible policy is to keep the growth of the financial sector, and in particular banks, in check. This requires an institutional framework that sets limits to growth, rather than micro-level regulation of banking behaviour. The institutional framework should address financialization: the continuous expansion of financial sector activities into the real economy. The Glass-Steagall-Act that had been in operation for 66 years was a successful institutional framework that made the financial sector more stable. As I have explained earlier, the banking lobby is too strong to put a similar law in place again. But there are other ways to increase the resilience of the FIRE sector. First, the prohibition for banks to trade assets for their own account. This prohibition is indeed in place in many countries now, but at the same time there are various risky activities in a non-supervised parallel banking sector referred to as shadow-banking. Hence, the regulation should be extended to and enforced in a wider circle than only to institutions with a banking licence.

Second, prevention of mergers and acquisitions of banks. An example of this is the 2015 law in the US that set an upper limit to the market share of banks in any lending market: mortgages, consumer credit or loans to small- and medium-sized businesses. This limit is a maximum of 10% market share. Such regulation prevents consolidation of the sector—the increase in the size of banks through mergers and acquisitions.

Third, the introduction of Central Bank Digital Currency (CBDC). Before internet banking, people kept part of their money in cash and used cash for payments in shops. Today, the share of cash holdings and cash transactions is much smaller. In Sweden, for example, only 10% of today's transactions are done with cash. Moreover, larger denominations (in particular the 500 euro bank note) are often used for illegal transactions in various criminal activities.[7] Today, for most day to day transactions and for almost all larger purchases, people use their bank accounts and digital transfers. As a consequence of the shift to digital money, banks have more money available to lend out, pushing up their leverage. With CBDC, people can store money and pay for purchases without need to deposit money on a bank account. This can be done just as easy as with a bank account and may be facilitated by a mobile phone App. A great advantage, similar to holding cash, is that when a commercial bank goes bankrupt one does not risk losing money. Moreover, the costly deposit guarantee system could be trimmed down. Finally, CBDC is not only a way to reduce the size of banks but also likely to reduce the instability of the banking sector by providing a safe haven and reducing transaction costs and interest rates for holders of digital cash. But more research and experiments need to be done before all advantages and disadvantages of digital cash will be understood. The Central Bank of Sweden is running an experiment with CBDC under the name of the e-Krona.[8] One potential disadvantage is that in case of a bank run people will shift on a massive scale from bank accounts to CBDC, which may trigger a series of bankruptcies. Of course, this is precisely one of the reasons to have CBDC, since it provides an incentive for commercial banks to behave less risky and to increase their buffers.

Lower Loan-to-Value Ratio

Various countries in the developed world allowed high loan-to-value ratios (ltv) for mortgages. In the Netherlands, this implied that buyers could borrow up to 110% of the market value of the house they bought. No savings were required, not even for the furniture and tv-set. In reaction to the housing crisis that followed the financial crisis, the Dutch government has reduced the maximum ltv gradually to 100%. But this still means that with the slightest decline in housing prices, mortgage debt is higher than the market value of the house and people are left with a net debt. Moreover, before the crisis interest-only mortgages were allowed and quite popular. Hence, until the end of the lending period, house owners did not pay back anything, and would pay back the loan with the sales of the house. Today, the government requires a repayment mortgage for at least 50% of the total amount of the mortgage.

Other countries have always considered such lenient lending policies as risky and have set a lower maximum ltv and lower shares of interest-only mortgages or they don't allow them at all. In the US, the average ltv is 75%, while the government-supported mortgage insurance agencies Fannie Mae and Freddie Mac set a maximum of 80%.[9] In the UK the maximum ltv is 90%, while in Germany it is 80%. If that ratio would have been the norm in the Netherlands, on average no mortgages would have been under water, because the average decline in house prices after the crisis was 20%. An additional advantage of a lower ltv is that the monthly expenditures are lower too, which provides some flexibility in household expenditures during bad times.

NOTES

1. https://www.fhfa.gov/SupervisionRegulation/FannieMaeandFreddieMac. Accessed on July 15, 2020.
2. Gary Dymski, Jesus Hernandez, and Lisa Mohanty, "Race, Gender, Power and the US Subprime Mortgage and Foreclosure Crisis: A Meso Analysis," *Feminist Economics* 19, 3 (2013): 124–152.
3. Deutsche Bank Research, *EU Monitor Financial Markets*, p. 5: https://www.dbresearch.com/PROD/RPS_EN-PROD/PROD0000000000443314/Large_or_small%3F_How_to_measure_bank_size.pdf. Accessed on July 15, 2020.
4. https://www.mx.com/moneysummit/biggest-banks-by-asset-size-united-states. Accessed on 15 July 2020.
5. https://www.theatlas.com/charts/B1_DhlILW. Accessed on September 19, 2019.

6. Hyman Minsky, "Comment on Ben Bernanke, 'Credit in the Macroeconomy'," *Hyman P. Minsky Archive*, Paper 361. http://digitalcommons.bard.edu/hm_archive/361. Accessed June 19, 2020.
7. Laure Lalouette and Henk Esselink, "Trends and developments in the use of euro cash over the past ten years" (Frankfurt: ECB Economic Bulletin, issue 6, 2018). https://www.ecb.europa.eu/pub/pdf/ecbu/eb201806.en.pdf?f0f55f1b4f767b3ac0030de809c181c3. Accessed on September 14, 2019.
8. "The Riksbank's e-krona project – Report 2" (Stockholm: Sveriges Riksbank, October 2018). https://www.riksbank.se/globalassets/media/rapporter/e-krona/2018/the-riksbanks-e-krona-project-report-2.pdf. Accessed on July 15, 2020.
9. Statista, "Average loan to value ratio in the United States, 2019, by state," https://www.statista.com/statistics/460677/average-ltv-in-the-usa-by-state/. Accessed on November 13, 2019.

Bibliography

Dymski, Gary, Jesus Hernandez, and Lisa Mohanty. "Race, Gender, Power and the US Subprime Mortgage and Foreclosure Crisis: A Meso Analysis." *Feminist Economics* 19, 3 (2013): 124–152.

Deutsche Bank Research. "*EU Monitor Financial Markets*." https://www.dbresearch.com/PROD/RPS_EN-PROD/PROD0000000000443314/Large_or_small%3F_How_to_measure_bank_size.pdf. Accessed on July 15, 2020.

Minsky, Hyman. 'Comment on Ben Bernanke, "Credit in the Macroeconomy," *Hyman P. Minsky Archive*, Paper 361, 1993. http://digitalcommons.bard.edu/hm_archive/361. Accessed on June 19, 2020.

Lalouette, Laure, and Henk Esselink. "Trends and developments in the use of euro cash over the past ten years." Frankfurt: ECB Economic Bulletin, issue 6, 2018. https://www.ecb.europa.eu/pub/pdf/ecbu/eb201806.en.pdf?f0f55f1b4f767b3ac0030de809c181c3. Accessed on September 24, 2019.

Sveriges Riksbank. "The Riksbank's e-krona project – Report 2." Stockholm: Sveriges Riksbank, October 2018. https://www.riksbank.se/globalassets/media/rapporter/e-krona/2018/the-riksbanks-e-krona-project-report-2.pdf. Accessed on July 15, 2020.

Chapter 3: John Maynard Keynes on Debt and Demand

THE PROBLEM

The macroeconomic causes of a financial crisis reflect a mutual reinforcement of two processes. This dynamic starts with a steady increase of asset values far beyond their real values. This increase of market value hides an underlying increase in private debt—of households and firms to which Minsky referred. Then follows the next process in which debts begin to constrain the real economy, resulting in contractions of various nonfinancial markets and subsequent disadvantages for nonfinancial firms and households. Keynes focused on the macroeconomic relationships between financial sector instability, debt and aggregate demand.

Bubbles

In the real economy, the relationship between price and value of goods and services is generally clear. The prices of fruit and holidays don't fluctuate much and when they do it is often very clear why. A price hike in kiwi's may be explained by a bad harvest in New Zealand while a sudden price rise of a safari may be the result of a scarcity of hotel rooms due to their popularity.

In the FIRE-sector, price hikes are generally less attributable to input costs or relative scarcity, as Minsky already explained. And that is why the market value of financial assets tends to be more volatile and why financial markets tend to suffer from bubbles. This is not only the case for pure financial assets such as shares or MBS or government bonds. It is also true for other assets in the FIRE-sector, such as houses. But the more abstract the asset, the weaker the relationship between price and value and hence, the higher the risk of bubbles. The stock exchange is a financial market that also can be overvalued as a whole—not just for a few companies. This is shown in Fig. 1 for the share prices of the S&P-500 in New York from its start in 1871 up to 2020. The

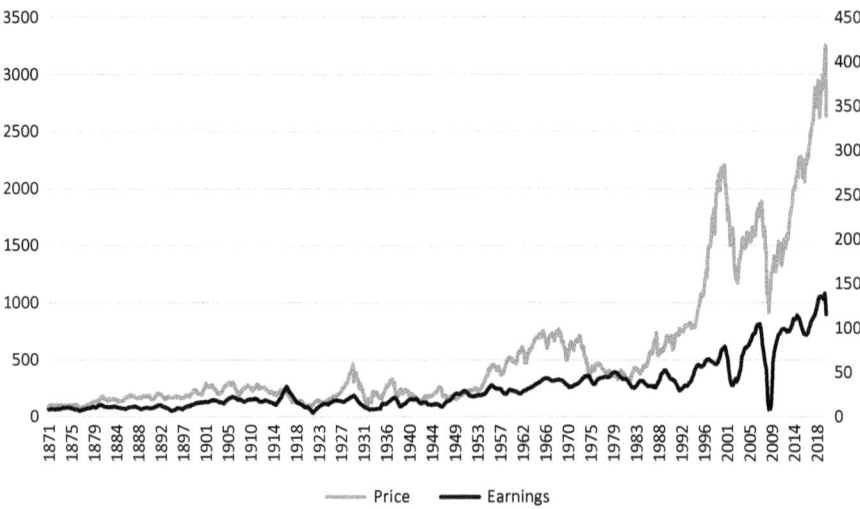

Fig. 1 Development of S&P-500 NYSE stock prices and earnings 1871–2015. (Source: author's calculations based on data provided by Robert Schiller, http://www.econ.yale.edu/~shiller/data.htm Accessed on June 18, 2020. Note: Left axis: real price. Right axis: real earnings)

light shaded line shows the real share prices, while the dark shaded line, which is much lower and fluctuates much less, reflects the earnings of the same shares. The diagram clearly shows four bubbles and their respective bursts: 1929, 1970s (oil crises), 2001 (the dot.com crisis) and 2008. But it also shows that since recovery started in 2011 in the US, prices have been growing fast again until the COVID-19 crisis.

Overvalued share prices have various origins, most of them psychological as Robert Schiller, who collected the data for the diagram, argues. But the bubble is also inflated as a consequence of the low interest rate policy of central banks. An unintended side effect of that monetary policy is that the interest earned on savings is negligible. And when the interest rate of government bonds is also low—which indeed has been the case for a long period of time now, money seeks higher returns on the stock exchange. Increased supply of portfolio investments on various stock exchanges increases share prices even further. Not only due to decisions made by the money managers referred to by Minsky, but also due to choices of households who ask themselves: "where could I put my money to see some returns?".

Unsustainable Private Debt

The price increases in the FIRE-sector not only generate inflated asset values on the balance sheets of nonfinancial firms and households. They are also often funded through debt. Banks were the champions of such debt-funding. Their holdings of financial assets such as derivatives were financed through short-term capital market trades, resulting in debt obligations with other banks. In the meantime, households funded their homes with mortgages over 100% of the market value of their houses—a practice that was allowed in the Netherlands until recently. This also implies a high debt-to-income ratio, making households vulnerable to pay-back risks due to unemployment, divorce or disability.[1]

The problem, however, also has a macroeconomic dimension. The debt-financed bubbles result in a mounting debt burden for the economy as a whole. This fuels economic growth based on fragile grounds: GDP-growth consists of an increasing part of investments based on unsustainable debts as well as consumer expenditures based on consumer loans. What is even more disturbing is a shift from investment in the real economy to investment in financial assets, which do not provide any expansion or technological advancement for manufacturing and employment. In the UK, this has resulted in the deindustrialization of publicly listed companies.[2] The lower the interest rate and the more favourable fiscal benefits for debt financing, the more loans are taken by households: from mortgages to credit card debt and from student loans to car loans. According to the IMF, the world average of private debt was 225% of global GDP and much higher for high-income economies (266%) than for low-income countries (77%).[3] Moreover, the IMF data show that this level of debt is 10% higher than at its previous peak in 2009. Figure 2 shows the global debt burden in 2017 for selected countries. The diagram makes clear that various developed countries have very high debt rates, in particular Ireland, Portugal and the Netherlands. When we look at household debt only, the Netherlands stands out with household debt at 105% of GDP. The majority of this debt consists of mortgages: total mortgage debt of Dutch households amounted to 726 billion euro in 2018.[4]

In the UK too, household debt is very high, namely 86% of GDP, second to the Netherlands. Like the Netherlands, this is related to mortgages. And these have increased with house prices over the past decades. Figure 3 shows a steady monthly increase of average house prices in the UK (lower line) and in London (upper line). The house prices in London are the highest for all regions in the UK, with an average house price of more than 470,000 pounds in 2019. The overheated housing market of London is not only clearly visible from the steep increase in the line but also from the small (15%) and short dip (one and a half years) during the financial crisis. For the rest of the UK it took eight years before house prices were back at the pre-crisis level of 2007.

From Private to Public Debt

In the US, the debt problem was quickly recognized as constraining economic recovery. Household debt resulted in lower consumer demand and the losses and debts of commercial banks led to a squeeze in credit for businesses. The Fed decided to engage in unconventional monetary policy. Not by further

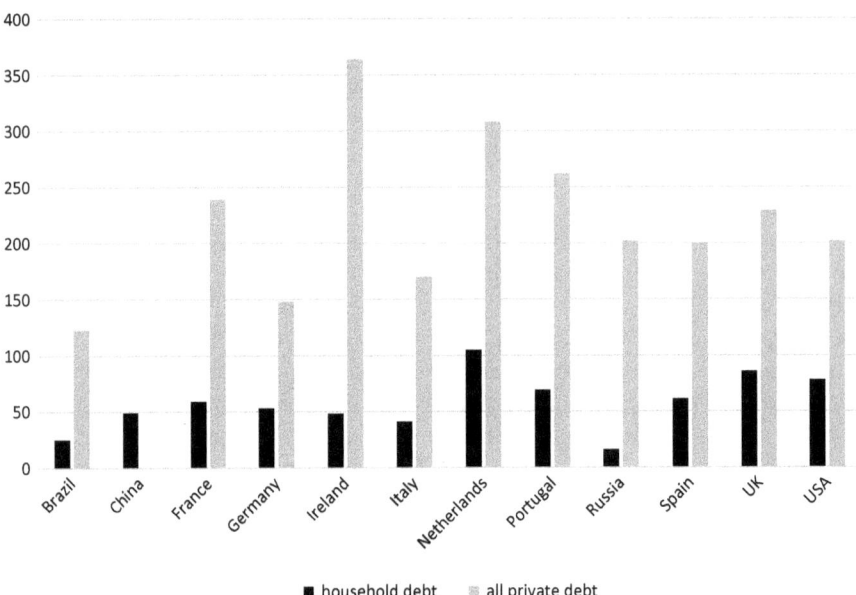

Fig. 2 Private debt as percentage of GDP, 2017. (Source: Calculated by author based on IMF, "New Data on Debt", 2 January 2019, https://blogs-imf-org.eur.idm.oclc.org/2019/01/02/new-data-on-global-debt/ Accessed on June 19, 2020)

lowering interest rates, which were already very low, but by quantitative easing (QE) of the money supply. This policy consisted of buying financial assets from banks, such as MBS and other securities, in exchange for dollars. This provided liquidity to banks, that they, in turn, could lend out to households and firms to stimulate economic demand. This policy can be regarded as a "no cost" alternative to fiscal policy. Because fiscal stimulation policy implies higher government debt and hence a public debt burden that weighs on future government budgets. QE, instead, brings money into the economy, through commercial banks, in exchange for toxic financial assets that are moved to the balance sheet of the Central Bank and out of economic circulation. The Fed can simply write-off these assets over time without any need to "pay" for this, because the Central Bank has the authority to create and destroy money "out of nothing". The QE-program of the Fed has pumped 3.5 trillion dollar in the economy between 2008 and 2015 alone, which has helped commercial banks to clean up their balance sheets and to start providing credit again.[5] Later, the Fed started buying US government bonds, helping the government to finance its deficit and the market to keep the interest rate relatively low. Thanks to this QE-policy, the US economy recovered from the crisis already in 2009 and has shown an average GDP growth rate of at least 2% per year since then.[6] But the massive scale and prolonged period of QE have also contributed to asset bubbles.

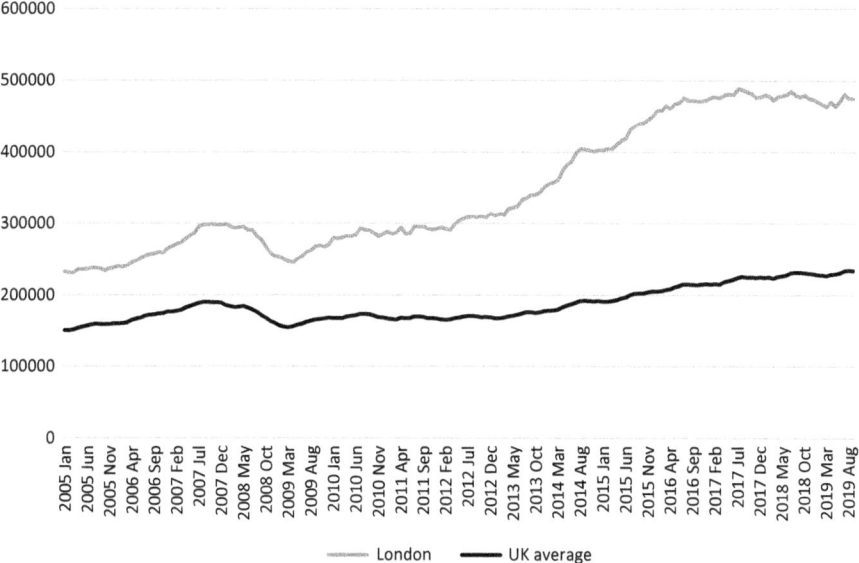

Fig. 3 Average house prices in the UK and London 2005–2019. (Source: Calculated by author based on data from UK House Price Index, Office for National Statistics, https://www.ons.gov.uk/economy/inflationandpriceindices/bulletins/housepriceindex/september2019 Accessed on June 19, 2020)

In the UK, the same unorthodox policy was followed, with the same effect, since 2016. Since then, the Bank of England has bought in particular government bonds from banks and other financial institutions such as pension funds, worth over 400 billion pounds. An assessment of QE policies by the Bank of England indicates that these policies have probably contributed to 1% increase in GDP in the various countries that have implemented these policies, but more at the beginning than at later stages of the QE-operations.[7] In the UK, as in the US, economic recovery started in 2009, but has remained only around 1% per year since. In the European Monetary Union, the ECB has hesitated for a long-time before it adopted the same policy in 2015. That was after several years of limited and unstable recovery of the EU and the unfolding of the euro crisis. Some governments in the Eurozone did not continue fiscal stimulation of their economies long enough for their economies to recover. Recovery in the Eurozone started in 2010 but in 2012 GDP growth fell below zero, while it recovered in 2013 and has been around 2% since 2014.[8] The ECB QE policy consisted largely of government bonds held by banks (in particular banks based in northern European countries such as Deutsche Bank), and importantly, government bonds of southern European countries (such as Greece).

Even though the QE-policy by the EU is massive, its effect on the eurozone economy has been limited, because commercial banks have been hesitant to lend out to households and businesses. They increasingly earn their incomes from charging user fees for their banking services and from—again—financial trading and less from the spreads of lending. Hence, the QE liquidity that the ECB is providing does not necessarily end up in credit, and hence, in consumer expenditure and business investment. Moreover, there is another weakness of the QE policy of ECB and that is linked to the euro crisis.

Whereas in the US, the Central Bank bought non-transparent securities from banks, the European Central Bank bought fully transparent government bonds. This means that the banks—the most important of them based in Germany and France—had bought Greek, Spanish, Portuguese and Italian bonds in full knowledge of what they bought. They did so because the interest rates on these bonds were high. Hence, they took the risk knowingly that the southern European states may fail to pay back their debt. But they reckoned that the ECB would not let any eurozone country down. And they were right. The ECB helped them getting rid of the risky bonds, which in a way was again a too-big-to-fail situation. Now, the banks were not saved by national governments but by the European Central Bank, which in fact bailed out the northern European banks while keeping pressure on southern European governments to pay back their debts, which are now in the hands of the ECB. So, a risky debt burden in the hands of banks now turned into public debt on the balance sheet of the ECB.

Households and Businesses on Hold

Also, in other European countries, the crisis was prolonged due to a mix of too limited fiscal stimulation policy, commercial banks' hesitance to provide credit, and high household debt. Since the recovery, unemployment rates have come down but are still high in various member states. In 2018, three countries had unemployment rates above 10%: Italy (10.6%), Spain (15.3%) and Greece (19.3%), while in France, the country of the yellow vests protests, the unemployment rate was 9%.[9] Another indicator of slow recovery in Europe is the high share of households with problematic debt. In the Netherlands, one in five households has problematic debts, which means that they are unable to pay them back.[10] In the UK, there are 1.6 million households in extreme problem debt according to the Centre for Responsible Credit, and 3.2 million households which pay more than a quarter of their income on consumer debt payments.[11] In fact, households in the UK and the Netherlands have the same high debt burdens as households in the PIGS-countries, both in 2007/2008 and in 2014/2015, according to the same report.

Economic recovery, hence, has not been robust in the European Union. One of the main reasons for this is that the members of the Eurozone have agreed in the Maastricht Treaty on the conditions for introducing the euro, that government deficits should not exceed 3% of GDP while government debt should not exceed 60% of GDP. However, during a crisis, this agreement prevents national governments to stimulate their economies with increased government expenditures when necessary. The US and UK were free of such binding constraints, so that they were able to stimulate their economies much better through fiscal expansion right after the crisis. Moreover, the state support to save banks required an enormous increase in government expenditure in Europe, which was so much that that support alone already took all the budgetary space available within the Maastricht criteria. Hence, governments were not allowed to borrow more to stimulate their economies with fiscal support. Instead, governments in continental Europe soon embarked on austerity measures in order to remain within the restrictive Maastricht criteria of public debt. This has particularly affected public expenditures on education and health, affecting predominantly the poorest households.

The Insight

The lesson to be drawn from the debt burdens before and after the crisis is not very different from the lesson that John Maynard Keynes learnt from the 1929 crisis. His key insight was not only about the origin of the crisis—a market bubble—but also about the recovery from it.

Bubbles

Financial bubbles are not new and have occurred well before the 1929 crash. For example, in the trade of tulip bulbs in the Netherlands in 1637. Traders from various countries exchanged bulbs as if they were bars of gold, hoping that very special breeds of tulips would make them a fortune—until some traders realized that the market prices were absurd and moved their attention to other assets.

Neoclassical economic theory assumes that prices reflect underlying asset values and that a sudden drop in market prices simply implies that new information is available about the true value of the assets traded. But Keynes found this assumption highly unrealistic. Where would this information come from and why so suddenly? And why then do prices decline often below the real value of an asset? Such price movements, Keynes thought, have an important psychological dimension. Thereby, he laid the foundation for the field of behavioural finance. His analysis of 1929 resulted in the detection of two mechanisms behind the crash. The first one is speculation, which he explained with the term animal spirits, or unfounded optimism. Investment in the real economy, whether in factories or houses, involves much calculated reasoning: cost accounting, consumer demand, wages and so on. But investment in financial assets depend for a large part on psychological factors, such as trust and expectations, or, to state it more bluntly, the primary motivations of fear and greed. Keynes was familiar with these motivations because he was a speculator himself. He knew like no other that investment behaviour is driven by optimism, hope, envy and stubbornness. Animal spirits indeed—rather than rational calculation and careful deliberation.

The second mechanism behind financial bubbles and bursts that Keynes discovered was herd behaviour. That is now a well-known concept in social psychology. Keynes saw that optimism in financial markets is contagious in a self-reinforcing dynamic of beliefs, information shared on the media, and actual behaviour of investors and traders. They simply tend to follow the buying and selling behaviour of others, assuming that they, perhaps, know more. Today, herd behaviour is amplified by powerful computers and fast internet connections, as well as the ease of trading, through index trackers and smartphones. As a consequence, in booming periods, financial markets attract more and more investors who all are willing to invest larger amounts of money in order not to lose out on opportunities to make good profits. In particular, when certain assets seem to promise high returns at low risk—from tulip bulbs in the seventeenth century to derivatives in the years leading up to 2007. But this herd behaviour is at the same time the source of instability on financial markets, Keynes found out. It amplifies the volatility of the boom and bust cycle. And this is the reason why asset prices decline below their real value during a market crash and why trade comes to a sudden standstill: it reflects pure panic in the herd of traders.

Keynes also found out how an economy can recover from serious crises. The connection between his insights about bubbles and economic recovery is debt. Because, as Minsky would later explore more deeply, bubbles are partially financed through debt rather than with savings or cash. Keynes has provided modern economics with three insights about economic recovery: debt burdens, purchasing power and the multiplier effect. They all consider the macroeconomic level, whereas his insight about bubbles concerned the micro economic level. The clear distinction between microeconomics and macroeconomics started with Keynes.

Debt Burdens

The first lesson from Keynes arises from a mismatch between saving (S) and investment (I). Classical economics held that they are always equal (S = I) because the market interest rate ensures that there is no excess saving or investment in the market: all savings are invested at the going interest rate. But the 1929 crisis demonstrated that this assumption was wrong. There was more invested than there were savings available. An increasing share of financial investment appeared to be financed by credit—hence, with debt. Keynes argued that savings do not depend on the market rate of interest—at least not for a significant part. That is because households and businesses save for sound economic reasons, and not so much in reaction to the interest rate as a financial incentive. They keep money aside for a rainy day or to bridge a time period between expenditures and earnings. Keynes explained that households have only two options for their income: spend or save. Obviously, the first has always priority in a market economy: it ensures consumption.

Keynes' insight that savings is the residual after consumption, also helps to explain why poor people save little and rich people save substantial amounts. This is not, he argued, because the rich are more rational but because the poor need all of their income for their daily livelihood. Due to this mechanism, when the economy is booming and hence household incomes grow quickly, more savings will be available for investment and at the same time credit will be available due to the optimistic expectations in a booming economy. And the higher one's income and savings, the higher one's credit rating and the more banks are willing to lend out. This induces an upward spiral of asset prices, volumes traded and debt. And when the bubble bursts, we see prices and volumes decline, but not debt. Hence, the dynamic is not symmetrical. Debt remains. Moreover, when asset values fall below the value of accumulated debt, the debt burden is unsustainable and will not be paid back on time—not even the interest rate, when the Minsky Moment is reached. Keynes' focus on debt rather than on interest rates is even more important today with a much larger FIRE-sector than in the 1920s and 1930s.

Purchasing Power

Keynes' second insight for economic recovery was also a deviation from neo-classical theory. He recognized that the enormous unemployment in the 1930s was not caused by unwillingness to work for the going wage rate. To the contrary—millions of impoverished unemployed men and whole families travelled around the US in search for a job, however dirty and badly paid. They were desperate and willing to work as day-labour for meagre wages. But the labour market does not respond to low wage offers during a recession. Keynes discovered that this is because demand for labour is *derived demand*: it is dependent upon the demand for consumer goods. When consumer demand is low, production will be below full capacity and some labour (and capital) will remain idle. This insight led Keynes to introduce the concept of *effective demand*. This is the level of demand for goods and services in an economy that is equal to supply. It reflects an equilibrium that is not necessarily at full capacity, where all labour supplied is being hired. This insight is reflected in the standard macro-economic equation:

$$Y = C + I + G + EX - IM$$

In other words, national income (Y) is determined by the sum of consumption (C), investment (I), government expenditures (G) and net exports (EX - IM). When purchasing power is low, and producer's confidence in the economy is low, and demand from abroad is limited, demand for labour will be limited too. Even if there are plenty of unemployed workers who are willing to work at, or even below, below the market wage rate.

The policy implication of a situation of low effective demand is that only one variable could make a difference, in Keynes' view: government expenditures

(G). By increasing public expenditures, the government can lead economic recovery and hence an increase in national income (Y). More generally, Keynes argued that the government should stimulate economic growth by increasing its expenditures during a recession. Similarly, during a boom, the government could reduce its expenditures (and thereby reduce the risk of inflation), with declines in public expenditures. Such fiscal policy implies an increasing public deficit and public debt during a recession, and a budget surplus and reduction of public debt when economies are booming. This is referred to as countercyclical fiscal policy. An additional advantage of countercyclical policy is that during a boom, government revenue will increase automatically due to higher tax revenues, while welfare expenditures will automatically decline because there is less need for income support for the unemployed. Hence, in good times, government receives the additional income that it had spent in bad times, so it is able to pay back the debt it had incurred during the last recession.

After the 2008 crisis, the governments of the US and UK have immediately applied Keynes' recipe and saw their economies recover relatively quickly. But in the eurozone the Maastricht criteria constrained the possibilities of countercyclical fiscal policy. As a consequence, recovery was slow and haphazard, with various European countries experiencing a double dip. If the ECB had started its quantitative easing policy six years earlier and if it had channelled its funds not only through commercial banks but also through the European Investment Bank (EIB), effective demand could have driven the recovery effectively. If ECB had bought EIB bonds, the public investment bank could have used the funds to invest in labour-intensive projects in the real economy. And it could have invested too in a new economic infrastructure for the twenty-first century, including renewable energy, sustainable agriculture and improved ICT. If Keynes had been alive today, he would probably have qualified the Maastricht criteria as unnecessarily harmful.

The Multiplier Effect

The third lesson about economic recovery is the multiplier effect. This relates to the increase in public expenditures, as discussed above. Keynes demonstrated that there is not only a direct effect of an increase in G on effective demand but also various indirect effects. These run through the other demand variables in the macroeconomic equation. A first indirect effect is through employment created through G, which will generate more income for households, which will be spent, at least in part, on consumer goods (C). These will induce more production (with a time-lag for the depletion of stocks), with investments (I) and again more employment, with a positive effect on consumption (C), and so on. The total effect on demand will therefore be two to even five times as big as the initial increase in public expenditures, Keynes argued. The same process allows for higher tax revenue from increases in labour income, profit income, and value added exchanged, which will make it relatively easy for the Minister of Finance to pay back the increased government debt. The only condition for this is not economic but political: the government should not give in to demands from society and lobby clubs to spend all the additional revenue in good times but use it to reduce government debt as well, although the timing of this may be flexible and depending on the strength of economic recovery and needs of a sustainable economy. For example, the zero-interest rate in the eurozone since the crisis makes government borrowing virtually free, which would make the necessary energy transition relatively cheap.

THE ECONOMIST

John Maynard Keynes (1883 Cambridge–1946 Tilton)

Keynes was born in a privileged family. His father, John Neville Keynes, was lecturer of economics at the University of Cambridge, where he himself would later be appointed as professor. His mother even was, for a short period, mayor of the same university town. John Maynard Keynes was a tall man with a wide interest beyond economics. At the age of 42, he married the Russian ballerina Lydia Lopokova. He was member of the famous Bloomsbury group of artists and intellectuals in London, where nobody had any problem with his somewhat unusual lifestyle.[12] He functioned as the chair of the Bank of England, speculated on financial markets, and was the founder of the World Bank and IMF right after the Second World War. Keynes was also a strong supporter of women's rights, for example in his book *The end of laissez-faire*. He was well read and dedicated himself to a wide variety of activities, from explaining colour blindness to saving a theatre.

It is therefore no surprise that also his economic thinking went against the flow of his days. "Economics is a moral science", he wrote in the preface to his influential book, *The General Theory of Employment, Interest, and Money*, which appeared in 1936. He pointed out that economics deals with people, wealth, poverty and progress and all these issues are discussed in different theories with different policy implications, working out differently for different social groups. Keynes argued that economics is never morally neutral—as if it would be possible to have one single objective analysis of economic issues, leading to an undisputed single policy option. Against the common view, Keynes argued that economics cannot be reduced to optimization problems. No wonder that it was Keynes who joked that if you put two economists in a room, you will get three different views. Indeed, he sharply criticized mainstream economics— just like Joan Robinson would do a few decades later. In the middle of a theoretical argument, he would write: "It may well be that the classical theory represents the way in which we should like our economy to behave. But to assume that it actually does so is to assume our difficulties away."[13]

The General Theory emerged from his analysis of the 1929 crisis and lack of recovery until the Second World War. In this book, Keynes introduced whole new concepts in economics, such as uncertainty, involuntary unemployment, effective demand, the multiplier effect and, of course, animal spirits and herd behaviour. The key message for policy makers was to ensure sufficient effective demand in the economy so that high rates of unemployment can be prevented. This advice was taken at heart by the Central Bank in the US where low unemployment ended up as one of the Fed's policy objectives. But elsewhere, keeping inflation low was often the only objective. He travelled to the US twice and met President Roosevelt and had, according to his biographer, an influence on the New Deal policy. Keynes saw the economy in a different way than most of his contemporaries, just like he viewed almost everything in his own way. He was an unconventional man and could be both charming and cheeky but was widely respected. He died of a heart attack at the age of 63. Through all his work as an economic adviser, he warned the world to be careful with economic ideas, because they may be very influential. As if he knew that his own theory would experience a remarkable revival 65 years after his death. As his biographer, Lord Skidelsky, phrased it in the title of his 2009 book: *Keynes, the Return of the Master*.

Reading Keynes
John Maynard Keynes, *The General Theory of Employment, Interest, and Money* (Cambridge: Palgrave Macmillan, 2018).

Reading About Keynes
Robert Skidelsky, *Keynes: The Return of the Master* (London: Allen Lane, 2009).

Practising Keynes

Stimulus Packages During Recessions

Keynes' policy proposal to help economies out of recession through increased government expenditures has become known as stimulus packages. As we have seen, these were implemented right after the financial crisis but were stopped too early out of fear of unsustainable public debt. And in the eurozone due to the tight Maastricht criteria for public finances. Fortunately, the COVID-19 crisis shows a different EU-response. First, European governments have each supported their economies during the crisis with huge subsidies to firms, in particular wage subsidies in order to prevent a high rise in unemployment rates. Second, EU-member states have agreed on a joint stimulus fund, to help in particular the weaker economies of the eurozone—including Italy, which was severely hit by COVID-19. The fund consists of 750 billion euro—half grants, half loans. Keynes would have argued for grants only, but the strong opposition from "the frugal four" (the Netherlands, Austria, Denmark and Sweden, with Finland joining later) resulted in a higher loan share, adding to the already high debt burden in the southern member states.[14]

This financial stimulus package is funded through a loan by the European Commission—a joint loan, backed by the strong economies of the eurozone, so that the interest rate will be low. In practice, this form of funding implies a kind of Eurobonds, even though that term is taboo in Brussels. And there are more advantages, in the line of Keynes' theory. First, the stimulus package will regenerate jobs, which will help to recover consumer demand and therefore GDP. The multiplier effect will help to spur economic recovery throughout the EU. Second, economic recovery in the EU will help EU-exports, because the large majority of these are within the EU. This will be particularly useful for net-exporting member states such as Germany and the Netherlands—the countries that are likely to be among the strongest contributors to the stimulus fund. Third, the unprecedented joint fund will help the EU to stand stronger as an economic community in a world in which the international role of the US declines and that of China is rising. Fourth, the stimulus package can be aligned with the EU's proposal for a Green Deal. Spending part of the fund on green investments will strike two birds with one stone. Examples are employment-generating investments in the European railway network, energy transition and the reconstruction and building of energy-neutral housing. Finally, with the prospect of continuing low interest rates (and low inflation rates) in the EU, borrowing for economic stimulus is a very low-cost economic policy, even if all money would be allocated through grants.

Debt Jubilee

The bible already mentions debt forgiveness. For small loans after every seven years and for agricultural land every fifty years (after 7 × 7 years). Today, the debt jubilee is reflected in bankruptcy laws for firms and individuals, and in (partial) debt cancellation in crisis situations for businesses, households and even whole countries. We have seen examples of partial debt forgiveness for countries during the 1980s' Latin American debt crisis, which started when Mexico announced that it could no longer pay back its debt. Most of the debts of Mexico and other Latin American countries where not cancelled, however, but paid back with new loans on favourable terms, with only a small percentage of debt being forgiven. An earlier case in point was Germany when it was defeated in the Second World War. The country was forced to pay reparations, but soon the neighbouring countries realized that this kept the German economy in a long recession and that it might—as it did in the 1930s—lead to political instability. Therefore, in 1953, the former allied forces decided to cancel 50% of the debt of the German government and German firms. In addition, the repayment of the other half was made dependent on Germany's export earnings. In this way, it was in the interest of the creditors to import goods from Germany. The policy change from revenge to forgiveness was the main driving force behind the *Wirtschaftswunder* that turned Germany in a few decades into the strongest economy of continental Europe.

In general, capitalist societies are strongly against debt jubilees. The main argument is that debtors have willingly taken the risk and should be kept responsible for paying back. This is a backward-looking argument. A forward-looking argument against debt forgiveness is that potential lenders will become hesitant to provide new loans, because they may not get their money back if debt cancellation becomes the new norm. Both these arguments are narrow, excluding morality, context and a long-term economic perspective. The international jubilee campaign (www.jubileedebt.org.uk) instead, argues for debt cancellation for developing countries that suffer under high public debt often entered into by nondemocratic governments. The jubilee campaign also refers to Europe, and the lack of any debt forgiveness for Greece for example, and it makes a plea for a relaxation of the Maastricht criteria, so that eurozone countries can stimulate their economies á la Keynes in times of deep recessions.

Interestingly, there are quite some differences in bankruptcy laws between countries. In the US, for example, it is relatively easy to make a new start after a financial breakdown of a business, and one can walk away from mortgage debt by handing in the home key at the bank. In Europe this is much harder. Even when a house has been financed with mortgage insurance, the loan provider insists on full repayment, also when the mortgage is under water, owners have become unemployed, divorced or their business has gone bankrupt. This is an interesting paradox: even though the United States' economy is considered to be the most capitalist economy of the world, its policies around financial mishap are closer to the biblical jubilee than that of many European welfare states. This example, and the post-war example of Germany, suggests that a more lenient debt policy is not only more human but can be economically wise as well.

Notes

1. Luis Jácome and Srobona Mitra, "LTV and DTI Limits – Going Granular," IMF Working Paper 15/154, 2015.
2. Daniele Tori and Özlem Onaran, "The Effects of Financialization on Investment: Evidence from Firm-Level Data for the UK," *Cambridge Journal of Economics* 42, 5 (2018): 1393–1416.
3. IMF, "New Data on Global Debt", https://blogs.imf.org/2019/01/02/new-data-on-global-debt/ Accessed on November 18, 2019.
4. https://opendata.cbs.nl/statline/#/CBS/nl/dataset/83834NED/table?ts=1574079777029.
5. https://www.cnbc.com/2017/11/24/the-fed-launched-qe-nine-years-ago%2D%2Dthese-four-charts-show-its-impact.html.
6. Andrew Haldane, Matt Roberts-Sklar, Tomasz Wieladek, and Chris Young, "QE: The Story so far", Staff Working Paper 624 (London: Bank of England, October 2016).
7. Haldane et al., "QE".
8. https://data.worldbank.org/indicator/NY.GDP.MKTP.KD.ZG?end=2018&locations=EU&start=2009. Accessed on July 15, 2020.
9. Eurostat. https://ec.europa.eu/eurostat/statistics-explained/index.php/Unemployment_statistics. Accessed 15-07-2020.

10. Divosa, "Armoede en schulden in Nederland" (Utrecht: Divosa, 2018), https://www.divosa.nl/pdf/%2D%2D_%2D%2Darmoede-en-schulden-nederland/pagina.pdf Accessed on November 19, 2019.
11. CfRC, "Britain in the Red – Why we need Action to Help Over-Indebted Households" (London: Trades Union Congress, 2016), https://www.responsible-credit.org.uk/britain-red-action-reduce-debt-burden/ Accessed on November 19, 2019.
12. Robert Skidelsky, *John Maynard Keynes 1883–1946: Economist, Philosopher, Statesman* (London: Penguin, 2005).
13. Keynes, John Maynard, *The General Theory of Employment, Interest and Money* (New York: Macmillan, 1936), p. 34.
14. The opposition was led by Dutch prime minister Mark Rutte, who used the misplaced metaphor of 'keeping one's household accounts in order' in his demands for structural reforms (such as a higher pension age) in the southern EU-member states. The rest of the EU, including Germany and France, criticized him for this. And rightly so.

Bibliography

CfRC. "Britain in the Red – Why we need Action to Help Over-Indebted Households." London: Trades Union Congress, 2016. https://www.responsible-credit.org.uk/britain-red-action-reduce-debt-burden/. Accessed on November 19, 2019.

Divosa. "Armoede en schulden in Nederland." Utrecht: Divosa, 2018. https://www.divosa.nl/pdf/%2D%2D_%2D%2Darmoede-en-schulden-nederland/pagina.pdf. Accessed on November 19, 2019.

Haldane, Andrew, Matt Roberts-Sklar, Tomasz Wieladek, and Chris Young. "QE: The Story so far." Staff Working Paper 624. London: Bank of England, October 2016.

IMF. "New Data on Global Debt." Blog, 2 January 2019. https://blogs.imf.org/2019/01/02/new-data-on-global-debt/. Accessed on November 18, 2019.

Jácome, Luis and Srobona Mitra. "LTV and DTI Limits – Going Granular." IMF Working Paper 15/154, 2015.

Keynes, John Maynard. *The General Theory of Employment, Interest and Money*. New York: Macmillan, 1936.

Skidelsky, Robert. *John Maynard Keynes 1883–1946: Economist, Philosopher, Statesman*. London: Penguin, 2005.

Statista. "Average loan to value ratio in the United States, 2019, by state." https://www.statista.com/statistics/460677/average-ltv-in-the-usa-by-state/ Accessed on November 13, 2019.

Tori, Daniele and Özlem Onaran. 'The Effects of Financialization on Investment: Evidence from Firm-Level Data for the UK.' *Cambridge Journal of Economics* 42, 5 (2018): 1393–1416.

Chapter 4: Frank Knight on Risk and Uncertainty

The Problem

The spread of risk is one of the core virtues of banking and finance. Don't put all your eggs in one basket is the guiding principle of portfolio investment. That is precisely why all financial institutions have a risk management department and sometimes also a chief risk manager on the board. Balanced risk is crucial for both the liquidity and the solvency of a firm. Do we have sufficient means to cover our obligations on a daily basis (liquidity)? Are our assets bigger than our liabilities (solvency)? Hence, it is wise to keep risk in check by making certain people responsible for risk management. This helps to prevent excessive risk taking when different departments, branches and traders of a bank each take risks that add up being more than the bank can safely handle.

Whistleblowers

What were the risk managers doing in the years leading up to the meltdown of 2008? Didn't they understand the risks of complex derivatives? Or did they lack oversight because banks had grown so big? Let us go over the answers step by step. Let's start with the whistleblowers among the risk managers. They were there, right in the very banks and supervisory agencies that were the key agents in the financial crisis, and they certainly have warned against excessive risk taking. Not just a few weeks before the crash. The key whistleblowers already sound the alarm bells a few years earlier, when the real estate markets and the derivatives markets skyrocketed, and when banks grew bigger and bigger through mergers and acquisitions as well as by trading for their own account. They may not have heard of Minsky but they spotted the building up of the Minsky Moment in those financial markets in which their institutions operated.

In 1997, the Chair of the US Securities and Exchange Committee, Brooksley Born, asked Congress to regulate the trade in derivatives. She did this because she was worried about the extensive risk that nonfinancial firms and local governments took with massive trading in derivatives. Already in 1994, Orange County, in California, went bankrupt as a consequence of such reckless speculation. Born recognized that the enormous growth in derivatives trading, largely but not exclusively consisting of small portions of subprime mortgage loans, meant risks that many buyers could not oversee. After the bubble burst, the balance sheets of numerous local governments and nonprofit organizations outside the US also appeared to be filled with such toxic assets. For example, Vestia, the biggest social housing association of the Netherlands in 2011, lost two billion euro on its derivatives portfolio. But Congress did not respond to Born's request for regulation. In 2006, another supervisor called for regulation. This time it was Sheila Bair, Chair of the US Federal Deposit Insurance Corporation (FDIC). She warned that an increasing number of households were unable to pay back their mortgages. That could mean that banks were risking severe losses and even bankruptcies, and as a consequence the pay-out of large sums of money from the FDIC to holders of bank accounts. Congress chose to ignore her plea for regulation. The third whistleblower was the chief risk manager of Lehman Brothers, Madelyn Antoncic. In 2006, she informed the board that the risk position of the bank was unsustainable. But the CEO ignored her notice and continued with the highly profitable derivatives trade until the very last moment. Antoncic was fired and replaced by someone without expertise in risk management. The rest is history.

Regulatory Capture

The crisis was clearly not caused by irresponsible risk managers and inattentive supervisors. It rather seems the case that the political climate was not ripe for bad news in times when financial markets were growing without limits. Markets were in the stage that Keynes recognized as exhibiting optimism and greed. And the lobby of the sector was so strong that regulation did not even make it to the political agenda—a phenomenon known as regulatory capture. That refers to the prevention of regulation by those interest groups who would suffer from the rules. Regulatory capture does not need to rely on fraud or bribery. It operates entirely legal and in public space. How was this possible? Well, surprisingly simple.

First is the revolving door principle between banks and supervisory agencies. Various former politicians and supervisors end their careers as board members of banks or insurance companies and the other way around. Examples are former Goldman Sachs banker Marc Carney who was appointed governor of the Bank of England, former Dutch Minister of Finance Gerrit Zalm who became the CEO of ABN AMRO bank after its nationalization, and former Goldman Sachs CEO Henry Paulson who was appointed as the US Treasury Secretary, while John Dugan worked for the Treasury and now serves as CEO of

Citigroup.[1] Countries appear to have only very limited regulation to prevent revolving door practices between the government and the business world.[2] This widespread practice not only enables regulatory capture but even institutionalizes it.

The second mechanism behind regulatory capture is ideological. It is the strong belief in markets as self-regulating and efficient and serving common interest. This ideology is particularly strong for financial markets, as we have seen in Chap. 2. That is because the mechanism of arbitrage is much faster and cheaper than in other markets. The trade in shares, currencies or derivatives involves gigantic volumes per day, driving down price differences across the globe within seconds. Such quick arbitrage is absent on many other markets. For example, labour markets, which display friction unemployment between labour supply and vacancies. On the car market, or drug market, international arbitrage is even prohibited, preventing a single international price for, say, a BMW or a cancer drug. But on financial markets arbitrage is so fast that profit making must come from volumes and not from significant margins per unit. So, if you would want to make a profit from trading in Japanese yen by buying in New York and selling in London, you would have to do this for a large volume, say a million yen at least, and within a second, otherwise your profit disappears through the arbitrage of other traders who fancy the same opportunity. Arbitrage is therefore the subject of a well-known joke among economists: 'Hey, there is a fifty-dollar bill on the street,' says a friend to an economist while walking the street together. 'No, that is impossible,' answers the economist. 'If it were true it would have been picked up already.' So, the only way to make money with currency trading is to trade not in hundreds or thousands but millions or hundreds of millions. The success of arbitrage is also its weakness. Arbitrage makes financial markets vulnerable to high volatility due to the large volumes traded and sudden changes in the behaviour of traders as soon as sentiments on markets change.

Of course, arbitrage is as old as financial markets—at least since the sixteenth century when banking and financial trading became popular in Europe. But when it is guided by computer algorithms the volatility of financial markets may become even bigger. The dominant theory of finance, the Efficient Market Hypothesis (EMH), does much more than describing and explaining what arbitrage does—it has been embraced by traders as the ultimate model of reality. The EMH explains the price of a financial asset from arbitrage of market prices that represent the underlying real value of each asset. Hence, if the price of a share of RBS would increase by 5% on a single day, this would imply that the Royal Bank of Scotland's book value has indeed increased 5% over that day—millions of pounds sterling. Or, alternatively, the value increase happened over a longer period but the information reflecting that increase came available a bit later, causing random noise in the value development of the share price of RBS. This example illustrates that EMH is based on two crucial assumptions. First, that all relevant information is translated in share prices and second that these adequately reflect underlying risks. This reliance on the EMH makes that traders trust in the transparency of markets: what you see (price) is what you get (a certain risk-return ratio). And by spreading risk—not putting all your eggs in the same basket—brokers, traders and investors are not likely to go bankrupt from trading. To the contrary, by spreading risk, one will have a mixed bag of high-risk-high-return and low-risk-low-return assets, while one's risk preference defines the ratio between the two types of assets in one's portfolio. In case the high-risk assets turn out worthless, you still have the returns from the low-risk assets. But that is the ideal world of markets—the one that Alan Greenspan, Chair of the Fed in the years running up to the crisis, later would admit to be false.

Assuming Away Risk

The consequence of the what-you-see-is-what-you-get message of the EMH is that the price developments on financial markets are regarded as a reflection of the real value of assets, subject to a random deviation due to random errors in information. The theory claims that average risk on financial markets is around zero. That is, some assets may be a bit overvalued whereas other assets may be a bit undervalued at any moment in time, but these random deviations will cancel each other out, according to the theory. The basic premise is that there exists no systematic over- or undervaluation. This is illustrated by Fig. 1, showing that the price development on financial markets only suffers from small random deviations from the market price. That is why this curve is also referred to as a random walk curve.

The consequence of this view is that investment in a mixed fund of stocks will generally generate the highest possible average returns. However, there are many individuals, traders and even hobbyists, who believe they can beat the

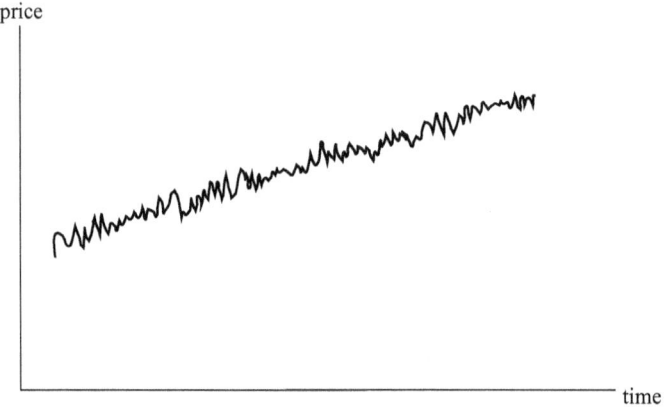

Fig. 1 The random walk of asset prices according to the EMH-theory. (Source: Author)

market and therefore make their own buy and sell choices—speculators, like Keynes in his days.

The problem of excessive risk has grown undisturbed from the turn of the millennium onwards, despite various high-level whistleblowers, because almost everyone active in the market believed that the non-systemic character of risk in combination with a mixed portfolio would prevent financial instability. This belief was only strengthened with the introduction of derivatives, which were supposed to spread risk within a single asset. Safer asset investment did not seem possible: first risk spreading within derivatives and then risk spreading by holding different types of derivatives. The party could not be spoilt by regulation thanks to the revolving door mechanism and the popularity of the EMH.

But this led to a systematic underestimation of real risk levels. Moreover, policy makers began to grasp that there is something else, even more erratic, that leads to high instability: uncertainty.

The Insight

Wasn't there any alternative to the EMH-theory in the years leading up to the crisis? And how strong was the EMH really? Did all financial economists really think that it was plausible that a nice straight upward line with some random noise would explain financial markets with nearly zero net risk? Did students believe it even though it clearly could not explain the crash of 1929 or the dot. com crisis of 2000? To be honest, I am still puzzled why the efficient market theory became so dominant and why its major proponent was awarded a Nobel Memorial Prize.

Of course, those who developed the theory between the 1920s and the turn of the new millennium also asked such questions. This resulted in an answer fully in-line with the idea of independent risk. The answer was, as we have seen in Chap. 3, that financial crises only happen as a consequence of exogenous factors. For example, political instability or an earthquake. Graphically, such shocks show as a sudden lower level of the same random walk line. This is shown in Fig. 2. The line discontinues at its old level and picks up again at a lower level—the break point representing the shock. In addition, the line may become less steep for a while, until all the ripple-effects of the shock have been absorbed by the market and asset price development is back to business as usual.

This explanation of financial crises was also accepted by traders, supervisors and politicians. Because it implies that market regulation to prevent crises would be of no use. If the shock comes from outside markets—exogenous—and not from market behaviour itself—endogenous—than regulation of financial markets is pointless.

And what about fast price increases? Where do these come from? This is more difficult to explain within the logic of EMH. How does one explain that during booms house prices rise faster than the developments that make up market prices (land, population growth, and building material)? EMH assumes that market prices and underlying asset values are in fact exactly the same, apart

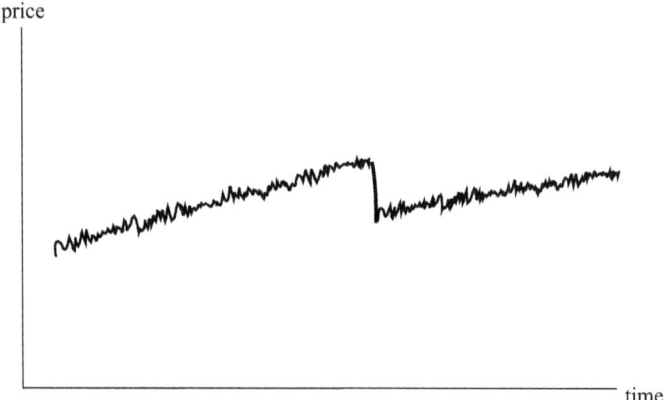

Fig. 2 The random walk of asset prices in EMH-theory with an exogenous shock. (Source: Author)

from some non-systematic deviations related to errors in information and individual risk perceptions. Hence, an unusual rise in market prices necessarily implies that the real values of these assets are increasing as well, without any bubble of overvaluation. In EMH, bubbles don't exist. A crash, hence, does not mean that a bubble bursts but that a shock from outside the market causes the market to shake and re-adjust to a lower price level. The examples that are often mentioned by EMH-theorists are the oil price shocks of the 1970s and 1980s, when the OPEC manipulated scarcity in order to increase its oil revenues. However, this seems to be an exception rather than the rule, as Keynes and Minsky already explained. But even there, so called petro dollars moved to US asset markets and helped to build bubbles. So, contrary to the message of EMH, financial crises generally arise from bubbles that burst based on dynamics within markets as a combination of sentiments, expectations, herd behaviour and increasing fragility due to increasing debt financing.

The most astounding is that the founder of the EMH, Irving Fisher, experienced himself that his beloved theory was proven wrong. On Black Monday, 28 October 1929, and the following day, Black Tuesday, he lost all of his wealth on the New York Stock Exchange and in addition a large sum of money he had borrowed from his sister-in-law. He was convinced that the stock prices reflected underlying values and that they would continue to rise. Eighty years later, his successor Eugene Fama still holds on to the same idea. According to him, the 2008 financial crisis was not caused by bubbles in the derivatives market and the housing market, but by a shock that quickly adjusted market prices to a decline in underlying values. But this does not explain the shock at all. Fama ignores the following key questions: how was it possible that values and prices could diverge so much? And where did the new information that caused the price adjustment suddenly come from? And why was the information not gradually incorporated in the price development by traders and brokers? And what was this shock? Fama's explanation suggests that there is no satisfactory explanation from the EMH. Robert Schiller, his rival and proponent of behavioural finance theory—which explains the crisis as the bursting of a bubble—in fact pointed this out in the *New York Times* five years after the bubble had burst. He remarked that what Fama's own investment fund information refers to as a 'risk premium' is exactly the same as the irrational behaviour causing bubbles ...[3]

Risk

A decade after the crisis, the EMH-theory, with its prediction that individual risk was neutralized at the market level, is no longer so dominant. Many economists admit that what happened in 2008 was indeed a bubble that burst, driven by irrational behaviour of investors and traders who suffered from overoptimism, wishful thinking, greed and herd behaviour. And when we acknowledge that bubbles are possible, that market dynamics can cause prices to rise faster than underlying values, we also have to admit that average risk on markets can increase. The more overvalued assets, the higher the risk that those assets cannot be sold against higher prices in the future.

The 2008 financial crisis has demonstrated that the probability of such losses was much higher than experts had imagined. Not one in ten thousand or so, but perhaps one in a hundred. This phenomenon of relative high risk for extremely high or low asset values is referred to as 'fat tails'. Figure 3 shows this in a diagram of a probability distribution. The normal bell curve distribution of values shows that for extreme values (very low or very high), probabilities that they will occur are very low (vertical axis). But the dotted curve shows a distribution that is less steep at both ends, with fat tails. That curve seems to be a better reflection of financial markets, where extreme values are much more likely to happen than in normal distributions. Compare this, for example, with

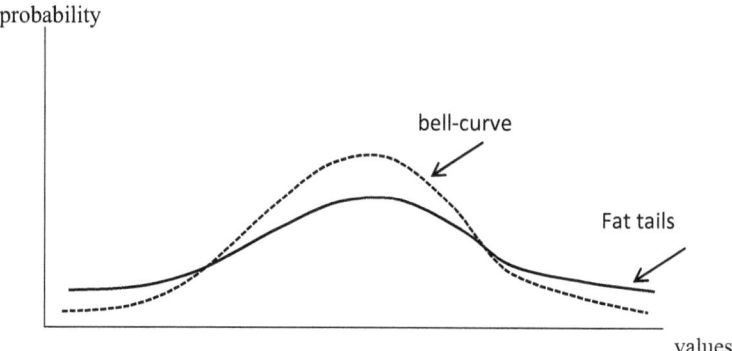

Fig. 3 Fat tail distribution with high risk of extreme values. (Source: Author)

the distribution of men's height, in which men shorter than 1.50 meter or taller than 2.10 meter are indeed very rare. Fat tails reflect the underestimation of the risk of individual assets, such as MBS, not only by individual traders and investors but also throughout the financial system. In other words, the individual risk positions of each of these investors are intertwined through futures markets in which assets play the role of securities. The result is systemic risk. This implies that if just a few financial institutions fail, they will pull down the rest of the financial system, with a series of bankruptcies as a result.

So, in fact, there are two problems with risk in financial markets. The one is a relatively high risk for extreme values to occur, and the other being systemic risk because of the entanglement of risky assets throughout the system due to securitization. How to prevent this to happen again? Well, we know from Marx that crises are an inherent part of capitalism, so it is impossible to prevent crises completely. But it is very well possible to reduce the size and impact of crises, as the long period between the Glass–Steagall Act and the repeal of this law has shown. Damage reduction can be done by a variety of regulatory measures, such as independent credit rating, more transparent financial products, a prohibition of sales commissions and bonuses in consumer markets, and limits to securitization. This, of course, requires regulation and strict supervision of new types of financial assets—exactly what Brooksley Born and Sheila Bair had asked for and what they are still pleading.

Obviously, risk reduction is only possible when types of risk and their probabilities are known. But that is not always the case and the 2008 financial crisis has illustrated this once again. The crisis made clear that financial market instability can lead to situations no one had even imagined. Investment banks and retail banks going bankrupt. Large consumer banks that had to be saved by the state. Consumers panicking about their savings and standing in long queues for cash machines. The interbank payment system that was threatened. Financial supervisory bodies asking themselves if bank clients could still use their bank debit cards in shops. And how long would the electricity network operate if money transactions would dry up?

Uncertainty

The name of the deeper problem of financial instability is not risk but uncertainty. This brings us to the lesson of this chapter: the crucial difference between risk and uncertainty. Risk refers to possible future states and the probability of each of these. This is like throwing a dice: the six possible states are known and the probability of each is clear. It is simply impossible, with a probability of zero, to throw number seven or eight—when you don't use the dice from the magic box of your children. The same counts for your house burning down in the next year. There are two possibilities: it does or it does not burn down. The same counts for every other house in the insurance portfolio of your insurance company. On the basis of fire statistics based on many years, the company has quite a good idea about the expected number of houses burning down each year and their average value. This probability results in a calculation of the insurance policy costs plus a profit margin, which together define what home owners will pay annually for their home insurance. Bad luck for an insurance company if one day a whole town burns down as a consequence of an earthquake that makes gas pipelines explode? No, not at all. Because such an occurrence is a combination of systemic risk (fire in a few buildings jumps to adjacent buildings) and uncertainty (the probability of an earthquake, e.g., in San Francisco, is not knowable). This is not risk but uncertainty. That is precisely why you can insure your home against risk (individual fire) but not against uncertainty (widespread damage due to a tsunami, nuclear disaster or earthquake). The small print of your insurance policy will show you these and any other imaginable and unimaginable disasters that fall under the rubric of uncertainty. The lesson about the difference between risk and uncertainty is that risk can be insured but uncertainty not, because damage costs of the latter simply cannot be estimated—there exists no probability distribution.

Uncertainty, hence, is the future state that you could not have known (a dice with an unknown number of sides) and about which you have no idea of probabilities to occur (a dice with an unknown shape). The lesson for financial market instability is that this not only results from intertwined risk but also from uncertainty. The first is manageable through risk spreading, transparency and insurance, but the second is not controllable.

The first economist who analysed this was Frank Knight. He obtained his PhD in 1917 on this very topic. The book, *Risk, Uncertainty and Profit*, that he published four years later has been cited over 24,000 times since its publication.[4] Knight came to the idea of the distinction between risk and uncertainty when trying to account for predictable and unpredictable sources of profit. In other words, he was interested in profit arising from smart entrepreneurship and profit from luck. Unfortunately, many of us tend to mix-up the two concepts of risk and uncertainty on a daily basis. For example, we would say that investing in production facilities in countries with civil conflict or an authoritarian regime is politically risky, whereas we actually do not know the possible consequences of such regimes on investments. So, what we actually mean is economic uncertainty, not economic risk.

In a nutshell, uncertainty implies market volatility that is unpredictable and its costs are impossible to estimate. It is precisely that feature of financial markets that leads to speculation and herd behaviour. When nobody is able to estimate chances of win and lose, it is simply sentiment that rules the market. As soon as a few traders no longer believe that price development is upwards, they will start selling. Hence, bubbles and bursts do not only arise from bad risk management but also from the fundamental uncertainty of the future value of financial assets. But spreading risk is insufficient to reduce instability. When volatility increases, people only trust their intuition and follow others hoping that they know better. Volatile markets are ruled by animal spirits, as Keynes already described—both in times of optimism and in times of pessimism.

The conclusion of Knight's analysis was that the large differences in profit margins between companies are the result of two factors. First the combination of risk and uncertainty. Second the extent of competition in a market. The fact that Keynes eventually became a rich man from his speculative activities is not only attributable to his smartness as investor but also to luck. He was the first to admit this. He was immediately convinced of Knights' analysis. That is precisely why he emphasized in his own work the role of uncertainty in financial markets and its consequences for the real economy, for example in consumers losing confidence and reducing their consumer expenditures and investors holding back new investments until consumer confidence would pick up again.

The lesson to be learnt about uncertainty in financial markets is that the spreading of risk, whether in individual portfolios or in the market as a whole, is not sufficient to reduce financial instability. The only thing that would help to diminish market volatility is simplicity and hard caps, as Keynes already recognized. This implies much higher buffers of banks (more equity capital), a prohibition of trading for one's own account for retail banks, a fence between investment banking and retail banking, a limitation to consolidation of the banking sector to prevent too-big-to-fail banks, strict regulation of derivatives and their use in securitization in the real economy, and a public safe haven for savings money with a subsequent reduction of deposit insurance for commercial bank accounts. The strange thing is, most of these policy measures are not new but were in place before the 1990s, when the banking sector was much smaller and much more competitive than it is today. It is possible to reduce the size, entanglement and power of the financial sector. But it will take time, dedication and political will to do so. Above all, it will take the burial of the belief in efficient markets and the idea that uncertainty is less relevant than risk.

The Economist

Frank Knight (White Oak 1885–Chicago 1972)

Frank Hyneman Knight was born as the eldest of eleven children. The family lived on a farm in the state of Illinois, and after his study of economics at the University of Tennessee and Cornell University in New York, he spent his career back in Illinois, at the University of Chicago. He married and had four children with his first wife and two children with his second wife, Ethel Verry. During much of their marriage, Ethel was the director of an orphanage in Chicago. Due to his long affiliation, Knight is sometimes referred to as one of the founders of the Chicago School of Economics. This school of thought is well known for its free market proponents and its aversion against the state. Over the years, free market economists like Milton Friedman, James Buchanan and Gary Becker became the exponents of the Chicago School. Today, Eugene Fama is one of its figure heads. But the theoretical difference between Fama and Knight can hardly be bigger.

Frank Knight first developed his insights on risk in his analysis of profit but later applied it to other economic questions, including the problem of high inequality. His study of inequality in wealth led him to conclude that an important source of this is inheritance law. This results in wealth accumulation not from one's own entrepreneurship but from sheer luck of being born in a family with property. In addition, he investigated the philosophical dimensions of uncertainty. He asked himself whether uncertainty has an ontological status: is it *real*? And he wondered if it can be observed empirically and measured. His conclusion was that uncertainty is a complex problem with subtle features. This led him to remark in his book *Freedom and Reform*, that we hardly know how much we know and whether our knowledge is correct: 'There is no visible boundary between knowledge, opinions, and ignorance.'[5] This is an interesting reminder for us, living in times of fake news, internet trolls, and those regarding solid scientific evidence as just another opinion.

Today, Frank Knight can be considered to belong to a small minority of economists interested in ethics. He was raised with a Calvinist attitude. This led him, for example, to consider labour not only as useful but also as valuable in a moral sense. Nevertheless, he objected against a Christian ethic and made this very clear to his students as well. The story goes that his students said among each other: 'there is no God but Frank Knight is his prophet,' according to James Buchanan, his student and later Nobel Memorial Prize winner, in the preface to Frank Knight's collected essays titled *Freedom and Reform*. Knight was also concerned with income inequality and the inability of markets to reduce it. In the book with the intriguing title *The Ethics of Competition*, he studied this problem. In this book, he developed an interesting view, very different from Chicago School economics that regards competition as a natural and beneficial phenomenon without any ethics involved. For him competition, just like cooperation, is not morally neutral and part of choices made by society. But Knight could also express his discontent with general misunderstandings of how markets work. In his 1950 presidential speech for the American Economic Association he expressed his irritation about the economic ignorance of the general public:

> Of late I have a new and depressing example of popular economic thinking, in the policy of arbitrary price-fixing. Can there be any use in explaining, if it is needful to explain, that fixing a price below the free-market level will create a shortage and one above it a surplus? But the public oh's and ah's and yips and yaps at the shortage of residential housing and surpluses of eggs and potatoes as if these things presented problems any more than getting one's footgear soiled by deliberately walking in the mud.[6]

Reading Knight
Frank Knight, *Risk, Uncertainty and Profit* (Eastford: Martino Fine Books, 2014 [1921]).

Reading About Knight
William Greer, *Ethics and Uncertainty: The economics of J.M. Keynes and Frank H. Knight* (Cheltenham: Edward Elgar, 2001).

PRACTISING KNIGHT

Following Frank Knight's suggestion to limit the consequences of fundamental uncertainty, the banking sector can be made more crisis-proof with two relatively simple policy measures: a strict separation between investment banks and retail banks, and higher buffers for all banks. Who could be against such safeguards? Unfortunately, the banking sector itself opposes both measures and has, over the past decade, successfully lobbied against these two measures. The reason is that their shareholders expect high dividends, their top managers expect juicy bonuses linked to the same profit rate, and clients are happy with the generous deposit insurance, and everybody expects the government to save the bank again in case of bankruptcy ... Moreover, these vested interests are strengthened by the revolving door between banks and the state, and by politicians holding on to the dogma of efficiency arising from unregulated markets.

Retail Banks and Investment Banks

The Glass–Steagall Act has functioned as intended for 66 years. The prohibition of universal banks (a combination of investment and retail bank in one) has prevented serious financial crises between 1929 and 2008. Its successor, the Dodd-Frank Act, was implemented in 2010. But is much weaker—courtesy of the banking lobby. Moreover, it is much less effective due to an overload of micro regulation and countless exceptions. The new banking regulation of Dodd-Frank with its 30,000 pages and so many rules and exceptions is very difficult to enforce, while the unavoidable inconsistencies enable banks and their lawyers to find escapes and continuously create new opportunities to grow their balance sheets, to take excessive risks and to trade in opaque derivatives. Sometimes, it looks as if the banking sector as a whole has become too big to fail. Those politicians and regulators who would genuinely like to see the sector operate on a smaller and clearly defined playing field seem to lose the battle. Moreover, the current trend worldwide is towards more consolidation, leading to even bigger banks, rather than to smaller and safer banks.

Buffers

Up to the 1990s buffers well over 10% were normal for banks. Today, most large banks regard 5% as the upper limit and the new international regulation of Basel III does not require more. Even more surprising is that the banking lobby managed to manipulate the new international regulation of Basel III in such a way that they are allowed to use their own confidential models of risk-weighing of their liabilities for the calculation of their buffers. This allows them, for example, to count mortgages as safe assets, so that these require less equity capital as a buffer. This is like students deciding for themselves what the weights are of the different parts of their exam for a course, for example essay, group work and multiple-choice questions. The problem with this is obvious: banks can manipulate, entirely legally, their buffers to their advantage, while central banks are unable to check the details of the internal risk-weighing models. As a consequence, uncertainty about banks' solvability is heightened rather than reduced in Basel III, despite the stress tests enforced by central banks.

The solution is twofold. First, simple universal leverage ratios at least up to 5–10% for all banks plus extra capital requirements for systemically relevant banks. Second, additional counter-cyclical buffers that banks can build up in good times and can rely on in bad times. One or both of these types of buffers may be enforced by requiring that banks are not allowed to pay out dividend and bonuses until the required leverage ratio has been reached.[7]

Notes

1. An inventory of the revolving door between banks and the government in the US can be found in: Elise Brezis and Joël Cariolle, "Financial Sector Regulation and the Revolving Door in US Commercial Banks," in Norman Schofield and Gonzalo Caballero (eds.) *State, Institutions and Democracy – contributions to political economy* (Cham: Springer, 2017, pp. 53–76).
2. Suzanne Mulcahy, *Lobbying in Europe – hidden influence, privileged access* (Berlin: Transparency International, 2015). https://www.transparency.org/whatwedo/publication/lobbying_in_europe. Accessed on January 14, 2020.
3. Robert Schiller, "Sharing Nobel Honors, and Agreeing to Disagree," *The New York Times*, 26 October 2013.
4. Knight's book was cited more than 24,000 times when I wrote this chapter: https://scholar.google.com/scholar?cluster=17701737638298991757&hl=en&as_sdt=2005&sciodt=1,5 Accessed on June 22, 2020.
5. Frank Knight, *Freedom & Reform – essays in economics and social philosophy* (Indianapolis: Liberty Fund, 1982 [1947], p. 80).
6. https://www.econlib.org/library/Enc1/bios/Knight.html. Accessed on July 15, 2020.
7. See, for example, a proposal: Goodhart, Charles and Dirk Schoenmaker, 'Automatic Stabilisers in Banking Capital,' *VOX*, 11 July 2019, https://voxeu.org/article/automatic-stabilisers-banking-capital Accessed on January 24, 2020.

Bibliography

Brezis, Elise and Joël Cariolle. 'Financial Sector Regulation and the Revolving Door in US Commercial Banks.' in Norman Schofield and Gonzalo Caballero (eds.) *State, Institutions and Democracy – contributions to political economy*. Cham: Springer, 2017, pp. 53–76.

Goodhart, Charles and Dirk Schoenmaker. 'Automatic Stabilisers in Banking Capital.' *VOX*, 11 July 2019. https://voxeu.org/article/automatic-stabilisers-banking-capital. Accessed on January 24, 2020.

Knight, Frank. *Freedom & Reform – essays in economics and social philosophy.* Indianapolis: Liberty Fund, 1982 [1947].

Mulcahy, Suzanne. *Lobbying in Europe – hidden influence, privileged access.* Berlin: Transparency International, 2015. https://www.transparency.org/whatwedo/publication/lobbying_in_europe. Accessed on January 14, 2020.

Schiller, Robert. 'Sharing Nobel Honors, and Agreeing to Disagree,' *The New York Times*, 26 October 2013.

Chapter 5: Barbara Bergmann on Gender Biases

THE PROBLEM

Have you noticed that the three key whistleblowers in the previous chapter were all women? Do you think that is a coincidence? Or that I, perhaps, have not mentioned their male colleagues?

The last mentioned is certainly not the case. If you search the internet for whistleblowers and the 2008 financial crisis, you will find the names of Sheila, Brooksley and Madelyn and not many more. Whether this is a coincidence, and that the well-known key players in financial fraud and disastrous financial losses tend to be all men, is in a way the topic of this chapter. Former EU commissioner Nelie Kroes and current ECB-president Christine Lagarde refer to this as the Lehman Sisters Hypothesis. This is the proposition that if women had been in charge of the banks, we would not have ended up in the worst financial crisis since 1929.

I have studied the empirical evidence related to this hypothesis.[1] Since then, I have been invited to speak about it across the world. I spoke at the headquarters of OECD in Paris and was invited to Reykjavik by an Islandic banker who safely steered her investment fund as a Lehman Sister through the turbulent crisis period when the three major banks in the country collapsed. At first sight, the hypothesis seems to be valid, but we should not rely on anecdotal evidence or get carried away by feminist wishful thinking. In this chapter, I will investigate the extent to which sex—the biological differences between women and men—and gender—the socially constructed differences of masculinity and femininity—have played a role in the financial crisis. I understand very well that some male readers may find this endeavour by me, as a female researcher and a feminist, suspect. That is why I have chosen to rely particularly on research published by men.

Let's start from the recognition that banking is man-made, well, human-made. Traders, investment bankers and fund managers make use of computer models but eventually bear the responsibility for the decisions to buy and sell. New financial products and services are imagined, created and tested by teams of experts and checked by supervisory bodies. These activities involve a number of crucial features. The most important are an adequate estimation of risk and how to deal with uncertainty; the extent to which bankers follow their moral compass; and the leadership that should guide financial decisions and prevent herd behaviour of too much optimism and pessimism. Interestingly, research shows gender differences but no sex differences in all these behavioural features.

Over the past twenty-five years the study of gender in economics has changed from a marginal topic studied almost exclusively by women to a mainstream topic drawing attention of an increasing number of men in an increasing number of economic areas—from household bargaining to international trade.[2] This has resulted in a great variety of publications on sex and gender differences in economic behaviour, but not always distinguishing between the two and often without sufficient foundation in feminist economic theory, which adequately distinguishes between sex and gender and explains why that matters.[3] The empirical studies of gender differences in economic behaviour include the analysis of fMRI-scans of men and women to games in single-sex versus mixed-sex settings, and from survey analysis to risk-experiments in a computer lab. I have reviewed many of these studies in relation to financial behaviour. And I have discovered some persistent and disturbing gender patterns. I will summarize these for the three topics involved in the Lehman Sisters Hypothesis: risk and uncertainty, moral compass and leadership.

Attitude Towards Risk and Uncertainty

In 2008, male fund managers lost twice as much money compared to their female colleagues. Among managers of Asian and American hedge funds, female managers generated 50–75% higher returns than their male colleagues between 2000 and the crisis. Another revealing result came from a study by a British wealth fund, which asked 2000 clients in 20 countries how they made their investment decisions.[4] The results indicated that female investors tend to behave in a more risk averse manner and show more self-restraint when markets are volatile. In such uncertain periods, they consciously skip the financial news, preventing themselves from selling stocks they would actually like to keep for the long term. The rich ladies keep their heads cool when markets are turbulent.

Many studies support the hypothesis that women take, on average, less risk than men.[5] In a stable market with low uncertainty, such an attitude results in lower average returns as compared to higher risk taking. But when uncertainty rules, women's attitude appears to be an advantage and leads to higher average returns on investment. Women tend also to behave in a more loss averse manner. Also, that attitude is an asset in turbulent markets. Hence, in the long run, women's average higher aversion to risk and loss, benefit their returns.

A famous study of gender differences in investment behaviour has analysed the portfolios of 35,000 American households. The study found that women obtained a small but statistically significant higher return on investment as compared to their male counterparts. This result was not only due to their choice of less risky firms in their portfolio, but also because they showed more patience. The men carried out almost half as much transactions as the women, because they tried to beat the market. This resulted in higher transaction costs and, as a consequence, a lower net profit as compared to the women who kept their heads cool. In other words, when a century ago factory workers handed in their weekly wage to their wives this was not such a strange practice at all. Apparently, both of them realized that this was the wisest way to manage the breadwinner's meagre earnings.

On financial markets, gender differences in risk and loss attitudes have even more potential impact than in the household. Because most decision making in financial markets is carried out by men, who dominate trading and strategy. The masculine risk attitude in finance is strengthened by the fact that many jobs in this sector are insecure in the financial centres of the world—one can be fired without notice, which reinforces a short-term risk-taking perspective. The reasoning in such jobs is that high risk favours a higher probability of profit *now*, whereas low risk helps to reduce a bank's losses *later*. The continuous threat of job loss in the financial sector turns out to be a risk-enhancing factor for banks and the financial sector as a whole.

But there is more. The gender difference in risk attitude even contributes to the volatility of financial markets itself. In other words, volatility is not just a natural characteristic of financial markets but may be increased by the choices made by traders. This is the outcome of an innovative study by a group of neuroscientists of 17 male traders at the London Stock Exchange (no women for the simple reason that they were absent in that trading department).[6] Al 17 men traded predominantly in German government bonds. Hence, they were watching, all day long, a computer screen with fluctuating interest rates of the various bonds. The researchers observed them during eight days, during which they took twice a day saliva samples, one in the morning and one in the afternoon. At the same time, the researchers noted down the interim results of the profit and loss accounts of each trader. The saliva samples were used to measure the levels of testosterone and cortisol of each trader. Testosterone is a hormone that correlates with self-confidence and risk preference. Cortisol is a stress hormone, that is influenced by uncertainty and can be found at similar levels in men and women.

The researchers discovered that traders who came in with higher testosterone in the morning made higher profits at the end of the day. The nickname for testosterone among top athletes as the winner's effect apparently holds also true on the stock exchange. But the cortisol effect was entirely different. Here, the causal relationship appeared to be the other way around. Irrespective of the cortisol level in the morning, cortisol shot up when a trader was making net losses during the day. Moreover, the data showed a strong correlation between the volatility in the rates of the bonds and cortisol levels at the end of the day, which sometimes increased by 500%. To summarize, higher testosterone seemed to predict higher profit and the stress caused by market volatility seemed to predict higher cortisol. The problem with testosterone is that continued high levels change it from a winner's hormone to excessive risk taking and impulsive behaviour. And the problem with continuous high levels of cortisol is that it generates anxiety. The implication for male-dominated financial markets may be that markets may rise quickly due to the winner's effect of testosterone, but also that they may collapse quickly after a period of high volatility due to the herd behaviour of anxious traders filled with cortisol. In other words, Keynes' concept of animal spirits seems to be at work much more literally than he had imagined. The neurologists concluded that the dominance of men in financial trading might contribute to the instability of financial markets. Women have, on average, lower levels of natural testosterone and women's bodies tend to react faster to stress than men's bodies with the love hormone oxytocin, which counteracts cortisol. Hence, women seem to have a double natural advantage over men: their testosterone levels make them less vulnerable to impulsive behaviour and their quick body reaction to high cortisol makes them less vulnerable to panic.

Moral Compass

There is a very interesting anthropological study of traders, written by a female anthropologist, which I nevertheless discuss here precisely because it shows so much sympathy for the male traders involved.[7] She made an ethnographic study of traders on the futures exchanges of Chicago and London, by working as a trader herself. She found out that traders love the kick of winning, the game of selling and buying, and that for that reason they reduce the trade to abstract, meaningless products and money to 'ticks'. They are not at all interested in the people behind the firms with whose money they are gambling or the population of countries whose bonds they buy at junk prices to claim the nominal value back later through lawsuits. In 2014, this happened, for example, to Argentina, which led to widely shared protests against so-called vulture funds. The anthropologist did an important discovery in Chicago and London. Successful traders appeared to switch off their moral compass when they entered the trading floor. She admitted that she was also affected by the trading game, trying to score and taking high risk to win—not only to make money but even as a goal in itself, just like in a real game—for example, the intrinsic value of playing a game of chess. Two Wall Street researchers recognize this behaviour, and both refer to it as hypermasculinity.[8] An excessive desire for risk, strong competition between traders, supported by a culture of contempt for real economic impacts, flavoured by rude language and offensive behaviour towards women. The anthropologist of the ethnographic study experienced this as well and eventually felt uncomfortable on a trading floor dominated by men.

In 2014, I conducted a survey on banking culture among 600 retail bankers of all top banks in the Netherlands. The results indicate that the average banker surely does have a moral compass and also that it is pointing at client interest. But what showed to be problematic was that the dominant culture made it often very difficult to really do justice to client interest. I will present some detailed results from my survey in Chap. 7. Interestingly, my results did not indicate any gender differences in the moral compass of the Dutch bank employees—neither in the ethics, nor in the application of the moral compass towards clients. This suggests that any gender differences found in finance might be limited to the typical top jobs of trading, investment and strategy. Ordinary bankers, male or female, generally keep their moral compass close at hand.[9]

Leadership

Men dominate leadership roles in publicly listed firms in all sectors, but the trend is showing a gradual increase in the share of women. But there is wide variation. The European Women on Boards Gender Diversity Index 2019 shows that for the 600 Europe Stoxx companies, 7% of chairs of boards are women and 5% have a female CEO. The three countries that top the ranking, Norway, France and Sweden, have 40% women on boards, whereas the bottom three countries, Poland, Switzerland and Luxembourg, have only 22% women on boards.[10] And although the UK is among the countries with the highest share of women on boards, only 8% of the CEOs of the FTSE 250 firms were women.[11] FTSE companies that have a female CEO and at least four female directors include Kingfisher, GlaxoSmithKline, Direct Line Insurance Group, Imperial Brands and ITV. Of the five firms, one is an insurance company and none is a bank. A study among 63 financial institutions in the UK has revealed that those with more women on their boards show significantly higher firm value. Diversity has become a business case, and not only women but also many men like to see more gender diversity in leadership positions. An online survey that I did in 2011 among financial professionals in the Netherlands showed that 81% of the men would like to see more women in top positions and 51% said that gender diversity may help to prevent a next severe crisis.[12]

The trends and views about female leadership are hopeful, in particular since male leaders tend to hold on to a narrow leadership style. And that is insufficient in todays' market environment that is not only affected by risk but particularly by uncertainty. Markets that are looking for new business models and firms that need or actively look for new business cultures. An interesting Europe-wide study among nearly one million companies compared firms with a male CEO and those with a female CEO.[13] Firms with a female CEO appeared to have significantly lower risk of bankruptcy due to higher solvability indicators. Other studies, carried out among firms in Europe, Canada and Israel, including over 2000 companies, also studied the impact of female leadership on business performance.[14] These studies indicate that companies with more women at the top show better financial results, although there are also smaller studies with inconclusive results. Interestingly, the threshold for positive impacts on business performance seems to lie around 30% women on boards, according to a study among 150 German firms—so having simply one or two women at the top may not be sufficient to generate the benefits of board diversity.[15]

How can we explain the gender differences in leadership that are emerging from research? First, there is a statistical explanation. Such a low percentage of women makes it very likely that those who manage to break through the glass ceiling are simply exceptional. Hence, the average performance of women on boards will be higher than the average performance of men. But there is also a more substantial explanation of the difference. Two American leadership researchers have investigated the whole range of relevant leadership competencies among 7000 leaders worldwide, a third of them women.[16] For every leader, approximately thirteen colleagues have rated the qualities of their leader. The result of these 90,000 assessments was that for 12 out of 16 leadership qualities, female leaders scored higher than their male counterparts. Three qualities did not show any significant differences between men and women. Only one quality, strategic perspective, showed higher scores for men, but only because more men than women occupied the very top positions. For a summary of leadership competencies and men's and women's scores, see Table 1.

The top ten qualities in the table are in many societies viewed as masculine (agentic) and the rows for these are bold. The bottom six qualities are in many societies generally viewed as feminine (communal), and these rows are italic. The surprising finding is this: women not only score significantly higher on all stereotype feminine qualities, but also on seven out of ten stereotype masculine qualities, such as being result-oriented and innovative.

The alarming finding is that male leaders have quite a limited menu of competencies in which they perform well, and these are stereotype masculine leadership traits. While female leaders appear to possess a broader set of qualities, covering both agentic and communal behaviour. This wider set of leadership competencies of female leaders is the most important finding of the study. Although the fact that female leaders score on average higher on most qualities than their male counterparts is an extra argument for equal hiring practices.

The Insight

Most academic research into gender differences in economic behaviour is carried out in the fields of social psychology and management studies. A key researcher in both these fields is Alice Eagly. She explains that male–female differences in economic behaviour tend to reflect stereotypes of masculine and feminine behaviour that are often no longer relevant in the real world.[17] According to Eagly, masculine behaviour can be summarized as agentic (active-oriented) and feminine behaviour as communal (connection-oriented). The origin of the gender difference lies in prehistoric times, when men often were

Table 1 Top 16 competencies, which top leaders exemplify most

Leadership quality	Men's score	Women's score	Statistically significant difference?
Takes initiative	48	56	Yes
Practices self-development	48	55	Yes
Drives for results	48	54	Yes
Establishes stretch goals	49	53	Yes
Champions change	49	53	Yes
Solves problems and analyses issues	50	52	Yes
Communicates powerfully and prolifically	50	52	Yes
Innovates	50	51	No
Technical or professional expertise	50	51	No
Develops strategic perspective	51	49	Yes
Displays high integrity and honesty	48	55	*Yes*
Develops others	48	54	*Yes*
Inspires and motivates others	49	54	*Yes*
Builds relationships	49	54	*Yes*
Collaboration and teamwork	49	53	*Yes*
Connects the group to the outside world	50	51	*No*
Average leadership quality	49	53	*Yes*

Source: Author, based on data from J. Zenger and J. Folkman, 'Are Women Better Leaders than Men?,' *Harvard Business Review*, 15 March 2012, https://hbr.org/2012/03/a-study-in-leadership-women-do Accessed on July 16, 2020

Note: Statistical significance of the differences between male and female leaders is 99%

hunters and made weapons, and women were often gatherers and caregivers for children and the ill. But today's society does no longer reflect this Flintstone-scenario, and the idea that our brains are still programmed for the old days has been refuted by recent research in evolutionary biology and psychology. Eagly therefore argues that our brains are much more plastic and they can adapt much faster to changing circumstances than previously thought. As a consequence, women and men are both very well capable of agentic and communal behaviour and of shifting between these two. The gender stereotypes of Fred and Wilma are social norms that form outdated behavioural constraints—for men and women alike.

Biosocial Theory of Gender Differences

The biosocial theory of Eagly leads to tree important insights. First, almost all types of behaviour can be observed regularly in both women and men, except those requiring much physical strength and typical boyish and girlish behaviour among adolescents. Thus, the large majority of behaviours show gradual gender differences and not systematic ones. Second, certain hormones correlate with agentic behaviour (testosterone and cortisol) or with communal behaviour (oestrogen and oxytocin). Since men have higher natural levels of testosterone and suffer from longer exposure to cortisol under stress than women, these two hormones seem to strengthen typical masculine behaviour in men. Act instead of reflect. Now instead of later. Cashing out instead of keep on playing. And since women have more oestrogen and more oxytocin in reaction to stress, these hormones seem to strengthen communal behaviour in women. Cooperation instead of competition. Deliberation instead of impulsive actions. Warning instead of ignoring. The third and last implication from Eagly's theory is the mutual influence between, on the one hand, physical differences between the sexes, such as hormones and neural networks, and on the other hand behavioural differences. Together, these insights make the old opposition between nature and nurture as the drivers of observed differences in the behaviour of men and women obsolete. When a man holds a baby in his arms, his testosterone goes down. When men are given a dosage of oxytocin, they become more cooperative. And when women are given a shot of testosterone, they become more effective in a short-term trading game.

The implications of all this for understanding economic behaviour and the behaviour of financial markets in particular is important. It is the subject of feminist economics—a field that started with an association and journal in 1994.[18] Its research takes into account the way in which gender stereotypes and gender relations affect economic behaviour. For financial services, it is both agentic and communal behaviour that is important. One needs to identify opportunities and steer around risk. And one needs to deliver services to clients that they need and will help them amidst uncertainties. Hence, financial service delivery requires diversity in financial decision-making: agentic and communal. Of course, men and women can both have a balanced mix of these characteristics, but in our gendered societies it will take many years, perhaps generations, before stereotype gender norms will be defeated. The implication from the research on gender and leadership is, both on grounds of justice and of effectiveness, that there is a strong need for a balanced mix of men and women on key financial positions. This requires an organizational culture, which does not reward stereotype masculine behaviour and excludes and ridicules stereotype feminine behaviour, but a culture that balances and values the whole spectrum of competencies necessary for adequate financial service delivery.

Feminist Economics

The field of feminist economics studies the two-way relationship between the economy and gender—in the household, the labour market, consumer behaviour, trade, finance and any other field of economics. Concerning the topic of this chapter, feminist economics addresses questions about masculine organizational culture, behavioural differences between men and women, and the glass ceiling and the gender wage gap. An increasing number of countries shows higher levels of education for women as compared to men while the gender gap in mathematics performance is gradually disappearing. Nevertheless, women have considerable disadvantages in economic life. Feminist economic theory explains why.

A first explanation is the prevailing distribution of roles in households, of male breadwinners and female homemakers or part-time workers. The traditional roles are transferred to the next generation through gender stereotype upbringing and the role models of the parents and many others, leading to stereotype preferences, aspirations and careers from generation to generation. This explains why change towards gender equality is so slow. Second, gender stereotype choices of school and profession, following the invisible yet normative blue and pink tracks from the baby-years onwards, reinforce the traditional role pattern. Typical feminine jobs such as secretary, primary school teacher and nurse have limited career perspectives. A secretary will not easily be promoted to director and a nurse cannot be promoted to medical doctor. The stronger the gender stereotypes in upbringing, education and expectations in society, the sooner boys and girls are likely to follow the respective blue and pink tracks in life. Third, the number of typical pink professions is much smaller than the number of typical blue professions, so that women compete for less typical feminine jobs, whereas they find entry barriers to typical masculine jobs. In many countries across the globe, the majority of women in the labour market has a pink job, following stereotypes about women's role in society as care givers. This makes competition for a job among women stronger as compared to men, who have access to much more jobs that are stereotype masculine jobs. Figure 1 shows that this crowding effect for women pushes women's wages down, as Barbara Bergmann has explained thirty years ago.[19] It is called the crowding theory of the gender wage gap. There is simply more choice among blue professions, with more employers, which provides more space for men to negotiate their wages. The first panel shows the gendered labour market for women, the second panel for men. If men and women would flow flexibly between stereotype masculine and feminine jobs, the same wage rate would

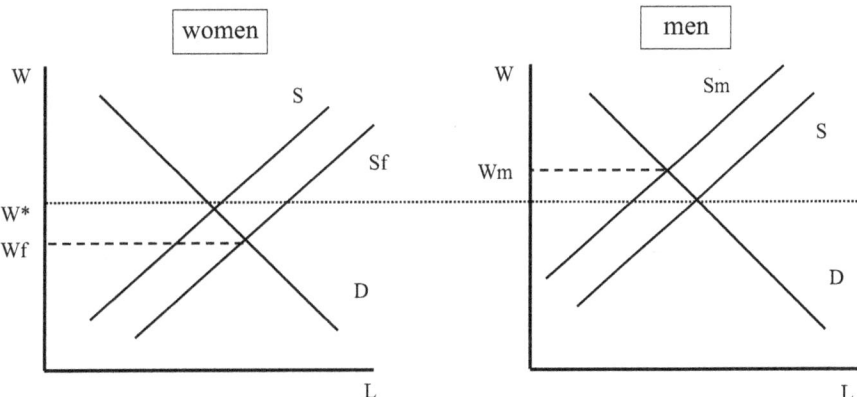

Fig. 1 Bergmann's crowding theory of wage inequality. (Source: Author)

obtain in both markets (W*). But women's labour supply is for a limited number of professions (Sf). The competition between women for this limited number of professions (where a few men are interested in) pushes their wages down (Wf), below the wage of a non-segregated labour market (W*). For men the opposite is the case. Men's labour supply is for a wide number of professions, which women are constrained to enter due to their typical feminine education or due to outright discrimination by employers. This wide availability of professions for men reduces men's labour supply per profession (Sm) and therefore pushes their average wages up (Wm), relative to the situation of no labour market segregation (W*), when women would massively move away from typical feminine to typical masculine professions. As a consequence, average women's wages (Wf) are below average men's wages (Wm).

Moreover, this does not necessarily imply that women working in blue professions will earn the same wage as their male counterparts—also there, gender stereotypes play a role. For example, the idea that men are more deserving than women due to their breadwinner's role, or the idea that women lack the qualities to be just as good as men in typical masculine jobs. This idea is irrational of course, considering that women often need to overcome prejudice to get a blue job in the first place. The passenger who insisted to leave the airplane when he heard the female pilot introduce herself not only made a fool of himself but also opted out of a flight that most likely had an above-average skilled pilot at the control stick.

The fourth feminist economic explanation is the self-reinforcing process of a pink upbringing and pink expectations in society about cooperative and connecting behaviour of women. This makes many women to accept a wage offer ('I've got the job, that's the most important!'), while men begin to negotiate ('Nice bid but let's try to get more out of it!'). Not that women are naïve, though. To the contrary, women know very well that when they start negotiating, they may be considered as bitches—going against stereotypes of femininity—which may negatively affect the relationship with their new employer. Interestingly, when women negotiate on behalf of someone else, they bargain just as tough as men do, and when job applicants are explicitly invited to negotiate, the gender wage gap disappears, according to an experimental study.[20] The problem, hence, is not that women cannot negotiate effectively, but that they are judged negatively when they do, while men are expected to negotiate and are regarded as self-efficacious when they do.

The gender stereotypes of men being agentic and women being communal constrain the careers and salaries of women, even of highly educated women. And even when their future boss does not hold traditional gender norms, women's anticipation of possible gender stereotypes working against them in their application process may constrain their equal position on the labour market. The same is true on other markets and economic interactions, which are equally unrelated to the lives of Fred and Wilma Flintstone. Women's economic disadvantages are clearly not caused by inherently lower ambitions or lower levels of education. They are the consequence of labour market segmentation and gender-based expectations. The theory behind this was first developed by Barbara Bergmann, and later elaborated, empirically tested, and complemented with other theoretical contributions in the field of feminist economics.

THE ECONOMIST

Barbara Bergmann (New York 1927–Bethesda 2015)

Barbara Bergmann was born in the Bronx, New York, as a daughter of East-European immigrants. She excelled in mathematics but did badly at all other school subjects. She was socially engaged and a proponent of decent social policy funded with tax money. Hence, she opted to study economics, like so many who were socially engaged and good in maths. When she was a student at Harvard in the 1950s, women were not allowed to enter certain spaces on the campus and they were required to sit exams separately from the men. Despite these challenges, she obtained her PhD in 1958 and was offered a job as senior economist at the White House. Later, she became professor of economics at the University of Maryland and the American University in Washington D.C.

In her book *The Economic Emergence of Women*, she argued that the main reason for the increase in female labour supply was that women's labour is simply too valuable to be restricted to the kitchen. In an interview she once told the interviewer that she had wanted to be a feminist already since the age of five. At that age, she had figured out that one needed one's own money to be independent, and when she would grow up, that is what she wanted—to be independent. That is the reason why she relied exclusively on economic arguments, and no equal-rights-language, when she studied the position of women. She used terms such as productivity, efficiency, free choice, market power and economic institutions. With this innovative approach to women's disadvantaged position, she became one of the founding mothers of feminist economics and of the International Association for Feminist Economics (IAFFE). The association soon had over 500 members, male and female, including several (male) Nobel Memorial Prize winners. The journal *Feminist Economics* made an enormous impact on the discipline and was the highest ranked new economics journal ever.

One of the most important contributions of Bergmann was the crowding theory of indirect discrimination in the labour market, mentioned earlier. It helped to explain the gender wage gap in situations where there was not direct wage discrimination of women as compared to men for the same jobs. The theory also helped to be useful to explain the lower wages of ethnic minorities, such as blacks in the US and Muslim immigrants in Europe. Her explanation referred to various forms of indirect, often invisible and intangible, forms of discrimination that constrain the choice of women and minorities towards a limited number of sectors. Jobs with low status and limited career opportunities, which results in crowding and strong competition, in particular from younger—and cheaper—generations. Barbara had experienced this herself when looking for a job after her graduation in 1948. The only job she could find was as a typist and she rightly judged that this was a waste of her talent and skills. It was right then that she decided to dedicate her life to research about women's economic position and that of other marginalized groups.

Bergmann was a warm person and I fondly remember a barbeque party in her garden after an IAFFE-conference. But she also could be a snappy debater. She labelled the theory of the family by Nobel Memorial Prize winner Gary Becker preposterous, exposing the breadwinner in his model as a dictator who had full control over the housewife through his financial power. The housewife in his model had no freedom of choice at all; she argued rightly and thereby laid the basis for the feminist household bargaining approach that is now the standard theory used in household research. A few weeks before her death in 2015, she sent a message to the feminist economic internet forum in which she expressed abhorrence of the fact that so many young women today wear ever higher heals. This, Bergmann argued, is not only bad for one's back, but also a sign of subordination to the male gaze. Together with a dozen other feminist economists I responded to this provocative remark. I openly wondered whether Bergmann would also reject lipstick, mini-skirts, or loose long hair—appearances that I sometimes choose to wear irrespective of the presence of any male gaze. Bergmann herself was usually dressed in unisex jeans and t-shirts with inevitable brown flat health sandals. Or, for special occasions, a wide, shapeless dress with flower print. She once surprised her audience when walking up to the podium of the main lecture hall of the University of Nebraska, grabbing the text of her speech from her bra. I keep missing her sharp analyses and ditto tongue.

Reading Bergmann
Barbara Bergmann, *The Economic Emergence of Women* (New York: Palgrave Macmillan, 2005).

Reading About Bergmann
Obituary in the *New York Times* (April, 11, 2015).[21]

Reading About feminist economics
Marianne Ferber and Julie Nelson (eds.) *Beyond Economic Man – Feminist Theory and Economics* (Chicago: University of Chicago Press, 1993).

Günseli Berik and Ebru Kongar (eds.) *Handbook of Feminist Economics* (New York: Routledge, 2021).

Practising Bergmann

The lessons to be learnt from systematic gender biases in economic behaviour have been put into practice in a variety of ways. A first example is through a balanced portfolio strategy. A second example is the removal of constraints for women to attain top positions and thereby to address gender inequality as well as contribute to better board decisions—a goal set by the 30% Club of CEOs and board chairs in the UK.[22] Whatever actions are taken by governments, firms and civil society groups, what matters is that they should address gender biases arising from ideology, stereotypes and outright discrimination. Today, extensive research has shown that here is no reason to accept gender inequality on the basis of presumed natural differences—whether based on the myth of hard-wired brain differences or arising from biased experimental research that does not include gender norms and stereotypes as control variables in the analysis of observed female-male behavioural differences.[23]

Investing Like a Girl

Warren Buffett attained an average return on investment of 19.4% over 50 years. That is exceptional, and he is among the relatively few who managed to make relatively constant earnings over time. How did he do this? According to a popular book about his approach, titled *Warren Buffett Invests Like a Girl*,[24] this is because he relies on a couple of stereotype feminine investment virtues:

- Modesty: he reinvests most of his profits, pays out a relatively modest income to himself and does not live in extravagant luxury.
- Cautious: he keeps a large buffer to absorb possible losses without risking bankruptcy or being forced to sell stocks at a loss.
- Independent: he does not like to borrow but invests from what he owns.
- Reflective: he invests not in bonds but in stocks that he carefully picks after extensive research.
- Patience: he keeps his stocks for the long term, even when a company he invests in passes through difficult times, ignoring peer pressure.
- Prudence: he also makes money from hedging and postponed income (which is a fiscal strategy, but at the same time he is known to be in favour of higher income taxes for the wealthy, including himself).

Perhaps an even more insightful example is the Islandic wealth investment fund Audur Capital, set up a few years before the financial crisis hit. The fund was initiated and led by two women who were fed up with the hyper-masculine financial culture of excessive risk taking, extravagant bonuses and careless short-termism they had experienced when working as financial specialists. The two directors wanted to do things differently. The business model was simple: you invest not for yourself but for your client; you are honest about risks and don't buy products you don't understand; and you work with clients who want to go for the long term and therefore have a distant earnings horizon. But just when they were doing quite well and expanding the business further, the crisis hit Iceland—harder than any other country. But, much to the surprise of their male competitors, their fund survived the financial breakdown amidst a collapse of financial firms in Reykjavik. How did they manage to do this? They had built a trust-based and transparent relationship with their clients, they did not award themselves bonuses, and they had not promised their clients extravagant returns. As a consequence, they made a decent profit and stable returns for their clients.[25]

Women on Boards

Norway was the first country to have a quota law for women on boards. A minimum of 40% of executive board positions should be held by women with a threat of forced dissolution of firms that do not abide by this law. In Germany, the voluntary targets for increasing the number of women on boards have been substituted by a law in 2016. Now, at least 30% of supervisory board positions in Germany should be held by women. Companies that do not meet this quota are not allowed to fill a vacancy with a man but should leave it open until a suitable female candidate is found. Such quota prevents companies to get away with 'we can't find suitable female candidates.' Indeed, that argument has proven to be nonsense. In the Netherlands, for example, the Minister of Education, together with the Chair of the national employers' association, has taken the initiative for a national data bank with female candidates that fulfil the minimum criteria for board positions. The data bank was filled with over a thousand high-profile women within a few months. In Kenya, public companies are required to have a minimum of 30% of either sex on their boards. This law is a genuine gender equality law because it is not restricted to women. Businesswomen in Kenya are lobbying to have the law extended to all business corporations, in particular publicly listed companies. An increasing number of countries have action plans and policies to increase the share of women on executive and supervisory boards of firms and the time has come to learn from each other's experiences in order to speed up progress.

NOTES

1. See my article on this: Irene van Staveren, "The Lehman Sisters Hypothesis," *Cambridge Journal of Economics*, 38, 5 (2014): 995-1014. See also my TedX Talk on the subject: https://www.youtube.com/watch?v=pcl0kEeN4mk Accessed on June 23, 2020.
2. For more information, see the website of the International Association for Feminist Economics (IAFFE) and its journal *Feminist Economics*: http://www.iaffe.org Accessed on June 23, 2020.
3. In a systematic review article, a colleague and I concluded that there is hardly, if any, evidence for sex differences in economic behaviour, whereas gender

differences reported are often small and the result of various contextual factors: Esther-Mirjam Sent and Irene van Staveren, "A Feminist Review of Behavioural Economic Research on Gender Differences," *Feminist Economics*, 25, 2 (2019): 1–35, https://www.tandfonline.com/doi/full/10.1080/13545701.2018.1532595. Accessed on June 23, 2020.
4. Susan Arterian Chang, "Outsiders and Outperformers: Women in Fund Management," *The Finance Professional's Post*, 04/05/2010, https://post.nyssa.org/nyssa-news/2010/04/outsiders-and-outperformers-women-in-fund-management.html Accessed on June 23, 2020. Barclays Wealth, *Understanding the Female Economy. The Role of Gender in Financial Decision Making and Succession Planning for the Next Generation* (London: Barclays Wealth and Ledbury Research, 2011), https://www.findevgateway.org/paper/2011/01/understanding-female-economy-role-gender-financial-decision-making-and-succession. Accessed on June 23, 2020.
5. For example: Daniela Beckmann and Lukas Menkhoff, "Will Women Be Women? Analyzing the Gender Difference among Financial Experts," *Kyklos* 61, 3 (2008): 364–384.
6. J. Coates and J. Herbert, "Endogenous Steroids and Financial Risk Taking on a London Trading Floor", *PNAS* 16, 105 (2008), pp. 6167-6172. John Coates, *The hour between dog and wolf: risk taking, gut feelings and the biology of boom and bust* (New York: Penguin Press, 2012).
7. Caitlin Zaloom, *Out of the Pits – Traders and Technology from Chicago to London* (Chicago: Chicago University Press, 2006).
8. Linda McDowell, "Making a Drama out of a Crisis: Representing Financial Failure, or a Tragedy in Five Acts", *Transactions of the Institute of British Geographers* 36, 2 (2011): 193–205. Melissa Fisher, *Wall Street Women* (Durham: Duke University Press, 2012).
9. Peter Agyemang-Mintah and Hannu Schadewitz, "Gender Diversity and Firm Value: Evidence from UK Financial Institutions," *International Journal of Accounting & Information Management* 27,1 (2019): 2–26.
10. EWOB, European Women on Boards Gender Diversity Index 2019, https://europeanwomenonboards.eu/wp-content/uploads/2019/11/Gender-Equality-Index-Final-report-vDEF-ter.pdf Accessed on June 24, 2020.
11. See the Female FTSE Board Report 2019: Susan Vinnicombe, Doyin Atewologun and Valentina Battista, "The Female FTSE Board Report 2019 – moving beyond the numbers" (Milton Keynes: Cranfield University, 2019), https://www.cranfield.ac.uk/som/expertise/changing-world-of-work/gender-and-leadership/female-ftse-index Accessed on June 24, 220.
12. Irene van Staveren, "Van financial professionals moet men geen hervorming van de sector verwachten," *MeJudice*, 4, 13 October (2011), https://www.mejudice.nl/artikelen/detail/van-financial-professionals-moet%2D%2Dmen-geen-hervorming-van-de-sector-verwachten Accessed on July 3, 2020.
13. Nick Wilson and Ali Altanlar, "Director Characteristics, Gender balance and Insolvency Risk: an Empirical Study," SSRN Working Paper, 30 May (2009), http://ssrn.com/abstract=1414224. Accessed on June 24, 2020.
14. Conference Board of Canada, "Women on Boards: Not Just the Right Thing ... But the 'Bright' Thing" (Ottawa: The Conference Board of Canada, 2002), https://utsc.utoronto.ca/~phanira/WebResearchMethods/women-bod&fpconference %20board.pdf Accessed on June 24, 2020. Credit Suisse Research

Institute, "Gender Diversity and Corporate Performance" (Zurich: Credit Suisse AG, 2012). Yowei Fang, Bill Francis, and Iftekhar Hasan, "More than Connectedness – Heterogeneity of CEO Social Network and Firm Value," Bank of Finland Discussion Paper no. 26, 2012 (Helsinki: Bank of Finland, 2012), https://helda.helsinki.fi/bof/bitstream/handle/123456789/7719/170822.pdf;jsessionid=E4F338E076C1DFDC60E9723F0ED58F23?sequence=1 Accessed on June 24, 2020. McKinsey & Company, "Women Matter – Gender Diversity, a Corporate Performance Driver", October 1, 2007, https://www.mckinsey.com/business-functions/organization/our-insights/gender-diversity-a-corporate-performance-driver# Accessed on June 24, 2020. Miriam Schwarz-Ziv, "Gender and Board Activeness: The Role of a Critical Mass," *Journal of Financial and Quantitative Analysis* 52, 2 (2017): 751–780.

15. Jasmin Joecks, Kerstin Pull and Karin Vetter, "Gender Diversity in the Boardroom and Form Performance: What Exactly Constitutes a "Critical Mass?", *Journal of Business Ethics* 118, 1 (2013): 61–72.
16. Jack Zenger and Joseph Folkman, "Are Women Better Leaders than Men?," *Harvard Business Review*, March 15 (2012), https://hbr.org/2012/03/a-study-in-leadership-women-do Accessed on June 24, 2020.
17. Wendy Wood, and Alice Eagly, "Biosocial Construction of Sex Differences and Similarities in Behavior," *Advances in Experimental Social Psychology*, 46, (2012): 55–123.
18. The International Association for Feminist Economics and the journal *Feminist Economics* can be found here: http://www.iaffe.org/ Accessed on June 24, 2020.
19. Barbara Bergmann, *The economic emergence of women* (London: Palgrave Macmillan, 2005).
20. Andreas Leibbrandt and John List, "Do Women Avoid Salary Negotiations? Evidence from a Large Scale Natural Field Experiment," *Management Science* 61, 9 (2014): 2016–2024, https://doi.org/10.1287/mnsc.2014.1994. Accessed on June 24, 2020.
21. Nelson Schwartz, "Barbara Bergmann: Trailblazer for Study of Gender in Economics, Is dead at 87." *The New York Times*, 11 April 2015. https://www.nytimes.com/2015/04/12/business/barbara-bergmann-trailblazer-for-study-of-gender-in-economics-is-dead-at-87.html Accessed 15 July, 2020.
22. https://30percentclub.org/. Accessed 15 July 2020.
23. Sent and van Staveren, "A Feminist Review".
24. Louann Lofton, *Warren Buffett Invests Like a Girl – and why you should, too* (New York: HarperCollins, 2011).
25. For an explanation of the business philosophy of Audur Capital, see the Ted Talk by one of the founders, Hella Tomasdottir: https://youtu.be/dsmgvr-cH94U. Accessed 15 July, 2020.

Bibliography

Agyemang-Mintah, Peter and Hannu Schadewitz. "Gender Diversity and Firm Value: Evidence from UK Financial Institutions." *International Journal of Accounting & Information Management* 27,1 (2019): 2–26.

Barclays Wealth. *Understanding the Female Economy. The Role of Gender in Financial Decision Making and Succession Planning for the Next Generation.* London: Barclays Wealth and Ledbury Research, 2011. https://www.findevgateway.org/paper/2011/01/understanding-female-economy-role-gender-financial-decision-making-and-succession. Accessed on June 23, 2020.

Beckmann, Daniela and Lukas Menkhoff. "Will Women Be Women? Analyzing the Gender Difference among Financial Experts." *Kyklos* 61, 3 (2008): 364–384.

Bergmann, Barbara. *The economic emergence of women.* London: Palgrave Macmillan, 2005.

Arterian Chang, Susan. "Outsiders and Outperformers: Women in Fund Management." *The Finance Professional's Post*, 04/05/2010, https://post.nyssa.org/nyssa-news/2010/04/outsiders-and-outperformers-women-in-fund-management.html. Accessed on June 23, 2020.

Coates, John. *The hour between dog and wolf: risk taking, gut feelings and the biology of boom and bust.* New York: Penguin Press, 2012.

Coates, John and Joe Herbert. "Endogenous Steroids and Financial Risk Taking on a London Trading Floor." *PNAS* 16, 105 (2008): 6167–6172.

Conference Board of Canada. "Women on Boards: Not Just the Right Thing ... But the 'Bright' Thing." Ottawa: The Conference Board of Canada, 2002. https://utsc.utoronto.ca/~phanira/WebResearchMethods/women-bod&fp-conference%20board.pdf. Accessed on June 24, 2020.

Credit Suisse Research Institute. "Gender Diversity and Corporate Performance." Zurich: Credit Suisse AG, 2012.

EWOB. "European Women on Boards Gender Diversity Index 2019." https://europeanwomenonboards.eu/wp-content/uploads/2019/11/Gender-Equality-Index-Final-report-vDEF-ter.pdf. Accessed on June 24, 2020.

Fang, Yowei, Bill Francis, and Iftekhar Hasan. "More than Connectedness – Heterogeneity of CEO Social Network and Firm Value." Bank of Finland Discussion Paper no. 26, 2012. Helsinki: Bank of Finland, 2012. https://helda.helsinki.fi/bof/bitstream/handle/123456789/7719/170822.pdf;jsessionid=E4F338E076C1DFDC60E9723F0ED58F23?sequence=1. Accessed on June 24.

Fisher, Melissa. *Wall Street Women.* Durham: Duke University Press, 2012.

Joecks, Jasmin, Kerstin Pull and Karin Vetter. "Gender Diversity in the Boardroom and Form Performance: What Exactly Constitutes a 'Critical Mass?'." *Journal of Business Ethics* 118, 1 (2013): 61–72.

Leibbrandt, Andreas and John List. "Do Women Avoid Salary Negotiations? Evidence from a Large Scale Natural Field Experiment." *Management Science* 61, 9 (2014): 2016–2024. https://doi.org/10.1287/mnsc.2014.1994. Accessed on June 24, 2020.

Lofton, Louann. *Warren Buffett Invests Like a Girl – and why you should, too.* New York: HarperCollins, 2011.

McDowell, Linda. "Making a Drama out of a Crisis: Representing Financial Failure, or a Tragedy in Five Acts." *Transactions of the Institute of British Geographers* 36, 2 (2011): 193–205.

McKinsey & Company. "Women Matter – Gender Diversity, a Corporate Performance Driver." October 1, 2007, https://www.mckinsey.com/business-functions/organization/our-insights/gender-diversity-a-corporate-performance-driver#. Accessed on June 24, 2020.

Schwartz, Nelson. "Barbara Bergmann: Trailblazer for Study of Gender in Economics, Is dead at 87." *The New York Times*, 11 April 2015. Https://www.nytimes.com/2015/04/12/business/barbara-bergmann-trailblazer-for-study-of-gender-in-economics-is-dead-at-87.html Accessed 15 July, 2020.

Schwarz-Ziv, Miriam. "Gender and Board Activeness: The Role of a Critical Mass." *Journal of Financial and Quantitative Analysis* 52, 2 (2017): 751–780.

Sent, Esther-Mirjam and Irene van Staveren. "A Feminist Review of Behavioural Economic Research on Gender Differences." *Feminist Economics*, 25, 2 (2019): 1–35. https://www.tandfonline.com/doi/full/10.1080/13545701.2018.1532595. Accessed 15 July, 2020.

Staveren, Irene van. "The Lehman Sisters Hypothesis." *Cambridge Journal of Economics*, 38, 5 (2014): 995–1014.

Staveren, Irene van. "Van financial professionals moet men geen hervorming van de sector verwachten." *MeJudice*, 4, 13 October (2011). https://www.mejudice.nl/artikelen/detail/van-financial-professionals-moet%2D%2Dmen-geen-hervorming-van-de-sector-verwachten. Accessed on July 3, 2020.

Vinnicombe, Susan, Doyin Atewologun and Valentina Battista. "The Female FTSE Board Report 2019 – moving beyond the numbers." Milton Keynes: Cranfield University, 2019. https://www.cranfield.ac.uk/som/expertise/changing-world-of-work/gender-and-leadership/female-ftse-index. Accessed on June 24, 220.

Wilson, Nick and Ali Altanlar. "Director Characteristics, Gender balance and Insolvency Risk: an Empirical Study." SSRN Working Paper, 30 May (2009). http://ssrn.com/abstract=1414224 Accessed 24 June 2020. Accessed on June 24, 2020.

Wood, Wendy and Alice Eagly. "Biosocial Construction of Sex Differences and Similarities in Behavior." *Advances in Experimental Social Psychology*, 46, (2012): 55–123.

Zaloom, Caitlin. *Out of the Pits – Traders and Technology from Chicago to London*. Chicago: Chicago University Press, 2006.

Zenger, Jack and Joseph Folkman. "Are Women Better Leaders than Men?" *Harvard Business Review*, March 15 (2012). https://hbr.org/2012/03/a-study-in-leadership-women-do. Accessed on June 24, 2020.

Chapter 6: Thorstein Veblen on Inequality

THE PROBLEM

Many economists and politicians hold on to the widespread misconception that rising income inequality is necessary for economic growth. They believe that innovation, entrepreneurship and labour productivity benefit from increasing income inequality because it would provide an incentive for hard work. Even worse, students are still being taught this myth. It is supported with simplistic thought-experiments. The first asks what hard-working employees or entrepreneurs would do if the marginal tax rate would be 75% or more. Obviously, the answer goes, they would reduce their efforts or move to a country without such a merciless equalizing policy. They would prefer going to places where people can benefit more from the fruits of their hard labour and ingenuity. The second thought-experiment asks the question what would happen if the government would hand out large sums of money to everybody below a certain income level. They would be very pleased to receive the hand-outs and not make efforts to get a job or start a business, right? The consequence, according to the two related thought-experiments, is that redistribution will make those with the most resources feel demotivated and those with the least resources lazy. The economic result is inefficiency, a decline in income, and eventually, misery. And all caused by a well-meaning government trying to reduce income inequality. The road to hell is paved with good intentions.

But it is a myth. Why? Because of two key ethical concepts that are relevant in economics: opportunities and equity. An economy without equal opportunities constrains human capital, entrepreneurship and productivity. Those who do not participate also do not contribute. Redistribution of resources is necessary to enable everybody to participate. Moreover, an economy that is perceived by many as unjust, because the rich protect their position through lobby and funding political campaigns, and because technological development and globalization destroys jobs at the bottom of the labour market, will create frustration and conflict. It will induce strikes and protests, as well as an illegal economy of crime, human trafficking and informality. And that is costly—it will constrain economic development for everyone.

The influential book *The Spirit Level*, by Richard Wilkinson and Kate Pickett, has demonstrated that countries with higher income inequality have lower levels of wellbeing.[1] This ranges from wellbeing indicators for infant mortality, obesity and teenage pregnancies to the number of homicides, mental health problems, drug abuse and distrust. Hence, high-income inequality not only is inefficient, but also has enormous negative social costs—not only on those lagging behind but also for society as a whole.

Increasing Income Inequality

What were the trends of income inequality just before the financial crisis hit? Since the 1980s, inequality has risen in the US, UK and many European countries, but also in countries such as China and South Africa. There are various measures for this, for example inequality in household income, inequality between capital and labour income, and inequality of wealth. Figure 1 shows the global decline in the labour share of income relative to the capital share (profit, interest and dividend). The trend from 1980 up to 2019 is clearly downwards, for both developed countries (dark shade) and developing countries (light shade). Only for the second group, the decline has stabilized after the financial crisis, showing a relatively small decline in labour income from 54 to 52% of GDP. But there, the labour share of income was already lower than in developed countries. In the latter countries, the labour share of income

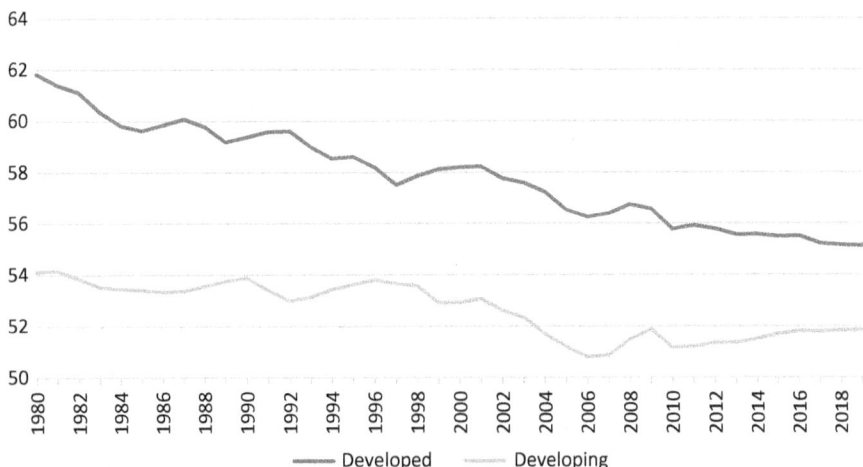

Fig. 1 Decline of the global labour share of income (% of GDP), 1980–2019. (Source: United Nations Global Policy Model and World Economy Database. Graph made by Jeronim Capaldo (UNCTAD))

declined more sharply: from 62 to 55% of GDP. Another interesting insight from the figure is that the biggest decline for both groups took place in the six years leading up to the crisis—between 2000 and 2006.

A different measure of income inequality is the Gini-index, which describes the distribution of household income. The Gini-index compares the incomes from the poorest to the richest households, measured in groups each consisting of 1% of all households. The higher the inequality, the higher the Gini-index. A Gini-index of zero means no inequality, whereas an index of 100 implies that the 1% richest households earn all the income while the other 99% earns nothing. Of course, these values are never observed in real-world economies. Generally, a value of 25 (e.g. for Denmark) or below is regarded as low inequality and values of 40 (e.g. for Turkey) and above tend to be regarded as high inequality. In developed countries, the Gini-index for disposable income has increased for almost every country since the mid-1980s. The highest increase in income inequality took place in Finland, Sweden, New Zealand, the UK and the US. The OECD-countries with the highest Gini scores are Mexico, Turkey and the US, all with an index at or above 40. A similar trend can be observed in developing countries. Figure 2 shows the trend for developing countries of the Gini-index (light shade) and compares it with the trend of the Globalization Index (dark shade), for the period 1992–2012. The left-hand axis is for the Globalization Index and shows an average increase from 47 to 62, whereas the

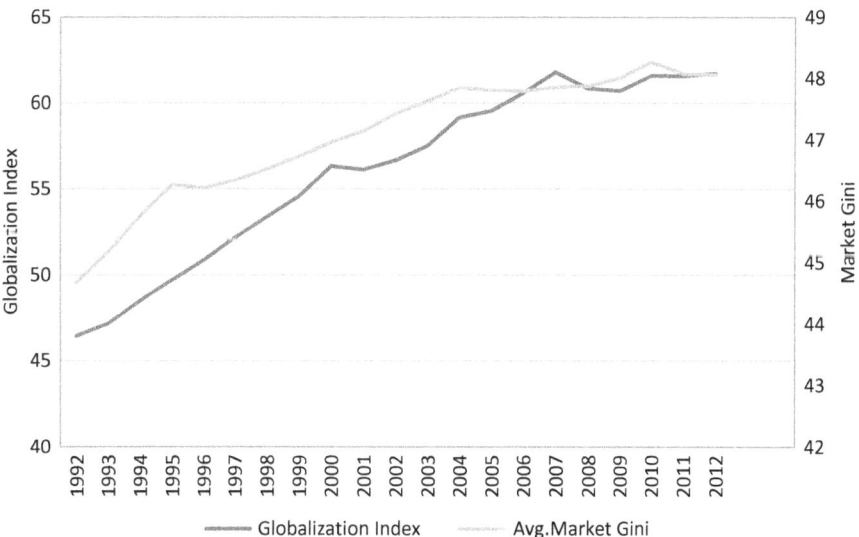

Fig. 2 Income inequality and globalization in developing countries, 1992–2012. (Source: Rolph van de Hoeven, 'Income inequality in developing countries, past and present', M. Nassanke and J. Ocampo (eds.) *The Palgrave Handbook of Development Economics.* Cham: Palgrave Macmillan, 2019: 335–376. Data based on SWIID and Globalization Index)

right-hand axis is for the Gini-index, demonstrating an average increase in income inequality from 45 to 48. The comparison suggests that the increase in globalization is neatly paralleled by an increase in income inequality in developing countries. Hence, even though globalization implies a shift of low-skilled jobs to developing countries, income equality has worsened in precisely those countries.

The trends in Figs. 1 and 2 suggest that there may be a relationship between the increasing inequality before the crisis and the outbreak of the crisis. If there is indeed a relationship, this would imply that the crisis was nourished by rising income inequality. Indeed, this is supported by some evidence. For this we turn to country-level data of the distribution of household income. Detailed data from the US indicates that the income of the bottom half of US households has not increased at all since the 1980s. This is shown in Fig. 3. The figure also shows that the bottom 20% of households even experienced a decline in their real incomes over a period of 30 years. And the next 20% of households saw their incomes remain the same. Only the next group, halfway the income distribution, saw their real incomes rise somewhat, but not more than 8% over 30 years. The richest 40% of households clearly benefitted (35%) from the economic growth since 1979. But the richest households benefitted the most. The top 1% saw their income increase by 185%. And the top 0.01% enjoyed an astonishing increase of 685%.

Nobody likes to pay taxes, but Americans seem to be particularly allergic to it. The American Dream of making it from newspaper boy to millionaire is widely shared even though the statistics show that upward mobility has become very limited over the past decades. It is that same dream of self-reliance and the reward of hard work with economic success, which prevents a rise in taxes in

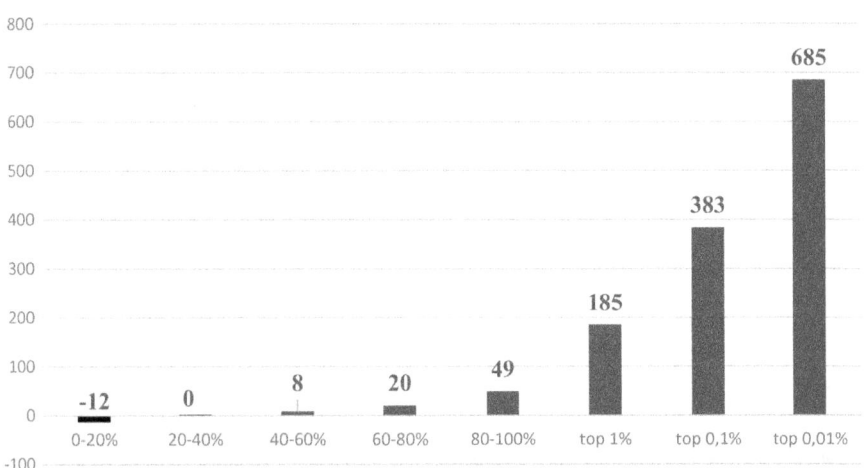

Fig. 3 Change (%) in US household income (1979–2012). (Source: Author, based on Andrew Sayer, *Why We Can't Afford the Rich* (Bristol: Policy Press, 2015))

order to support the poorest half of the households with health insurance, equal access to education and decent social housing. To the contrary, taxes have declined since the 1980s and in particular for the wealthy. Why did this happen when the result was not widespread upward mobility but increasing inequality and income decline for the bottom 40% of households? Why did the majority of voters accept a tax reform favouring the rich? The answer lies in the myth with which this chapter began. The idea that prosperity for all is only possible with rising inequality.

At the same time, there is widespread dissatisfaction among the working class. Paradoxically, this has not resulted in a reversal of the inequality trends. Under President Barack Obama, health care insurance was extended to millions of poor Americans. But this was insufficient to turn the tide. The widespread tax relief policy of 2011 benefitted the rich much more than the poor, as is shown in Table 1. One-third of tax relief measures reached the bottom 80% of households whereas two-thirds ended up in the top 20%. The richest 0.1% received 108 billion dollar benefits of a total of 939 billion tax benefits. That is 12% of all tax benefits for a group making up of only 0.1% of the population. Perhaps it is no surprise then that the impoverished white lower class voted for Donald Trump as the apparent embodiment of the American Dream (although he inherited his wealth from his father and has not shown much entrepreneurial success himself). The lower classes (in particular of white voters) lost trust in the Democrats and old politics—and not without reason, as the tax relief policy carried out under Obama indicates. They wanted their dream back, with jobs in coal mines, steel factories and the car industry. The growing economy since the recovery from the crisis, with expanding employment and tough trade policies against China, strengthens their belief in their cherished dream of social mobility and the accompanying myth of prosperity requiring inequality.

Also, elsewhere, the lower and middle classes saw their income share decline over the past few decades. A recent OECD study summarizes it as follows: 'The middle-income group has grown smaller with each successive generation. 70 percent of the baby boomers were part of the middle class in their twenties,

Table 1 Tax relief policy in the US, 2011

	0–20%	20–40%	40–60%	60–80%	80–99%	Top 1%	Total (billion US dollar)	Total (%)
Breaks	0.7	6.8	11.2	14.8	50.7	15.9	526	100
Deductions	–	0.7	3.8	14.2	54.9	26.4	147	100
Refundable credits	19.7	38.6	20.4	14.1	6.8	–	122	99.6
Capital gains taxed lower than wages	–	0.2	0.0	2.8	21.0	75.1	78	99.1
Other provisions	0.4	3.4	8.0	14.0	42.0	32.1	66	99.9
Total							939	100

Source: Author, adapted from the *New York Times*, 13 April, 2012. Based on data from the Tax Policy Centre

compared to 60 percent of the millennials. The baby boom generation enjoyed more stable jobs during their working life than younger generations.'[2] And the income inequality between the top 10% and the bottom 10% has increased markedly. While the ratio of the richest to the poorest 10% was 7 to 1 in the 1980s, it is now 9.5 to 1. Hence, not only the American Dream is increasingly unattainable, but upward mobility and its middle-class aspirations appear to be an empty promise for more and more young people throughout the developed world.

Credit for the Poor

The growing dissatisfaction among the bottom 50% of US households called for a policy response. From the turn of the new millennium, a typical capitalist response was found, through de Fed: cheap credit for the poor. By providing poor households access to capital, they could become homeowners. The Fed kept interest rates low, which allowed poor black families, Latino's and lone mothers to share in the American Dream. For example, home ownership among single mothers doubled in 20 years' time. The lenders earned commissions on the large number of mortgages, whereas the top bankers earned fat bonuses as a reward for the rapid increase in annual revenues. The banks made a safe bet, because the two national mortgage guarantee funds Fannie Mae and Freddie Mac backed the subprime loans.

But when it went wrong, it became clear that banking on inequality is not a viable business model. Half of the new mortgages since the year 2000 were not used for buying a home but instead to pay the bills, compensating for the lack of income growth of lower class families.[3] The loans were used by the bottom 50% of households to pay school fees, hospital bills and medication. A quarter of all mortgages ended up in the poorest 40% of households located in poor neighbourhoods. Hence, rising inequality and the delusion of the cheap credit policy were among the key economic developments leading up to the crisis. The American Dream that was sold to the economically weakest groups in society by the government and implemented by willing banks, was built on sand. Increasing inequality cannot be solved by credit in fragile markets suffering from elevated uncertainty and extremely risky bubbles. As if you try to cure someone's headache by distracting her with a funny story before knocking her out with a punch.

Increasing Inequality in Wealth

Did the financial crisis have a big impact on wealth? The answer is yes for the short run but no for the period after the recovery. One would expect that in particular the wealthy, those with assets, real estate and large savings, have suffered most from the crisis. But while this was true during the crisis itself, the wealthy recovered quickly due to rising equity values, moving portfolio investments to emerging economies, shifting to other assets such as gold, and the enormous increase in real estate values everywhere. Whereas many of those without sources of wealth other than a home with a high mortgage have not recovered yet from the crisis.

Recent data from the OECD shows that wealth inequality is twice as high as income inequality.[4] Across the OECD, the wealthiest 10% of households hold over 50% of total net wealth. And when wealth inequality is measured as the share held by the top 10%, the three most unequal countries are the US, the Netherlands and Denmark. The lowest wealth inequality is found in Poland, the Slovak Republic and Japan. Even more worrisome is that the Netherlands and Denmark are also the countries with the highest share of household debt relative to their incomes and assets. Around 25% of the households in these two countries have negative net-wealth. Fifty per cent of these concern home-owners with a higher mortgage debt than the market value of their homes. The other half consists of renters, who have accumulated debt unrelated to real estate. Such a high share of households having negative net-wealth points at startling financial vulnerability.

Wealth taxes have reduced over the two decades leading up to the crisis, according to the OECD.[5] There are three major forms of wealth tax: corporate income tax, dividend tax and net wealth tax. Corporate income tax rates have come down from an average of 47 to 25%, and taxes from dividend income have reduced from 75 to 42%.[6] In the OECD, only four countries had net wealth taxation in 2017. The others have only some form of taxation on net increases in wealth. As a consequence, the total revenue from wealth taxes is low, ranging from 0.5 (France) to 3.7% (Switzerland) of total tax revenues. And despite a substantive increase in wealth before and after the crisis, wealth tax revenue has not increased in OECD-countries. This is partially due to tax evasion and tax avoidance.

Protest: Us Versus Them

The 2007 financial crisis gave birth to the Occupy Wall Street movement, which quickly spread throughout the Western world. I remember having been invited by Occupy Rotterdam to talk about capitalism and Marx for the first time in my life. When the recession was over the movement disappeared. Discontent, however, remained. In various countries, lower income groups were dissatisfied but did not take to the streets. Instead, they voted for populist parties—in the Netherlands, Italy, Spain and Hungary—or for populist leaders of traditional conservative parties promising them to get their old factory jobs back, as in the US and the UK.

In France, however, a new social movement emerged in 2018: the yellow vests (*gilets jaunes*). It is a loosely organized movement based on online organization, without formal leadership and with flexible terms of participation. What unites the movement is the rejection of elites, the rejection of tax increases affecting the lower classes more than the higher classes, such as petrol tax and rising prices of costs of living, and, finally, the declining opportunities for social mobility despite the economic recovery. In addition, the yellow vests protestors are angry about tax cuts for the rich, in particular the reduction in wealth tax by president Emmanuel Macron in 2017. A recent OECD report about social mobility has calculated how many generations it takes to increase one's income from the bottom 10% of the income distribution to the mean income level.[7] The OECD-average is 4.5 generations. But in France, it takes 6 generations to move from the bottom to halfway the income distribution. Social mobility is far out of sight for younger generations in developed countries, in particular in France.

Social mobility in terms of earnings, occupations and education is high in Scandinavia, but low in many continental European countries. Social mobility measured as growth in individual earnings is especially low in France and Germany. This reflects how those at the bottom of the income ladder perceive their situation—and they are right in their claims of injustice and disrespect. The same OECD report also shows that those whose incomes have deteriorated have the feeling that their voice is not heard by politicians. In France for example, 40% of those whose income worsened felt that their voice was ignored, compared to only 20% of those who saw their income increase. An interesting analysis of the yellow vest movement shows the alternative way that these French people found to express their voices across the country—urban and rural alike.[8] A recent study explains the persistence of the movement with external and internal factors. The external factors are the legitimacy obtained in the light of harsh police reactions and the common anger against the elite. A key internal factor is solidarity emerging between very different social groups, ranging from unemployed and low-wage workers to self-employed and peasants, creating an 'us' versus 'them' dynamic. What they all share is their victimhood of increasing inequality, insecurity and limited social mobility.

The Insight

Let us start with the lessons learned from the crisis by a very wealthy American businessman. Nick Hanauer, one of the founders of Amazon.com and of 30 other companies, makes part of what he himself defines as 'the 0.01 percent filthy rich Americans'.[9] He has revealed that he was a mediocre student, that he does not understand computer programming and that he does not put in more effort than the average American. But he does like to take risk and has a nose for where economic developments go—he says that he sees over the horizon a bit faster than others do. And what does he see now? Pitchforks. He worries about widespread popular resistance that may turn out to be more violent than the protests of Occupy Wallstreet or the yellow vests. He worries not because he wants to protect his wealth but because he admits that the current level of inequality is socially unsustainable. With further increasing inequality, capitalism may even slide back into feudalism, he fears. And get back to a rentier economy, which extended well into the twentieth century, when the elites did not invest in productive assets generating employment but lived off the returns on their property.

Hanauer pleads for higher taxation of the rich and a decent minimum wage for employees at the bottom of the labour market. In 2013, he proposed a minimum wage of 15 dollar per hour, which was at that time twice the average minimum wage across the US. Economists, policy makers and many others thought that was a ridiculous plan and again, the myth about inequality and prosperity was brought in. They replied that such a high minimum wage would make employees lazy and lead employers to replace them by machines or move jobs elsewhere. Despite the critique, the minimum wage rate was introduced in Seattle. Since then, the city has remained among the fastest-growing local economies of the US. Hanauer refers to Henry Ford, who claimed that his workers should earn enough to be able to afford a T-Ford themselves. Hanauer could also refer to Keynes who made the same demand-side argument back in 1936. He explained that prosperity does not arise from building new factories but from higher earnings by consumers allowing them to purchase the goods produced by these factories. Hanauer was a bit bolder and claimed that when employees would earn twice as much, they would also spend twice as much. But not himself, because he already owns three homes, an airplane and a yacht and cannot go out for dinner or get a haircut more often than he already does, he acknowledges. He ends his letter to his fellow-filthy-rich-Americans acknowledging that their class is not superior but simply has had much luck—as Frank Knight had argued already about business success in the context of uncertainty.

The Leisure Class

Nick Hanauer grants that economic inequality is an economic problem that may result in destructive social dynamics. Hence, he recognizes what the founder of institutional economics already argued over a century ago. Thorstein Veblen became famous with his biting analysis of the rentier economy, *The Theory of the Leisure Class*, which was published more than a century ago.[10]

This bold social scientist observed high-income inequality in Europe and the US that did not seem to arise from hard work and entrepreneurship by the top earners and the lack of it by everyone else. He argued that the rentiers—in particular large landowners—did not provide any useful contribution to the economy. To the contrary, these wealthy men were proud to belong to the leisure class, and they emphasized the leisure time of their wives, who were not supposed to do any paid or unpaid work. At most, upper-class women were allowed to engage in charity, as the complement of their husbands' engagement in speculation or politics. In his article titled *The Barbarian Status of Women* Veblen already referred to the phenomenon of a trophy wife—not at the arm of a popular football player, but at the side of a man seeking public admiration of his status expressed with plenty leisure time spent at the horse races.[11]

The leisure class, Veblen observed, collects trophies such as extravagantly dressed women, luxury gadgets and big estates. And they are able to maintain that position because others, in the middle class and even in the lower classes, are furtively jealous. As a consequence, the wealthy generate a social norm to which a large part of society aspires and what Veblen calls an institution. This insight would become the start of institutional economics, which studies the effect of institutions on economic behaviour but also the influence of economic behaviour on the emergence, continuation and change of institutions. The earlier mentioned study of Wilkinson and Pickett about the social consequences of inequality, illustrates how widespread the institution of economic status has become in a country like the US. Approximately 13% of Americans live below the poverty line, but 80% of them have air-conditioning and 75% of them own a car, while at the same time their health status, life expectancy and food intake are significantly less than those who are economically better-off. The entrepreneurs and workers, who are the main contributors to productive activity, nevertheless are strongly influenced by the institutions of the wealthy class, who take their decisions on rents from their armchairs. Veblen therefore also refers to them as the pecuniary class: the leisure class which invisibly sets the rules of the game by receiving income from pecuniary activity and consuming it in extravagant ways.

It should be noted, that Veblen's critique of the rich class should not be confused with Marx' critique of capitalists. Whereas Marx criticized entrepreneurs for their exploitation of labour, Veblen admired entrepreneurship and criticized those who did not invest their wealth in factories, technology and other productive investments. He noticed that not only workers but also the petty bourgeoisie, artisans, salespeople and the self-employed were constrained by the pecuniary activities of the leisure class, depriving the economy from capital for productive investment. He even labelled the pecuniary activities as 'economic sabotage'. Moreover, Veblen claimed that armchair finance supports economic concentration and stifles healthy competition. As a consequence, he argued—echoing Marx—the bargaining power of capital over labour increases and real wages decline. The resulting economy, Veblen said, was a credit economy, in which finance is the driving force, dominating the real economy. The 2007 financial crisis arose from an abundance of credit, which was largely invested in non-productive activities, supporting Veblen's theory of the rentier class and the institutionalization of its social status.

The lesson that can be learned from Veblen is that economic inequality doesn't generate prosperity. Wealth inequality is not necessarily efficient and does not necessarily generate entrepreneurship, but may result in market power, short-termism and unproductive investment. In addition, the conspicuous consumption belonging to a pecuniary lifestyle of the happy few sets the norm for the rest of society. In the century after Veblen's death, the mechanisms behind this process have been unravelled by institutional economists.

Inequality as a Break on the Economy

An IMF-study shows that generally, a decrease in the Gini-index is paralleled by an increase in economic growth.[12] Only in case of very strong income redistribution there is no longer a contribution to growth, the IMF-calculations demonstrate—but there is no country on earth that shows such a negative relationship between equality and growth. This implies that the relationship between the two factors is generally positive—as is illustrated in Fig. 4.

The key mechanisms behind the negative relationship between inequality and growth are the following. First, the accumulation of wealth signals status, not investment. Think, for example, of large landowners such as the owners of haciendas in Brazil, who leave a significant part of the land idle. This is a modern reflection of Veblen's leisure class: such showing off of unproductive wealth signals status. Second, the inequality of land and other tangible assets, excludes whole groups from effective participation in the economy. A lack of agricultural land or education or access to affordable credit results in underutilization of human resources and hence, low levels of productivity. Moreover, low health status and unaffordable health insurance deteriorate this situation. Third, the wealthy can buy political influence to protect their interests. This enables them to bend formal institutions to fit their interests, for example the tax system or claiming private benefits from innovations generated with public funds. The tax reductions that coincided the increasing Gini indices of income and wealth were already discussed in this chapter. And the enormous profits made by the big tech companies such as Google and Apple are examples of the capture of public investments by private companies for their own benefit.[13]

The fourth mechanism behind the negative relationship between inequality and growth is the discouragement of hard work of those who do not see their incomes rise whereas they see the earnings of those above them increase without more effort. Why would one continue to work overtime and invest in knowledge and personal development if there is no reward for it, relative to the

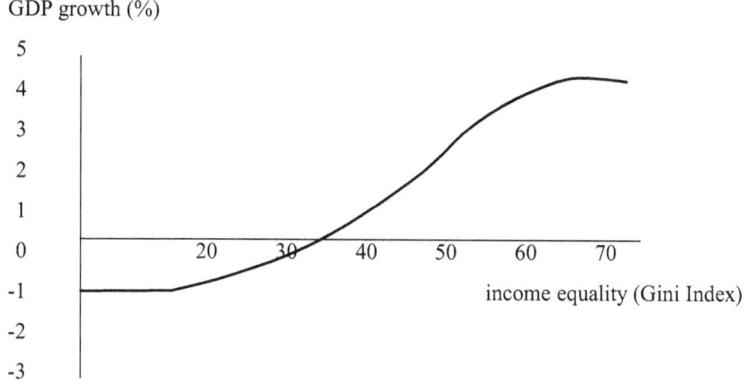

Fig. 4 The relationship between equality and growth. (Source: Author)

rewards that others get? When top bankers receive fat bonuses even though they had to rely on state support? It does not feel right. Even for bankers. When the CEO of ABN Amro bank, Gerrit Zalm, announced a 100,000-euro salary raise for the board, he received scorn not only from politicians and society, but also from ABN Amro Bank employees. They had not received a salary raise in five years. But they were the ones facing customers complaining about the high earnings at the top of the bank. Such blatantly unfair salary policy does not motivate to put in the extra mile for one's employer. The fifth mechanism is that growing inequality generates conflict. Strikes by dissatisfied workers, as they pop up even in a country such as China. Riots and looting in cities as far away as London and Buenos Aires. Flows of immigrants who do not see any future for their families in their own country, risking their lives in the deserts of northern Mexico or on the Mediterranean Sea. The sixth and final mechanism behind the negative relationship between inequality and growth is the purchasing power that Henry Ford and Nick Hanauer and Keynes talked about. More purchasing power for the rich does not generate much domestic demand for consumer goods. But more purchasing power for the poor immediately results in more demand for food, clothing, transportation, medication, and much more—benefitting domestic industry and retail firms. Unless the poor are heavily indebted—in that case they will first reduce their debt, with which they, unwillingly, stimulate the pecuniary profit machine instead of the real economy.

And this closes the circle. As long as the pecuniary economy—the FIRE sector of Minsky's analysis—remains dominant, inequality will rise and, eventually, economic growth and wellbeing will stagnate.

The Economist

Thorstein Veblen (Cato 1857–Menlo Park 1929)

Veblen was born on a farm in the state of Wisconsin and was the son of Norwegian immigrants. He started various studies at different universities across the US before opting for philosophy. He obtained his PhD in philosophy in 1884 at the University of Yale. The next seven years he tried to get an academic position as a philosopher and spent much of is his time reading—philosophy, but also in the social sciences. Eventually, he decided to study economics and obtained an appointment as lecturer at the University of Chicago. He remained there for 14 years. Disappointed about not receiving a promotion, he moved elsewhere. But he remained unsuccessful at other universities as well.

The reason may lie in his critique of the emerging and popular paradigm of neoclassical economics, led by economists such as Alfred Marshall and Leon Walras. For example, he labelled neoclassical economists, who assume that people always strive for happiness, hedonistic economists. He himself rejected that one-dimensional view of human beings, which he described as 'the hedonistic concept of men is that of a lightning calculator of pleasures and pains.'[14]

In addition, he hated to come to department meetings, didn't care much for being on time for his class and he abhorred grading work. He gave an average mark to every student, irrespective the quality of the work they turned in. To make matters worse, his students walked out of his classes because he used to be grumbling and take intellectual deviations that only his own mind could follow. The story goes that in the end, only one student remained.

Thorstein Veblen's personal life was equally chaotic. He did not make his bed or clean his home, and only began dishwashing when no clean plates and mugs were to be found and the dirty dishes had formed a dangerously balancing heap on the kitchen table. His furniture consisted of carton boxes and when he worked at the University of Missouri, he rented the basement of the house of a colleague, which he entered and left through the window. All boards of the universities he was employed at, reached a point at which they found ways to say goodbye to him. Not only because of his criticism of his fellow economists and his careless attitude towards teaching, but also because time and again he had affairs with his female students or the wives of his colleagues.

But Veblen was also the founder of a whole new school of economic thought: institutional economics. He was inspired both by Charles Darwin's evolution theory and by the pragmatic sociologists, such as Charles Pierce, who was among his former lecturers in philosophy. At first sight, this is a surprising combination of theories, which in his days could lead to appalling theories such as eugenics, which was supported, for example, by Chicago School economist Irving Fischer.[15] But the lesson that Veblen took from Darwin was a completely different one. He applied the idea of adjustment to one's environment to the economy, in which he noted that firms were doing exactly the same every day with the same result: survival of the fittest. Veblen's school of institutional economics demonstrated that economic institutions were driving much of the behaviour of firms, employees, investors and consumers. And it could explain why some institutions would support efficiency, for example public schools, while other institutions would reinforce the power of a dominant interest group, such as social status.

Veblen understood the dynamics of economic institutions through its substantial effect on economic behaviour: 'The growth and mutations of the institutional fabric are an outcome of the conduct of the individual members of the group, since it is out of the experience of individuals, through the habituation of individuals, that institutions arise; and it is in this same experience that these institutions act to direct and define the aims and end of conduct.'[16] Although today, when we speak of institutions we think about organizations and formal regulations, for Veblen institutions were primarily intangible, driven by habit, envy, status and other motivations. Hence, institutions refer to a wide range of social norms, including habits, beliefs and routines as well as organizations, laws and rules. His interest in institutions emerged from his insight that the social norms of the leisure class had considerable influence on economic variables, such as consumption and investment. It was precisely that understanding, which led him to study this class as a rentier class of men and women spending their time in idleness, simply living off the rents from the property accumulated by earlier generations. In *The Theory of the Leisure Class*, he noticed that this class expressed its status through conspicuous consumption instead of entrepreneurial activity. Today, such conspicuous consumption is identified as the Veblen-effect, referring to consumer goods not so much for their use-value but for status-signalling. This involves the seemingly irrational choice for expensive goods for which cheaper alternatives are available at the same level of quality. Gucci sunglasses, for example, or Luis Vuitton handbags. But we also refer to the Veblen-effect when the quality of a good is unknown or difficult to assess. In such instances, consumers tend to regard the higher price alternatives as signalling higher quality. For example, in the case of more expensive restaurants in an unfamiliar town or German cars instead of French or Korean ones even though the quality of these automobiles hardly differs anymore. Brands and marketeers capitalize on the Veblen-effect by appealing to the status of the higher-priced good. In the Netherlands, for example, a radio commercial for Opel cars (Vauxhall in the UK and Chevrolet in the US) was German spoken, suggesting that the General Motors brand is a German car, simply because it is produced in Germany.

Despite the fact that Thorstein Veblen was not a good teacher and all his consecutive employers wanted to get rid of him, he gradually became well-known as the founder of institutional economics whereas his innovative concepts, such as rentier economy, hedonistic calculus and conspicuous consumption, have been adopted throughout economics, sociology and political economy. It would take another century before Nobel Memorial Prizes would be awarded to institutional economists—Douglass North in 1993 and Oliver Williamson and Elinor Ostrom in 2009. Veblen died three months before Black Friday—just too early for an undoubtful sharp analysis of the destructive role that the financial elite had played in the 1929 crash and the lengthy depression that followed.

Reading Veblen
Thorstein Veblen, *The Theory of the Leisure Class. An Economic Study in the Theory of Institutions* (New York: Macmillan, 1899).

Reading About Veblen
Stephen Edgell, *Veblen in Perspective – His Life and Thought* (Armonk: M.E. Sharpe, 2001).

Practising Veblen

Limits to Bulging Earnings

The marginal rates of income taxation have come down considerably over the past few decades. The marginal rates varied between 70% and even 90% in

Europe and North America in the 1970s. But today, the myth about inequality and prosperity has driven them down to less than 50% (from an OECD-average of 66% in 1981 to 43% in 2016).[17]

There are basically two stages at which income inequality can be reduced. The best known and universally applied is at the second stage: taxation of earned income. This results in income redistribution after taxes, referred to as the secondary income distribution. In order to curb the current trend, the marginal rate of income taxes should go up again. This could be done in such a way that not the middle class is the target but the wealthy—say those earning three times the modal income and more, or the top 20% of the income distribution. This can be achieved by a combination of a higher marginal rate, a higher tax benefit at the bottom, and less tax deductions for the rich, such as fiscal benefits of interest paid on debts. Of course, tax raises should conform to two criteria for their effectiveness: international coordination to prevent tax evasion and tariffs that do not exceed the limit beyond which net tax revenue will decline due to lower income generated. The first criterion could be met through concerted action in international fora such as the EU and the OECD. The second one by simultaneously enable fairness in tax collection (by addressing tax evasion) and in fiscal spending (by transparency, curbing corruption and inefficient spending, and by demonstrating the common good served by public goods).

The first stage of income redistribution concerns the primary income distribution—where earnings are made. This involves raising minimum wages, which has been done already to some extent in the US and Germany without negative effects on employment. But it can be implemented more widely. For example, in the Netherlands, youth between 15 and 23 years old have traditionally been excluded from adult minimum wage policy and earn much lower minimum wages. A new law now gradually reduces the age limit for the minimum wage. Since 2019, youth from 21 years and above should earn the legal adult minimum wage of 9.54 euro per hour. The minimum wage for 18-year olds is 4.77 euro per hour and for 15-year olds only 2.86 euro per hour.[18] When my son had a side job in the local supermarket at the age of 15, filling stocks, he did not care much about that wage and simply enjoyed the work with his co-workers and earning some pocket money. When, two years later, my daughter got the same job, she was appalled by the meagre wage rate and quickly managed to find a better-paid job in the main shopping centre, handing out discount-flyers and trying to talk customers into the spectacles shop that hired her for twice as much as her brother had earned at the same age.

Next to increasing wages at the bottom, top incomes need to be capped, because it is predominantly the fast rise of top incomes that cause the rising inequality between the top and the bottom of the income distribution. After the financial crisis, the EU has agreed on a bonus cap of 100% of fixed salary for the financial sector (in the Netherlands the Minister of Finance has reduced the cap to 20%). But this is a rather weak measure. Banks are now using the back door by raising fixed salaries of top bankers. However, not all banks join the rat-race for status. For example, the cooperative bank Caja Laboral in Spain sticks to the rule of the Mondragon Corporation that it is part of. That rule implies that the salary of the CEO should not be more than 6.5 times the salary of the least earning employee. And the Dutch Triodos Bank, operating in five European countries, lives by the rule that the CEO earns no more than ten times the least earning employee. The additional benefit of such limits at the bottom and top of banks is that it forces them to reflect on status and legitimacy, both in their relationship to society and to their own employees. And this, in turn, is likely to benefit a company's culture and performance.[19]

Wealth Tax

Given the fact that in most countries, wealth inequality is higher than income inequality, it is odd that so little attention goes to wealth tax. Since the ratio of capital income over labour income has been increasing over the past few decades, it is even more inconsistent that income tax rates—which largely concerns labour income—are higher than the various types of wealth tax rates (on dividend, profit, inheritance or property). The first Nobel Memorial Prize winner in economics (1969), Jan Tinbergen, already argued for shifting taxation from labour to capital. Today, new voices have joined the plea for wealth tax. One of them is the French economist Thomas Piketty, with his two thick books about wealth inequality: *Capital in the Twenty-First Century* (published in 2014) and *Capital and Ideology* (published in 2019).[20] Obviously not every member of the leisure class applauds these books and their influence, but now that even some filthy rich men such as Nick Hanauer and Warren Buffett are willing to pay higher tax rates, time seems ripe for tax reform addressing the growing inequality.

The OECD reports discussed in this chapter recommend the following net wealth tax design rules: relatively low but progressive rates, limited exemptions and deductions, determination of the tax base on market values of assets, and transparency. In addition, they recommend inheritance tax. These are important not only to address income and wealth inequality but also to address the reduced social mobility of the lower and middle classes. But inheritance tax rates tend to be low, with high thresholds and numerous exemptions and opportunities for evasion. That is why the British economist Tony Atkinson made a proposal to replace this tax with two innovative fiscal instruments. The first being a progressive rate on the receiver's side: the more money one already has received from inheritances, the higher the tax rate, up to 100%. This is an incentive to bequest one's wealth, or at least part of it, to people who would otherwise not receive wealth at the death of family members. The second innovative idea is reversing a bequest to a subsidy for everyone upon birth or, in the version proposed by Piketty, when reaching adulthood. This would imply an inheritance tax rate of 100%, providing the state with a wealth fund from which the child subsidy or adulthood subsidy could be funded. This subsidy could then function as capital to be invested in education and personal development, for example setting up a business or buying a home.

NOTES

1. Richard Wilkinson, and Kate Pickett. *The Spirit Level: why more equal societies almost always do better* (London: Allen Lane, 2009).
2. OECD, "Under Pressure: The Squeezed Middle Class" (Paris: OECD, 2019: 13). http://www.oecd.org/social/under-pressure-the-squeezed-middle-class-689afed1-en.htm. Accessed on July 15, 2020.
3. See, for example, an insightful study on the subprime crisis and poverty by Gary Dymski, Jesus Hernandez and Lisa Mohanty, 'Race, Gender, Power and the US Subprime Mortgage and Foreclosure Crisis: a Meso Analysis,' *Feminist Economics*, 19, 3 (2013): 124–151.
4. Carlotta Balestra, and Richard Tonkin, "Inequalities in Household Wealth across OECD countries: evidence from the OECD wealth distribution" (Paris: OECD Statistics Working Papers 2018/01, 2018), https://doi.org/10.1787/7e1bf673-en Accessed on March 2, 2020.
5. OECD, "The Role and Design of Net Wealth Taxes in the OECD." OECD Tax Policy Studies no. 26 (Paris: OECD, 2018). http://www.oecd.org/ctp/the-role-and-design-of-net-wealth-taxes-in-the-oecd-9789264290303-en.htm. Accessed on July 15, 2020.
6. OECD, "Under Pressure: The Squeezed Middle Class" (Paris: OECD, 2019: 13) http://www.oecd.org/social/under-pressure-the-squeezed-middle-class-689afed1-en.htm. Accessed on July 15, 2020.
7. OECD, "A Broken Social Elevator? How to Promote Social Mobility" (Paris: OECD, 2018). http://www.oecd.org/social/broken-elevator-how-to-promote-social-mobility-9789264301085-en.htm. Accessed on July 15, 2020.
8. Jolanda Jetten, Frank Mols, and Hema Preya Selvanathan, "How Economic Inequality Fuels the Rise and Persistence of the Yellow Vests Movement," *International Review of Social Psychology* 33, 1 (2020), doi: https://doi.org/10.5334/irsp.356 Accessed on July 15, 2020.
9. Nick Hanauer, "Ultra-rich man's letter: 'To my Fellow Filthy-Rich Americans: the Pitchforks are Coming'," *Top Info Post*, 30 June 2014, http://forerunner-chronicles.com/ultra-rich-mans-letter-fellow-filthy-rich-americans/ Accessed on July 15, 2020.
10. Thorstein Veblen, *The Theory of the Leisure Class. An Economic Study in the Theory of Institutions* (New York: Macmillan, 1899).
11. Thorstein Veblen, "The Barbarian Status of Women," *The American Journal of Sociology*, 4, 4 (1899): 503–514.
12. Jonathan Ostry, Andrew Berg and Charalambos G. Tsangarides, "Redistribution, Inequality and Growth" (Washington, DC: IMF Staff Discussion Note, 14 February 2014). https://www-imf-org.eur.idm.oclc.org/external/pubs/ft/sdn/2014/sdn1402.pdf. Accessed 15 July, 2020.
13. Mariana Mazzucato, *The Entrepreneurial State. Debunking Public vs Private Sector Myths* (London: Anthem Press, 2013).
14. Thorstein Veblen, *The Place of Science in Modern Civilization – and Other Essays* (New York: B.W. Huebsch, 1919, p. 73).
15. Anne Cot, "'Breed out the Unfit and Breed in the Fit': Irving Fischer, Economics, and the Science of Heredity." *The American Journal of Economics and Sociology* 64, 3 (2005): 793–826.
16. Veblen, *The Place of Science in Modern Civilization*, p. 243.

17. OECD, "Net Wealth Taxes," 2018.
18. https://www.uwv.nl/particulieren/bedragen/detail/minimum-jeugd-loon Accessed on March 13, 2020.
19. I studied this relationship with data from a survey among Dutch bankers (of which I will say more in Chap. 9). Irene van Staveren, "The Misdirection of bankers' Moral Compass in the Organizational Field of Banking", *Cambridge Journal of Economics*, 44, 3 (2020): 507–526, https://doi.org/10.1093/cje/bez052. Accessed on March 13, 2020.
20. Thomas Piketty, *Capital in the Twenty-First Century* (Cambridge, MA: Belknap Press, 2014). Thomas Piketty, *Capital and Ideology* (Cambridge, MA: Belknap Press, 2020).

BIBLIOGRAPHY

Balestra, Carlotta, and Richard Tonkin. "Inequalities in Household Wealth across OECD countries: evidence from the OECD wealth distribution." Paris: OECD Statistics Working Papers 2018/01, 2018) https://doi.org/10.1787/7e1bf673-en. Accessed 2 March 2020.

Cot, Anne. "'Breed out the Unfit and Breed in the Fit': Irving Fischer, Economics, and the Science of Heredity." *The American Journal of Economics and Sociology* 64, 3 (2005): 793–826.

Dymski, Gary, Jesus Hernandez, and Lisa Mohanty. "Race, Gender, Power and the US Subprime Mortgage and Foreclosure Crisis: a Meso Analysis." *Feminist Economics*, 19, 3 (2013): 124–151.

Hanauer, Nick. "Ultra-rich man's letter: 'To my Fellow Filthy-Rich Americans: the Pitchforks are Coming'." *Top Info Post*, 30 June 2014 http://forerunnerchronicles.com/ultra-rich-mans-letter-fellow-filthy-rich-americans/ Accessed on July 15, 2020.

Jetten, Jolanda, Frank Mols, and Hema Preya Selvanathan. "How Economic Inequality Fuels the Rise and Persistence of the Yellow Vests Movement." *International Review of Social Psychology* 33, 1 (2020) https://doi.org/10.5334/irsp.356 Accessed on July 15, 2020.

Mariana Mazzucato. *The Entrepreneurial State. Debunking Public vs Private Sector Myths* (London: Anthem Press, 2013).

OECD. "Under Pressure: The Squeezed Middle Class" (Paris: OECD, 2019: 13) http://www.oecd.org/social/under-pressure-the-squeezed-middle-class-689afed1-en.htm. Accessed on July 15, 2020.

OECD. "The Role and Design of Net Wealth Taxes in the OECD." OECD Tax Policy Studies no. 26 (Paris: OECD, 2018a). http://www.oecd.org/ctp/the-role-and-design-of-net-wealth-taxes-in-the-oecd-9789264290303-en.htm. Accessed on July 15, 2020.

OECD. "A Broken Social Elevator? How to Promote Social Mobility" (Paris: OECD, 2018b). http://www.oecd.org/social/broken-elevator-how-to-promote-social-mobility-9789264301085-en.htm. Accessed on July 15, 2020.

Ostry, Jonathan, Andrew Berg, and Charalambos G. Tsangarides. "Redistribution, Inequality and Growth" (Washington D.C.: IMF Staff Discussion Note, 14 February 2014). https://www-imf-org.eur.idm.oclc.org/external/pubs/ft/sdn/2014/sdn1402.pdf. Accessed on 15 July, 2020.

Piketty, Thomas. *Capital in the Twenty-First Century* (Cambridge MA.: Belknap Press, 2014).
Piketty, Thomas. *Capital and Ideology* (Cambridge, MA.: Belknap Press, 2020).
Staveren, Irene van. "The Misdirection of bankers' Moral Compass in the Organizational Field of Banking," *Cambridge Journal of Economics*, 44, 3 (2020): 507–526, https://doi.org/10.1093/cje/bez052. Accessed on March 13, 2020.
Veblen, Thorstein. *The Theory of the Leisure Class. An Economic Study in the Theory of Institutions* (New York: Macmillan, 1899a).
Veblen, Thorstein. "The Barbarian Status of Women," *The American Journal of Sociology*, 4, 4 (1899b): 503-514.
Veblen, Thorstein. *The Place of Science in Modern Civilization – and Other Essays* (New York: B.W. Huebsch, 1919, p. 73).
Wilkinson, Richard, and Kate Pickett. *The Spirit Level: why more equal societies almost always do better*. London: Allen Lane, 2009.

Chapter 7: Amartya Sen on Financial Capabilities

THE PROBLEM

An uncertain financial context and the fragility of financial markets are clearly not enabling factors for sound financial decision making. Consumers are used to handle risk and banks are helpful by providing risk profiles from which their customers can choose. But how to deal with uncertainty? Banks do not give much advice other than warnings in small print. Often, bankers themselves think exclusively in terms of risk and not uncertainty. Good bankers are skilled in calculating the risk of a variety of investment projects and are able to estimate closely the probabilities of profit and loss for the bank as well as for their clients, although they may underestimate the effect of fat tails and systemic risk. But from the previous chapters we know that dealing with uncertainty requires different skills, including financial intuition, self-restraint, patience, long-term perspective, information sharing, and healthy buffers and other back-up options. In addition, risk and uncertainty require sufficient decision-making space in order to be able to make sound financial choices.

What about the decision-making space for bankers and consumers? This chapter will first go into the room for manoeuvre for financial professionals at the supply side of the market who offer financial products and services to clients who are generally not much interested in the details of it. After this, I will discuss the demand side of the financial market, with the consumer's need for payments, savings, credit and investment. This consumer is not necessarily an individual or household but may as well be a firm, association or government agency. But first, I will focus on the financial professional, zooming in on bankers in the Netherlands, whom I surveyed six years after the nationalization of ABN AMRO Bank.

The Curtailed Banker

I developed a questionnaire, on behalf of the Dutch think tank the Sustainable Finance Lab (SFL), for ordinary bank employees of all major banks in the country.[1] The online questionnaire was returned by over 600 bankers who were employed mainly at the lower and middle ranks of banks such as ING, ABN AMRO Bank, Rabobank and SNS. The respondents are the people one speaks to in person or on the phone and who are dealing with one's day-to-day financial business. For example, bank cards, mortgages, car loans and savings deposits.

For two years, I had been preparing myself with emails, phone calls and meetings with top managers of the main Dutch banks—HR directors, economists at the bank's research departments and even board members. I had hoped to reach a high number of bankers through the intranet of the banks themselves. But the first bank refused to cooperate with us right after the first meeting. They were also not interested in a short presentation about the need for a change of the Dutch banking culture after the crisis. Two other banks had doubts and were afraid for negative media coverage if the survey results would entail material that might give a negative impression of their bank. They both eventually declined to participate, after two years. I was very disappointed about this refusal of cooperation with a think tank consisting of a dozen well-respected economics professors who had joined efforts on a voluntary basis with the sole purpose of stimulating the Dutch financial sector to become much more resilient and sustainable. Of course, I could understand the hesitation about media coverage of the survey results, which undoubtedly would pick on findings that would turn out not so flattering for the already damaged image of the big banks. But the study on banking culture was not meant to be self-congratulating. It was a necessary instrument for the important and urgent task of cultural change and regaining society's trust in banks, which was—and still is—less than 50%.

The two banks with whom I had had various interactions about the questionnaire both wanted influence over the questions I would ask. I agreed with hesitance and added some questions while adjusting others—as long as they reflected the hypotheses that I had derived from the theoretical framework about banking culture and the behaviour of bank employees. It was only after these two years of fruitless interactions that it dawned on me that it all was a strategy of putting the whole thing off. Both banks told me that they would only participate directly in the survey if I agreed not to make the results public—either through the media or through academic publications. Of course, I did not accept this condition. Later, they both informed me that they had started an internal program of cultural change and that therefore, my survey would be redundant.

In the end, only one of the four banks agreed, which was clearly insufficient for a sector-wide survey. Fortunately, we found a back door through cooperation with the labour unions and a TV news show. They appeared to have a similar plan for a survey, following up on the persistent negative image of bankers since the crisis. They were interested to find out if there was something in the banking culture that could explain what had gone so wrong and continued to cause moral outrage and distrust, other than simply the idea that bankers are greedy and careless persons. I made new adjustments and added some questions to cover labour union concerns, and we sent the questionnaire off in 2014 to the 7000 bankers, who were members of labour unions. The sample of 617 bankers who had anonymously filled in the full online questionnaire was representative for all bankers who were members of a labour union (about 10% of all bankers). By comparing their key characteristics (age, sex, salary and bank where they were employed), I was able to confirm that this sample was not significantly different from the banker's population as a whole. And as expected, the respondents did not give typical labour union answers to the questions: for example, the large majority agreed with their salary level and the social plan for labour redundancy.

I presented the survey results at the headquarters of the only bank of the big four that had not declined to cooperate with us on the survey. The bank—to state it in a way that reflects the hyper-masculine culture so well—which had the balls to face the publication of possible negative findings from the survey. I presented the results in Amsterdam in front of an audience of over 500 bankers, followed by an engaging discussion with the board member for HR—also a woman. Two women on the stage openly discussing the sensitive issue of banking culture at the headquarters of a major bank—who's the weaker sex?, Barbara Bergmann could have asked. Below, I will summarize some of the findings of the survey, focusing on the capabilities of bankers to serve the interests of their clients.[2]

To my own surprise the large majority of the bankers agreed that serving client interest is the main goal of a bank. To check this answer, I also asked, elsewhere in the questionnaire, what was the main motive driving the respondents. Again, serving client interest came out first. Of course, the weakness of surveys, even when implemented online and anonymously, is that they may trigger socially desirable responses. But if we would deduct 10% of the affirmative reply, the positive response would still be over 75%. Another set of questions was about the perceived constraints to serve client interest in their day to day practices. One of these appeared to be high work pressure (82% of the respondents mentioned this). When we asked if the respondent feels a tension between the financial products offered on the one hand and serving client interest on the other hand, 49% answered that this was indeed sometimes the case, while 12% said that this was often the case. Of course, these were typical responses that most of the banks would not like to hear—let alone to have out in the media. The most contentious question was about products sold that one felt uncomfortable about—clearly not serving client interests. However, only 5% responded 'yes'—not to be applauded, nor a sign of bankers being all greedy and careless. Of course, that percentage may be underreporting so that the real incidence may be quite a bit higher. More importantly, however, was the question why so many bankers feel a tension between products and client interest and why some are even tempted to sell products that they know are not in the interest of their clients. Work pressure was already mentioned, but this is insufficient as an explanation. Over the years, academics have experienced more and more work pressure, with increasing student numbers, rising demands for public lectures and social media activity, and rising standards of academic publications and competition for limited research grants. But this does not necessarily result in cheating (although there are proven cases of plagiarism and fraud at universities). Next to work pressure, the academic world experiences an increase in chronic overtime and burn-outs but a persisting commitment to quality teaching and scientific research. In banks, work pressure could not be the only explanation of the gap between a commitment to serve client interest and the practices of doubtful service delivery.

I suspected two possible mechanisms for the constraints to serve client interest: detached leadership and detailed performance measurement. Three quarters of the respondents agreed that their leadership talked about the importance of serving client interest. But only one quarter noticed that their leaders put this into practice. In other words, there appeared to be a huge gap between the walk and the talk of the leadership of banks. Moreover, a quarter of the respondents said that their managers were not open to criticism and that they did not receive feedback other than about their targets. Hence, leadership in banks appeared to be largely top-down and driven by targets. Indeed, three quarters of the bankers stated that their performance was measured by targets and that many were financial targets. What was most revealing was that 63% stated that the targets constrain client interests. When asked whether they are motivated by targets, most of the respondents denied this was the case. This points at a second gap: while 74% stated to be monitored by targets, only 14% felt motivated by targets.

So, what does motivate bankers? As indicated before, serving client interest is an important motivator. That is not so strange, given the fact that banking implies financial service delivery—if one does not like to serve clients, banking is not the right profession to choose. To be honest, the profession has changed from the 1980s onwards and has moved away from the core business of helping clients with their basic financial needs with tailor-made personal advice based on mutual trust in a long-term relationship. But my survey results indicate that the large majority of ordinary retail bankers are still committed to good financial service delivery and that they possess a decent moral compass—see Table 1.

There does not seem to be much wrong with bankers' moral compass. Most of them are ordinary people with a feel for numbers. But how much space do bankers have to really use it in their job? In order to find out, I asked about their autonomy and the extent of trust among colleagues—see for the results Table 2. The answers were sobering. About 25% said they experience no autonomy to take decisions on their service delivery, while 28% stated they do not experience any space for taking initiative in service delivery. My question about mutual trust revealed a third glaring gap in banking culture. A small majority

Table 1 Banker's moral compass

	Yes	Neutral	No
Leaders talk about client interest	76	13	11
Leaders implement client interest	28	30	43
Financial targets are in the interest of clients	11	25	63
I feel motivated by performance targets	14	27	59

Source: author, based on: Irene van Staveren and Rens van Tilburg, Bankers Focus on Clients—But What Do Banks Do? (Utrecht, Sustainable Finance Lab, 2015), https://sustainablefinancelab.nl/wp-content/uploads/sites/232/2015/06/SFL_survey2014_ENGLISH_EA.pdf, accessed on June 24, 2020

Table 2 Bankers' space to use their moral compass

	Yes	Neutral	No
I have autonomy	42	33	25
I have space for own initiative	45	27	28
I experience trust in my team	62	20	18
I experience trust in my bank	16	39	45

Source: author, based on: Irene van Staveren and Rens van Tilburg, Bankers Focus on Clients—But What Do Banks Do? (Utrecht, Sustainable Finance Lab, 2015), https://sustainablefinancelab.nl/wp-content/uploads/sites/232/2015/06/SFL_survey2014_ENGLISH_EA.pdf, accessed on June 24, 2020

of 62% experience trust in their own team but only 16% experience trust in the bank as a whole.

Wait a minute. If one clearly possesses a moral compass and is driven not by targets but by adequate service delivery, but the organizational structure and hierarchy make it very difficult to use this compass, how on earth can employees be responsible bankers? When high work pressure, inconsistent and nonresponsive leaders, mutual distrust and a long list of targets take up much of one's time and effort, how can bankers be expected to really serve client needs and gain back society's trust? And how can individual bankers counter the dominant trend towards ever more detailed performance targets in such a top-down organizational field?

I have carried out some quantitative analysis to find out if the increased government regulation has enabled bankers to use their moral compass. The hypothesis was that banks seek legitimation from society after they had to be saved with tax-payers money and as a reaction to low trust from society. The results of the regression analysis do not support the hypothesis—regulation may be a response to the seeking of legitimation, but it does not provide bankers with more autonomy to use their moral compass.[3] Variables for regulation did not show any correlations. For example, support for the banker's oath that the Dutch government had made obligatory after the crisis, did not show any positive (or negative) effect on the use of the moral compass. Also, support for increased regulation showed no correlation, and neither the tighter rules of banks to address moral dilemmas. On the other hand, the limited space for own initiative, performance targets and variable pay were all negatively correlated with the use of one's moral compass. The conclusion that follows is that the banking culture, with its targets and distrust, discourages bankers to use their moral compass and that banking regulation is unable to counter that destructive culture.

The Opportunistic Financial Consumer

In today's globalized and digitalized society, consumers have to make many choices every day. Choices in shopping, subscriptions, credit card limits, pension investments and savings. In addition, governments have reduced welfare policies over the past few decades and even more so since the financial crisis. Citizens have been confronted with increasing insecurity in terms of their incomes, health care, housing and pensions. Together, the endless consumer choices and increasing uncertainty about livelihoods today and tomorrow, result in everyday decision-making stress—the paradox of choice, as Barry Schwartz calls it.[4] The way consumers try to deal rationally with this is to rely on the principle of opportunity costs. Going for option A implies foregoing options B, C and the rest. But what if the rest is too much to take into account? Or when knowledge about options is limited? Or when you do not really know what you want with so much commercial pressure around? Or when you have no idea about the proper time horizon for your choice for a new cell phone or car loan?

Our financial choices are influenced by many variables. On the supply side, for example, by commercials, discounts, teaser rates and branding. But there is also social influence. From peer groups, expected (gender) roles and social norms, including the Veblen-effect discussed in the previous chapter. Moreover, the norms are continuously shifting upwards, to more stuff and more spending. And the classes shift along in their consumer behaviour. Half a century ago, the middle classes in Europe and North America looked down upon the whole grain bread consumed by farmers, whereas now they are prepared to pay four times as much for artisan sourdough bread, whereas the poor purchase less healthy and cheaper white bread. Also, we often have no idea that our choices are shaped by whole industries simply because of the widespread occurrence of oligopolies, which not only make us believe there is a real difference between Pepsi and Coke but also make us pay much more for it compared to a fully competitive sector.

For financial choices the additional difficulty is the ubiquity of uncertainty next to risk. Can I afford my mortgage if I lose my job? Can I sell my house upon divorce? Is it worth it to take a disability insurance when I am self-employed? Credit circumvents the opportunity costs for consumer decisions: now, it is possible to go for options A and B too! The temptation to borrow is difficult to resist when the expected satisfaction today is high and the costs are somewhere in the future. In addition to all these behavioural dimensions of consumer choice, there is the secular trend of increasing materialism and social identities that are ever tighter connected with it. Consumer goods and the lifestyles affiliated with them turn our social identities more and more into economic identities. I buy, therefore I am. This trend even gets under the skin. Think about the increasing social acceptance of plastic surgery for beautification—from eyelids to bottoms—and botox injections in foreheads and lips. Looking younger or becoming a look-alike of a celebrity is simply for sale. The age of consumerism goes along with an increasing fixation on money. This causes that gnawing feeling that you rob yourself when you do not buy that super discount item (which you don't need) or if you do not spend a whole weekend at the kitchen table comparing offers of insurance policies (even if the price difference is less than five or ten euro per month). Many of us are so much concerned with discounts and cost reductions that it even leads to irresponsible financial behaviour. Think about the Icelandic bank Icesave, which provided online savings accounts in the UK and the Netherlands with a higher interest rate (5% instead of 4% at domestic banks). This was reckless—not only from the side of the bank but also from the side of savers who had not put in any effort to find out about the quality of the bank and its risk levels. They simply had looked for the highest possible savings rate around. When the bank collapsed, it was the Icelandic taxpayers who in the end had to bail out these opportunistic foreign savers, forced by the governments of the Netherlands and the UK.

Other times, financial consumers do not actively chase bargains—if it takes too much time or effort. We give up, stick to what we already have (status quo bias) or the better half of ourselves realizes that life should be more than spending our limited free time on endless cost-benefit analyses. Indeed, most of us are not maximizers but satisficers. Good enough is fine. That explains why many people do not have an orderly financial administration while at the same time they tend to be over-insured. Who knows the interest paid on one's credit card last month? Or how much the income difference of one's pension is between retiring at the age of 63 or 67? Or even how much you spent on buying clothing and shoes over the last year? Researchers in the field of financial consumer behaviour know all the traps of our financial ignorance. For example, we suffer from optimism bias (underestimating costs), confirmation bias (only seeing what we want to see), cognitive dissonance (impulsively buying stuff that does not match our values and commitments) and too short time horizons (impatience). We could all save lots of money if we would invest in acquiring some useful financial capabilities. But most of us don't realize that or don't care. And that has dear consequences—in particular when dependent on the financial advice of professionals who are discouraged to use their moral compass.

The Insight

Both the curtailed banker and the opportunistic financial consumer are held hostage in a one-dimensional system of short-term monetary gain and status seeking. And both know—at least many of them—that this reduces their personality and social life to who they can be and probably want to be in all their roles in life as a parent, child, friend, employee, livelihood-maker, neighbour, club member, investor and more. The financial crisis and the lack of systematic change since then reveals a moral vacuum in our economic behaviour and a lack of meaning in our economic lives, as professionals and as consumers.

This is a problem that resides at a deeper level than most economists study: it is all about ethics: the meaning and purpose of economic life. What drives choices? Whose interests do they serve? How is the rest of life affected by economic behaviour? And should we—and can we—reflect on a different ethical framework for our economic life? Are alternatives feasible? In other words, is it possible to make the supply and demand for goods and services consistent with underlying shared values?

Consistent and Meaningful Choices

It would take an economist who was also trained as a philosopher to reach this deeper level of economic analysis: Amartya Sen, the Nobel Memorial Prize winner of 1998. For his analysis of the role of ethics in economics, Sen focused on two key concepts: rationality and capability. He defined rationality as consistent choices in relation to one's goals. This consistency helps to shape one's identity and to make choices in line with it. In particular the alignment of more immediate goals—buying good and affordable food—and more distant goals—following a healthy lifestyle in line with sustainable agriculture—is how Sen connected the economic with the ethical, through the idea of commitment. His definition of rationality as consistent choices is very different from one concerned with cost-benefit analysis. For cost-benefit analysis one needs to be fully informed about all possible states of the world, whereas Sen's understanding of rationality is more in line with a context of uncertainty, in which decision making is necessarily contextual rather than detached, and thereby it is partially qualitative (moral, social, cultural) instead of exclusively quantitative. Sen's definition of rationality is closely related to one's social identity beyond economic status, and it is clearly different from the lightning calculus of neoclassical economics, which Veblen had criticized so much.

Sen has provided fundamental criticism of the use—in fact the abuse—of the ethical theory of utilitarianism in neoclassical economics. In the early nineteenth century, Jeremy Bentham had developed this ethics as an argument for the greatest happiness for the greatest number. But a century later, neoclassical welfare theory removed the heart from Bentham's theory. Whereas for Bentham, maximum welfare would be achieved by redistributing marginal utility from the rich to the poor until everyone's marginal utility would be the same and thereby maximized for society as a whole, welfare theory does not allow redistribution. Instead, neoclassical welfare theory holds that free markets achieve maximum welfare with the status quo of the distribution of resources, because redistribution would result in disincentives to produce—the well-known myth that I discussed in the previous chapter. Moreover, neoclassical theorists argued that it is impossible to compare utilities between persons, because utility is an entirely subjective concept, even though they use income as a proxy measure. According to welfare theorists, the law of diminishing marginal utility may only be applied at the individual level and not at societal level. For example, if you already had two cups of coffee you may get more marginal utility from eating a cookie next, than from another cup of coffee. But, as Bentham has explained, it is at the societal level that utilitarianism delivers maximum welfare by taxing those with more food or land and giving it to the poor, whose marginal utility would be significantly higher from an additional unit of land or food than the utility decline of the wealthy. This is because the rich will hardly miss the decline in their abundant resource-set, whereas for a poor person, having a piece of land may make the difference between a decent livelihood and destitution for a whole family, while in addition, the small plot will generally be used more productively than when it makes part of a large estate. Sen has therefore argued that neoclassical welfare theory has become a defence of the status quo for the wealthy, rather than a theory understanding welfare improvement for all, as Bentham had imagined. According to Sen, economists should either apply utilitarianism wholesale, at the individual and the aggregate level, or use a different ethical foundation for welfare economics. He has opted for the second alternative with his capability approach.

Capability is defined as the skills and opportunities enabling a life which one has a reason to value. This is a very different notion than the key idea of utility maximization in neoclassical economics. Sen illustrates the idea of capability with the difference between fasting as being hungry. The first is a capability, connecting a commitment to a spiritual value or a valued lifestyle on the one hand, with the mental skills to act in line with that commitment on the other hand. The second situation, hunger, is the absence of the capability to being well fed. It is not a choice at all but reflecting a lack of opportunities. This difference illustrates that the capability approach is not about *what* one chooses but about being able to *make meaningful choices*, that is, choices that are consistent with one's values, commitments and identity. And this, Sen argues, depends not only on one's internal capabilities such as talents, virtues and skills, but also on the choice context which should enable people's capability expansion. For capability expansion, the context should entail sufficient and meaningful options to choose from. And not, as he said in another telling example, meaningless options such as slicing up your toes.

Together, these two key concepts of Sen's economic thought—rationality as consistency in choices and capability expansion as meaningful choices—provide logic and meaning to economic behaviour and financial decisions. They make the implicit relationship between economic behaviour and ethics explicit—since economic choices are not morally neutral: they affect real people in real societies differently. When we start looking carefully at economic behaviour from the perspective of the capability approach, we notice that some financial professionals and consumers already act according to this alternative view, right in the shadow of capitalist markets. The forced redundancies in the banking sector have made some ex-bankers to make a radical career-shift. You can find them today as teachers, nurses or people managing green energy start-ups: professions that give them the opportunity to align their economic behaviour with their values. Fortunately, also some banks are moving, slowly, towards more socially responsible activities. A friend of mine has managed a few years back to shift to a newly created job in the bank to help borrowers with problematic debts. She feels much happier and useful today than in the 25 years as account manager in the same bank, when she offered the type of loans that some of her clients today realize they should never have taken.

Also, some financial consumers make deliberate different choices than following purely quantitative cost-benefit accounting. For example, they no longer want their economic life being dominated by money and materialism and embrace values of social and ecological sustainability. The 62 banks that have created the Global Alliance for Banking on Values serve more than 67 million customers, and their number is growing fast.[5] These financial consumers try to align their values with where they put their money as savers and investors or as borrowers. Although the savings rate that the customers of these banks receive is a bit below average and the interest they pay on their loans is a bit above average, the total return on investment of sustainable banks tends to be slightly above that of non-sustainable banks.[6] Value-based banking has shown to be a viable business model but can only operate with customers who seek meaningful choices rather than the highest possible interest rate on their savings.

There are two more factors that support capability expansion, namely resources and institutions. These two complete the capability approach: people have meaningful goals in their lives and try to make consistent choices to achieve these by employing the necessary resources in a particular institutional context, leading to the expansion of their capabilities.

Resources and Institutions

When we think about resources in an economic context, we immediately think of income and capital. In a market-based economy, this implies access to decent employment with living wages and, for entrepreneurs, access to credit at reasonable interest rates. In turn, access to decent employment also requires access to free primary and secondary education and affordable tertiary education. While access to credit is insufficient for successful entrepreneurship without business skills such as accounting, market analysis and supply chain management. But access to decent employment and business credit also requires economic conditions that involve sufficient demand for labour and sufficient market development for the sales of goods. As Keynes taught us, a thriving economy is one where demand is not constrained but enabled by purchasing power of those producing the very goods that need to be sold in order to generate employment. Consumer demand and employment are interdependent in the domestic economy.

But there are more resources than income and credit, and, indirectly, education and training. Resources include access to internet and news media and to social life and a backup structure in case of a livelihood shock, for example disease and disability or damage to property from floods or fire. Public healthcare and social insurances, therefore, are also important resources for the expansion of people's capabilities. While for the effective use of financial resources, we also need relevant information about risk and uncertainty—related to opportunities, challenges and backups. These are all helpful to build resilience in an uncertain financial market context and to enable personal efficacy in dealing with financial matters. This calls for financial literacy for young people, to be taught in schools. It should include the basics of risk calculation, interest and inflation and the potential costs of uncertain events. And it should help build resilience against the temptations of easy money and status goods. Do you really need that product? Do you want to have it to address some personal need or rather to address a want derived from your peer group? Is it that bad to ignore a too-good-to-be-true bargain? How long does it take to repay a debt plus interest and how much is that in total?

Another way in which people's resilience and efficacy can be strengthened is through nudges.[7] These are tools to enable you to stick to the choices that are in line with what you really value. Think about self-nudges, such as the habit of not going to the supermarket when you have an empty stomach. Or think of public nudges, such as speed bumps in residential areas. Some nudges are geared towards strengthening people's financial capabilities. In the UK, for example, letters announcing a fine to owners of vehicles who have not paid vehicle taxes are more effective when including an image of the vehicle within the letter.[8] This attracts the attention of the reader and makes the idea of losing the vehicle more salient. Research by the UK Behavioural Insights Team (BIT) has shown that this nudge has increased fines paid on time from 40 to 49%, reducing additional costs for the offenders. Other financial nudges have been suggested in various countries, such as an automatic text message from the bank in case of overspending. Or what about an App which shows on a daily basis what the actual costs of one's credit card are, or a tool that automatically shifts a salary raise to one's savings account? So, nudges and financial literacy are two types of resources that may increase people's financial capabilities, but back-up options are equally important, including a humane personal bankruptcy law and decent unemployment benefits, to prevent strangling debt to continue for years, limiting a wide range of capabilities.

The institutions related to Sen's capability approach are, just like those described by Veblen, both formal (laws and rules) and informal institutions (social norms and personal habits). These may be enabling, such as carefully designed nudges and financial education programmes, which help the expansion of capabilities. But there are also disabling institutions, as Veblen already noticed, and also Barbara Bergmann has pointed out. One of the disabling institutions that Sen mentions is the internalized social norm of adaptive preferences. Adaptive preferences refer to changes in consumer choices away from one's own needs towards socially desirable choices. In poor households in India, Sen observed this phenomenon among women who gave the best food to their husbands and even took pride in it. In more affluent contexts that are strongly influenced by consumerism, adaptive preferences may lead to over-borrowing, over-expenditure and overall short-termism in economic decision making. Hence, some institutions may constrain people's capabilities in direct but also in subtle, indirect ways.

Consistent Decision Making in a Meaningful Context

For a financial sector contributing to the needs and values of households and firms, the financial capabilities of both bankers and consumers need to be strengthened. This will enable both sides of the market to treat money and finance as what they really are: means and not ends. At the supply side, bankers should be given the autonomy and trust by their leadership to be conscientious service providers, navigating their interactions with clients with their moral compass. This implies that they should be able to advise against the short-term interest of the bank, to say "no" in case of over-borrowing without being punished with a lower performance score by their manager. Therefore, the top-down performance measurement and ranking needs to be replaced by horizontal qualitative peer assessment and feedback. The abolishment of the rank and file culture will not only enable the ethos of bankers, and therefore better financial service delivery, but also their productivity.[9] Destructive competition stifles creativity, mutual trust and cooperation. When bankers are really allowed to be autonomous professional financial service providers, clients would be enabled much better to build their own financial capabilities. In an enabling institutional context, both sides of the market benefit through capability expansion. Imagine markets to respond not to destructive competition and markets in which money remains a means and not more—in that way markets will be a useful mechanism for the expansion of capabilities of everyone, instead of being put at the forefront of economic growth policies. And that is the greatest insight of Amartya Sen's capability approach: putting means and ends right again.

In capitalism, and neoclassical economic theory as the framework to describe and to optimize it, the accumulation of money and goods is the end of entrepreneurship. The behavioural drive of many workers and consumers has been aligned with this end over the past two centuries so that the system is solidly geared towards ever more GDP growth. The capability approach does not obey this meaningless mechanism even though it puts great emphasis on freedom.[10] Instead, it is concerned with what people are able to do and be, in line with their values—both individually as well as collectively in their various social roles as family members, friends, neighbours, co-workers, creators, and so on. And whether that leads to GDP growth or not is not relevant. Because we would navigate our economies on a different national compass, determined by the key capabilities that people will define for themselves based on their values—through public discourse, as Sen advises.[11]

The Economist

Amartya Kumar Sen (1933 Santiniketan)

Amartya Sen was born in a middle-class family in what is now the Indian state of West Bengal, bordering Bangladesh. His father taught chemistry at Dhaka University (in the city which later would become the capital of Bangladesh) and his mother went to the same university as Sen would go later, in Santiniketan. When Sen reached the age of nine, a famine broke out, in which three million poor people died. The middle classes, and even the lower classes with employment or land, had no shortage of food—it was the landless and other vulnerable groups who could not afford to buy food anymore. The famine made a great impression on the child and influenced his choice to study philosophy and economics in order to understand the processes leading to poverty and hunger. In 1959, he obtained his PhD in Cambridge, under the supervision of the post-Keynesian economist Joan Robinson. Almost 25 years later, he received an Honorary Doctorate from the Institute of Social Studies, where I work. That was long before I met him. In 1994, I sent him my first academic publication, in which I applied his capability approach to women's reproductive health. Several weeks later, I received a friendly and personally signed letter in response, in which he thanked me for the interesting article and wished me success in my research. What a surprising kindness in the often so harsh world of economists. In 1998 Sen would receive the Nobel Memorial Prize in economics, and since 1995, the United Nations publishes annually the Human Development Report, which is the macro-level reflection of his idea of capability expansion.[12] I still have the letter, to cheer me up after receiving an unfriendly review letter on an article submitted to an economic journal. Later, we met a few times—in a workshop organized by the journal *Feminist Economics* honouring his work, and at an international conference of feminist economists, where he gave a keynote speech. Also, in person, he appeared to be very friendly and supportive to me and to all the young economists around.

When employed at Oxford, and later at Harvard, his star was rising particularly in development economics. One reason for this was his analysis of the Bengal famine. He explained that the death of millions of poor people was not caused by market failures, as some economists had argued. It was not the consequence of a monopoly, for example, or because of pricing policy enforced by the state. To the contrary, Sen showed, there was sufficient food to feed everybody. The cause of the famine was not a market failure but rather the result of the perfect functioning of markets, which allowed rice traders to sell their stocks to the highest bidders. And these were outside West-Bengal, and partially even outside India. The origin of the famine was a lack of purchasing power among the lowest classes—the lower caste groups in West-Bengal. They had no money, no land and no employment due to a lack of demand for labour. Sen's study demonstrated that well-functioning markets could be paralleled by terrible poverty and therefore that an economy requires more than markets to deliver wellbeing for all. The same point had been made by Adam Smith 200 years earlier, as we will see in Chap. 9. Sen argued that markets are insufficient but also that government support is necessary but not always sufficient. Equally important are social norms and social cohesion in society, which provide communities with the resilience to collectively ensure a basic minimum livelihood for the weakest groups. Sen has criticized neoclassical economics for rejecting government support because it would interfere with markets. And he has criticized them too for rejecting the idea of endogenous and changing preferences, influenced by norms and values, because it would destroy the neat mathematical framework of utility maximization of given preferences under fixed budget constraints.

Amartya Sen's out-of-the-box economics has led him to study the economy as embedded in social and moral relationships, just as Smith, Marx, Veblen and Keynes had done before him. He argues for substituting the idea of utility maximization with the idea of capability expansion. And that requires, next to markets, also public services, providing basic entitlements to everyone. This necessitates sufficient tax revenues, as Adam Smith already wrote. By contrasting the ethics of neoclassical economics (a crippled form of utilitarianism) with the ethics of the capability approach (related to Aristotle's virtue ethics), Sen makes clear that it is not the case that his theory is normative while neoclassical theory is positive—*both* theories have inescapable ethical dimensions. This argument illustrates that Sen is not only an economist but also a philosopher, and that is sometimes helpful in arguing against the inconsistencies and misconceptions of an economic theory. He argues that also mainstream economic theory takes a moral position—the position of libertarianism in which individual freedom is deemed more important than human dignity. And in which redistribution is regarded as robbery and unemployment is judged as a choice. His critique, however, does not imply that Sen would want to abolish markets. Not at all. He wants markets to function for everyone instead of only for those with sufficient purchasing power and lucky enough to find employment or to possess wealth. He argues that when markets do not benefit everybody, they need to be complemented with entitlements that allow those who are excluded from or exploited by markets to have the necessary resources to live a life in dignity.

The interesting thing is that this insight is already present in one of the most famous and influential economic articles ever: the mathematical proof in which Kenneth Arrow and Gerard Debreu showed that free, competitive markets lead to an equilibrium that reflects the most efficient allocation of resources in an economy.[13] The Nobel Memorial Prize winning economists noted that the model only works if everybody has access to markets and sufficient resources to trade. This sounds reasonable—how else can the weaker groups in society survive? If they are excluded from markets because they do not have any resources to trade, they will die or find illegal ways to scramble together a livelihood.

Most likely the state will support them with tax money but that affects the equilibrium that the model describes.... Precisely because of this precondition of market efficiency, Sen argues that a marked-based economy will only function properly when everybody has sufficient tradable resources or other entitlements. This is not a human rights argument, as some critics believe, but the consequence of a core market logic, as Arrow and Debreu already have shown.

Sen's capability approach can be applied both at macro-level and at micro-level. He earned his fame in the 1970s with his article about the rational fool.[14] In that article, he illustrates the inconsistency of the neoclassical economic definition of rationality as individual utility maximization at the micro-level. Walking on the street, a stranger asks Sen for directions to the railway station.

> 'There,' I say, pointing at the post office, 'and would you please post this letter for me on the way?' 'Yes,' he says, determined to open the envelope and check whether it contains something valuable.[15]

This famous example shows that if economic theory relies on such a notion of rationality, it reduces people to fools who have no idea of what it is to be human in a social context. Sen's alternative view of rational economic actors is one of consistent behaviour based on shared social values, including honesty. Without honesty and trust, markets, governments and communities would not function at all. Violence and chaos would reign. Hence, we are back to the two basic concepts of Sen's alternative approach to neoclassical economics: rationality and capabilities.

Perhaps, we should consider Amartya Sen as the keeper of integrity in economics. But he himself would reject such a label. He simply attempts to be a good economist. At the age of 23, he was made chair of the economics department of the newly founded University of Calcutta. And he considered it as completely normal that his much older rivals protested against his appointment. Now, at the age of 86, he is still travelling and giving public lectures. When I asked him how he copes with the jet lags at his age, his response was that he stopped calculating time differences and adjusts his watch to the local time wherever he arrives. He could not have provided me with a better illustration of his down-to-earth mentality. For me, he sets an example of a good economist—both as a person and through his contribution to the discipline.

Reading Sen
Amartya Sen, *On Ethics and Economics* (Hoboken: Wiley, 1987).

Amartya Sen, *Development as Freedom* (New York: Knopf, 1999).

Reading About Sen
Lawrence Hamilton, *Amartya Sen* (Hoboken: Wiley, 2019).

The website of the Nobel Prizes contains an autobiography: https://www.nobelprize.org/prizes/economic-sciences/1998/sen/biographical/.

Practising Sen

Professional Ethos as a Capability

Most firms are organized as hierarchies and have a top-down governance structure. The economic logic of this is that it reduces transaction costs. Hierarchy prevents continuous negotiations, price setting, comparing alternatives and hiring and firing employees on a daily basis. But the downside of top-down companies is costly as well, as the anxiety and distrust in the dominant banking culture demonstrates. Across the world, there are entrepreneurs who run their firms differently. Not as hierarchies but as communities. An example of such a business philosophy and practice is the Semco-model, developed by the Brazilian entrepreneur Ricardo Semler in his machine factory. The firm has grown from ninety to five thousand employees with a good and stable profit rate, since he started to experiment with his radical idea of horizontal organization.

The Semco-model is a democratic form of governance, with employees selecting their own hours of work and to some extent even their own salaries and having a voice in all key company decisions and real-time insight in the firm's accounts.[16] It is characterized by a horizontal structure which stimulates autonomy and trust, in which self-organizing teams have a greater sense of responsibility and respond in more flexible and innovative ways to change than in hierarchies. The idea is that employees should be taken seriously in their professional capabilities and that an enabling, trusting company structure allows them to develop their professional ethos, which makes for better products, better services, higher productivity and happier workers.

In the Netherlands, ZLM insurance in the city of Goes, in the south of the country, is a medium-sized mutual insurance company that follows similar principles. For ten years in a row, it has been awarded the first prize for the most customer-friendly insurance company, and it has been awarded the first prize for the best employer (of middle-sized companies) at least three times.[17] ZLM values personal relationships with clients. When a client moves to a different part of the country, ZLM sees no other option than to terminate the contract. Quality is valued over quantity. The insurer does not have an HRM department. The 200 employees have lots of freedom and responsibility for good service delivery. There are no performance targets. The only thing that matters is client satisfaction. Even when it implies giving up some profit: a few years ago, the company decided to end a profitable passenger insurance policy because they realized that a small extension of the standard car insurance policy would provide the same result at lower cost for customers. The client satisfaction results of ZLM are not very different from those of its competitors when it comes to questions like friendliness on the phone or answering one's questions. But ZLM does make a difference with its scores on being heard, taken seriously and treated fairly. At the same time, the employees report being very satisfied with the open work atmosphere and benefits such as the annual trip with all employees and their partners instead of bonuses for the top managers. Are they very special people over there in Goes? No, they are no saints. But they are selected primarily on their service-skills and caring attitude. Many have a background not in bookkeeping—the firm provides trainings to strengthen these skills—but in the hospitality industry. Teams select their new colleagues themselves—they have to in the absence of an HRM department, and the key selection criterion is a match between the values of the company and those of the applicant. If they match, ZLM is confident that the moral compass of the new employee is aligned with the firm's values of service delivery, trust, responsibility and teamwork.

Local Trading Based on Local Capabilities

The entitlements that Sen referred to, which provide everyone with tradable resources on markets, do not necessarily need to come from the state. In welfare states, social benefits play the role of entitlements. But in low and middle-income countries, this is often not possible, at least not at a sufficient level and for the population as a whole. Sometimes, local initiatives emerge in which the capabilities of people in a community are used to build a local trading system to sustain livelihoods during difficult times, which in turn help to strengthen other capabilities, such as being well-nourished, have self-confidence and being healthy. When these local initiatives also use their own money, they are referred to as community currency systems. Some of these are temporary, sustaining livelihoods during economic crises, while others have existed for decades alongside the regular market based on national currencies controlled by central banks.

An example of a temporary community currency system that helped, at its height, two and a half million people to sustain their livelihoods during a deep recession, is the Red de Trueque in Argentina, in the period 2000–2004. The initiators invented a new currency, called the little tree (arbolito in Spanish) named after the tree printed on a piece of paper. Trading took place in 5000 local trading communities, first in Buenos Aires and later throughout the country, through a registry of goods and services supplied, from home-made meals to haircuts and from car repairs to psychological help. This enabled the participants, who were mainly women from the lower-middle class, to compensate their loss of income in the regular economy between 25 and 50%.[18]

Another example of a community currency comes from the UK. There, community currencies often go by the name of LETS (Local Employment Trading Systems), which make explicit that not the local currency is the measurement rod of exchange but the fact that people's capabilities are translated in local employment for which there is local demand through the purchasing power provided by the currency. LETS are often set up for marginalized groups, such as long-term unemployed people with limited formally recognized skills. Another variation is time banks, in which labour time is the currency to be exchanged, again, building on people's capabilities to provide services in their communities. In Switzerland, the oldest local currency was established in 1934, called the WIR. It particularly served to boost local entrepreneurship. Today, another local currency in Switzerland even makes use of blockchain technology: the Léman.

Hence, there is much variation in local community currencies, but what they all have in common is that they are complementary to the regular currency and to regular markets from which marginalized groups of people are excluded. Community currencies serve to strengthen local economies in an inclusive way, based on the capabilities of local entrepreneurs, the unemployed, retired persons on a small pension, and those who reject the regular economy and want to build a more engaged local community.[19]

Notes

1. See for the website of the Sustainable Finance lab: https://sustainablefinancelab.nl/en/. Accessed on July 15, 2020.
2. See also my article: Irene van Staveren, "The Misdirection of Bakers' Moral Compass in the Organizational Field of Banking," *Cambridge Journal of Economics* 44, 3 (2020): 507–526. https://doi.org/10.1093/cje/bez052. Accessed on July 15, 2020.
3. Van Staveren, "The Misdirection of Bankers' Moral Compass."
4. Barry Schwartz, *The Paradox of Choice – Why More is Less* (New York: Harper Collins, 2004).
5. http://www.gabv.org/the-community/members/banks. The network includes, among others, City First Bank in the US, the Ecological Building Society in the UK, Ekobanken in Sweden, Caja Arequipa in Peru, North East Small Finance Bank in India, and Centenary bank in Uganda.
6. KKS Advisors, "Do Sustainable Banks Outperform? Driving Value Creation through ESG Practices" (London: Deloitte, 2019). http://www.gabv.org/wp-content/uploads/Do-sustainable-banks-outperform.pdf. Accessed on May 13, 2020.
7. For a good introduction of nudges, see Richard Thaler and Cas Sunstein, *Nudge: Improving Decisions about Health, Wealth and Happiness* (New Haven: Yale University Press, 2008).
8. The Behavioural Insights Team, "EAST – four simple ways to apply behavioural insights" (London: Behavioural Insights/Cabinet Office, n.d.). https://www.behaviouralinsights.co.uk/wp-content/uploads/2015/07/BIT-Publication-EAST_FA_WEB.pdf. Accessed on June 25, 2020.
9. Jan Woike and Sebastian Hafenbrädl, "Rivals Without a Cause? Relative Performance Feedback Causes Destructive Competition Despite Aligned Incentives," *Journal of Behavioural Decision Making* (no volume and number mentioned) 2020: 1–15. https://doi.org/10.1002/bdm.2162. Accessed July 15, 2020.
10. Together with a colleague, I have criticized this emphasis on freedom in the capability approach. We argue that the approach does not need this as the single overarching value: Des Gasper and Irene van Staveren, "Development as Freedom? And As What Else?," *Feminist Economics* 9, 2–3 (2003): 137–161.
11. There are alternative national wellbeing measures to support this, such as the Human Development Index (UNDP) and the Better Life Index (OECD).

12. The report is published by the UNDP, which also publishes national human development reports, containing a wide variety of data about trends in human capabilities: http://hdr.undp.org/.
13. Kenneth Arrow and Gérard Debreu, "Existence of an Equilibrium for a Competitive Economy," *Econometrica* 22, 3 (1954): 265–290.
14. Amartya Sen, "Rational Fools: A Critique of the Behavioural Foundations of Economic Theory," *Philosophy and Public Affairs* 6, 4 (1977): 317–344.
15. Sen, "Rational Fools," p. 332.
16. https://semcostyle.com/.
17. https://www.zlm.nl/.
18. A colleague of mine, from Argentina herself, has studied the Red de Trueque and has published her results in various articles. For example: Georgina Gomez, "What was the Deal for the Participants of the Argentina Local Currency Systems, the Redes de Trueque?," *Environment and Planning* A 42 (2010): 1669–1685.
19. There is an online open access journal on community currencies, with interesting research from across the world, the *International Journal of Community Currency Research*: https://ijccr.net/. Accessed on July 15, 2020.

BIBLIOGRAPHY

Arrow, Kenneth, and Gérard Debreu. "Existence of an Equilibrium for a Competitive Economy." *Econometrica* 22, 3 (1954): 265–290.

Behavioural Insights Team. "EAST – four simple ways to apply behavioural insights." London: Behavioural Insights/Cabinet Office, n.d. https://www.behaviouralinsights.co.uk/wp-content/uploads/2015/07/BIT-Publication-EAST_FA_WEB.pdf. Accessed on June 25, 2020.

Gasper, Des, and Irene van Staveren. "Development as Freedom? And As What Else?," *Feminist Economic* 9, 2–3 (2003): 137–161.

Gomez, Georgina. "What was the Deal for the Participants of the Argentina Local Currency Systems, the Redes de Trueque?," *Environment and Planning A* 42 (2010): 1669–1685.

KKS Advisors. "Do Sustainable Banks Outperform? Driving Value Creation through ESG Practices." London: Deloitte, 2019. http://www.gabv.org/wp-content/uploads/Do-sustainable-banks-outperform.pdf. Accessed on May 13, 2020.

Schwartz, Barry. *The Paradox of Choice – Why More is Less*. New York: Harper Collins, 2004.

Sen, Amartya. "Rational Fools: A Critique of the Behavioural Foundations of Economic Theory." *Philosophy and Public Affairs* 6, 4 (1977): 317–344.

Staveren, Irene van. "The Misdirection of Bakers' Moral Compass in the Organizational Field of Banking." *Cambridge Journal of Economics* 44, 3 (2020): 507–526. https://doi.org/10.1093/cje/bez052. Accessed on July 15, 2020.

Thaler, Richard, and Cas Sunstein. *Nudge: Improving Decisions about Health, Wealth and Happiness*. New Haven: Yale University Press, 2008.

Woike, Jan, and Sebastian Hafenbrädl. "Rivals Without a Cause? Relative Performance Feedback Causes Destructive Competition Despite Aligned Incentives." *Journal of Behavioural Decision Making* (no volume and number mentioned) 2020: 1–15. https://doi.org/10.1002/bdm.2162. Accessed on July 15, 2020.

Chapter 8: Gunnar Myrdal on Social Vulnerability

THE PROBLEM

People in vulnerable economic positions are the end station of the financial risk flowing from banks and brokers down to borrowers. At the bottom of the income distribution risk accumulates: unemployment, unsustainable debt, lower welfare benefits, a credit crunch, declining demand for goods and services from small-scale entrepreneurs and eventually bankruptcies. These risks for those who are least capable of dealing with its downsides are all side effects of a financial crisis and are particularly felt when the crisis is followed by a deep and long recession. On top of this, households at the bottom of the income distribution—not only the bottom 10% but in countries such as the US even the bottom 40%—have no savings at all or not more than a month's wage to fall back upon. This is not only problematic in case of the economic risks mentioned above during a crisis and recession, but also in case of the normal uncertainties of life (illness, disability, divorce, unplanned pregnancy, etc.).

The consequence is a severe lack of economic resilience for the bottom quarter to half of the income distribution, even in the richest countries of the world. Even in economic prosperous times, there are vulnerable groups in society who depend on social welfare or a minimum wage job. They often have problematic debt and no resources as fallback. But during a crisis, the whole economy suffers, including government revenues, export earnings and aggregate demand, so that support for disadvantaged groups is constrained. Higher public expenditures and increasing public debt are always a temporary solution. Hence, when there is a lack of resilience among large groups of the population and in addition a lack of resilience at the macroeconomic level due to strict budgetary rules, economies may remain unnecessarily long in a recession with equally unnecessary suffering of the most vulnerable households.

In this chapter, I will zoom in on two vulnerable groups with examples from South Korea and the Netherlands: the care needs of the elderly and the financial dependence of women.

Elderly and the Care Crisis

South Korea was not only affected by the 2008 financial crisis but even more so by the 1997 Asian financial crisis. Two decades after that severe crisis and a decade after the global financial crisis, South Korea is experiencing a care crisis. The country is rapidly aging and has the lowest fertility rate of all OECD countries.[1] The extremely low birth rate of 1.05 per woman is sometimes referred to as a birth-strike by Korean women in the age-group between 20 and 40 years old. That age-group is generally well educated and many of these women participate in the labour market, experiencing great difficulty in combing their work—in a culture of structural overtime—with the care for children and the elderly. Even women without a paid job find it increasingly difficult to provide extensive care for their parents and parents-in-law, in particular when they live far away. Moreover, cultural change has led to a shift in traditional family values towards individual freedom and gender equality and away from the social norm that women are expected to take care of their aging parents and parents-in-law. As a response to the care crisis, South Korea has implemented a long-term care policy and insurance system as well as a livelihood security policy. But these fall short of the enormous need for care by the elderly in the country, who increasingly live alone with very limited pensions.

The statistics of the living conditions of the elderly in South Korea are grim. The suicide rate is the second one in the OECD, after Lithuania, and it is rising and particularly high among the elderly. At the same time, the share of elderly with self-reported good health is among the lowest in the OECD. Moreover, the country has the lowest score of social support experienced by the elderly (63% stating they have some form of social support).[2] A survey among 162 elderly Koreans (average age 76 years) living alone indicates that 24% suffer from depression and 8% suffer from suicidal ideation.[3] In this sample, only 36% of the elderly experience social support, the majority from neighbours. Those with social support suffered less from depression and suicidal ideation, indicating that the mental health problems of Korean elderly may be related to the widespread lack of social care—precisely the reason why Koreans speak of a care crisis. The lack of social support seems even more pressing in rural areas, according to a survey among 408 elderly living at home.[4] About 21% (more women than men) appear to be in the category of social frailty (including not going out and talking to people). Also, the study shows a significant overlap between social frailty and physical frailty (including exhaustion, weakness and weight loss).

In addition, the poverty rate among Koreans of 65 years and older is the highest of all OECD countries: 44% can be considered poor (with the poverty line set at 50% below the median disposable income).[5] This extremely high poverty rate among the elderly is three times the OECD average. A large survey among almost 40,000 elderly Koreans illustrates the shortcomings of the livelihood security system: only 10% of the elderly are beneficiary of this policy. In 2008, a basic old-age pension was introduced, but this policy is also not sufficiently helping poor elderly people, particularly not those with disabilities (16% of the elderly), who face higher health care expenditures.[6] Another study with a large sample of Korean elderly has analysed the effects of the 2008 long-term care policy on the mortality rate among the elderly population (over 65 years old).[7] The findings were twofold. First, a quarter of those with medium disabilities and 20% of those with severe impairments did not make use of the health care services targeted at them, due to an inability to pay the fees. Second, those with lower incomes had a much higher mortality rate than those with higher incomes. Moreover, those with home-care services (as compared to institution-based care) appeared to be the most vulnerable. Finally, there is not only a relationship between the wellbeing of the elderly and low incomes but also with income insecurity. A study making use of longitudinal data of Koreans aged 60 years and older has found that depression among the elderly was related to income insecurity for those who do not live with their children.[8] The care crisis in South Korea, hence, indicates that the resilience of the elderly is weak and that this is particularly challenging in times of crisis.

Financial Dependence of Women

The poverty rate in the Netherlands peaked in the year 2013 at 7.5%.[9] This peak was a direct consequence of the recession that followed upon the financial crisis. It has declined to 5% in 2017 and has remained there (to increase again due to the COVID-19 crisis).

Poverty varies with age. Children as well as frail elderly persons with high health care expenditures are the age categories that suffer the most from poverty. About 10% of children under the age of 12 live below the poverty line. Almost 50% of migrant families live below the poverty line. The majority of the poor is female, in particular among single parents, due to the relatively low number of hours worked by adult women. Almost 13% of single parents live below the poverty line: 15% for single mothers as compared to 7% for single fathers. The labour force participation of women in the Netherlands has increased steadily over the past decade, but the number of hours of paid work among women remains low.

The Netherlands is the European champion of part-time work. In 2017, 71% of working women had a part-time job.[10] The average hours worked by men was 39 but for women only 28 hours per week. Indeed, many women have a small part-time job of 1–2 days per week. In addition, twice as many women than men do not participate in the labour market. Almost 20% of Dutch mothers do not have a job. As a consequence of the non-participation and widespread practice of part-time work by women, 40% of Dutch women are not financially independent, against 20% of men. Financial independence is defined as earning at least a fulltime minimum wage.

The statistics reflect clear gender inequality in financial vulnerability. About four in ten marriages end in divorce, and separation is even higher for those living together without being married. Women's low financial independence is due to a traditional division of labour in the household in which women take care of the large majority of housework and childcare. This gender division of labour implies a relatively high risk of poverty at any time in their adult lives. Moreover, when unemployment rates are high during a recession, it is even more difficult to find a fulltime job after divorce when one has limited work experience. But the recognition of the problem of financial dependence is surprisingly low among the women themselves. A study among young Dutch women found that the majority does not see any problem at all, assuming they will not be the one to get divorced. More than 80% of the respondents have not discussed the issue with their partner at all.

But the problem is not simply caused by a too romantic attitude of young women. The deeper problem is the entrenched gender norm of women's responsibility for the household. Only 15% of households distribute unpaid care evenly between the partners—in the other 85% of households, women do the main share of unpaid work.[11] This results in a catch-22 situation in which women work part-time in the labour market so that they can combine paid work with their household responsibilities and in which men are not prepared to do more housework because they bring in most of the income. The institutional context also favours the traditional gender norm: schools are open to noon on Wednesdays and to three o'clock on the other days. Childcare is expensive, so that most working mothers stay at home in the afternoons. This practice reinforces the norm that mothers make better care givers than fathers. When my children were small, I was the only fulltime working mother and one day the gossip reached me that some of the other mothers felt sorry for my children that they had such an absent mother, even though my children enjoyed going to after-school childcare and I worked at home on Wednesdays so that I could facilitate friends to come over and play with my children. I was labelled a bad mother.

The institutional setting of the male breadwinner and female housewife/part-time worker results in a situation in which women are stuck in a disadvantaged bargaining position in the household. That position may not necessarily leave them with more total hours of paid and unpaid work as compared to their male partners, but it clearly leaves them with less income, less bargaining power, and less resilience in case of negative life events and economic crises.

The two examples above of groups that have limited resilience in times of crisis point out two things about capitalist market economies. First, not everybody has the resources and skills that are required to adequately deal with the uncertainties around one's livelihood. Frail health and divorce, for example, can make an enormous difference in the wellbeing of individuals and their families, even in welfare states with social insurance and social welfare policies.

Second, resilience depends on a combination of individual skills and resources on the one hand and social institutions on the other hand. But in modern economies formal institutions rely more and more on self-efficacy of citizens, represented by social policies that require fees and own contributions to be paid for health care services. At the same, time, informal institutions still rely on traditional gender norms, which expect women to be the main unpaid care givers in households and for relatives in need of care. This institutional contradiction results in a lack of resilience among large groups of the population. Moreover, the share of people living with insecure livelihoods is growing due the increasing share of workers without fixed contracts in many countries. This expanding group is labelled as the precariat—those who earn a living but without livelihood security in case of unemployment or illness. The label refers to Marx' notion of the proletariat, the factory workers across Europe and the US with insecure labour contracts and no economic security whatsoever. Today, the precariat represents a growing group of flexible workers across the world without access to social security and with limited access to welfare benefits. Guy Standing, a labour economist, has described this group of flexible workers as having no occupational identity, working in low-paid jobs with volatile earnings, that demand their availability in their free time, often working below their level of education and with debts from periods of unemployment or illness.[12] It is such precariousness that is often not on the radar screen of economists, but of sociologists, political scientists and social psychologists.

The Insight

Crises are part of life. The human condition faces the basic uncertainties of illness, disability, divorce, single parenthood, and frail health in old age at the individual level, and earthquakes, floods and pandemics at the aggregate level. The COVID-19 crisis that hit the world in the spring of 2020 is an extreme example of such an exogenous but wide-ranging crisis. It started as a health crisis, spreading across the world, and soon resulted in a worldwide economic crisis due to the Great Lockdown that followed. But, as I have argued, economic crises are often man-made, which is the case of financial crises following financial bubbles. All three types of crises—noneconomic, economic and financial—demand resilience from individuals, households, firms, and institutions. It was the Swedish economist Gunnar Myrdal who developed an eye for the importance of resilience in economic life. He did an extensive social economic study of racial discrimination in the US during the Great Depression in the 1930s. That study opened his eyes to the economic precariousness of large groups of people.

Myrdal's insights were twofold. First, the dynamics of modern market economies resemble not equilibrium, as mainstream economic theory assumes, but 'cumulative causation', as he labelled it. Instability instead of stability, disequilibrium instead of equilibrium. Indeed, this was a verbal characterization of what later would become known as systems theory in physics and mathematics.

Much later, these ideas were reintroduced in economics from mathematics through the method of nonlinear economic dynamics.[13]

During the Great Depression, the American economy was clearly out of balance, with huge unemployment across the nation, a free fall of financial markets followed by an extensive slump, and high rural-urban migration of poor landless peasants looking for work. Instead of an equilibrium in the labour market, in which there would be no excess supply at the going wage rate, Myrdal observed a very low demand for labour, low confidence among investors and consumers, and widely felt uncertainty and insecurity, which fed each other in a vicious circle. The accumulation of negative economic effects through supply and demand side factors in all types of markets. The downward spiral stopped only when the US joined the Second World War, which resulted in a huge increase of military production whereas the army recruited young men who received an income that they spent on consumer goods for their families. It was, ironically, the war which resulted both in supply-side stimulus of the economy (through military production of weapons and soldier wages) and in demand-side stimulus (through the spending of wages by soldiers). The second insight that Myrdal developed from his analysis of inequality and discrimination in the US economy, was that well-meaning social and economic policies may have unintended consequences for the most disadvantaged groups. This is what economists today refer to as perverse effects (or negative externalities of policies). Myrdal observed these first in the US and later in a study carried out in India.

Cumulative Causation

In short, cumulative causation refers to a chain of effects of an economic phenomenon—often negative effects. These include feedback effects, which tend to reinforce the dynamics. And that was precisely what Myrdal observed in the case of labour market discrimination. Cumulative causation reinforces advantages for the already advantaged and disadvantages for the already disadvantaged. This increases existing inequalities, with richer regions, countries and groups benefitting and poorer regions, countries and groups losing out. Not, however, because of some force of nature, but because of the power dynamics that connect the two sides of the same dynamic. Just like the growing inequality in capitalism as explained by Marx or the discrimination of women in the labour market and the household as explained by Bergmann and the status effects of a rentier economy as described by Veblen. The value added of Myrdal's concept of cumulative causation is that he focused not on the outcome but on the process, pointing at the interrelatedness of the growing benefits for some and the accumulating disadvantages and insecurity for others. Figure 1 shows the idea of cumulative causation with the example of racial discrimination—the topic Myrdal studied in the US. The graph shows two inter-related circular processes, each with their own dynamic but also feedback effects from the other dynamic. The diagram makes immediately clear that the

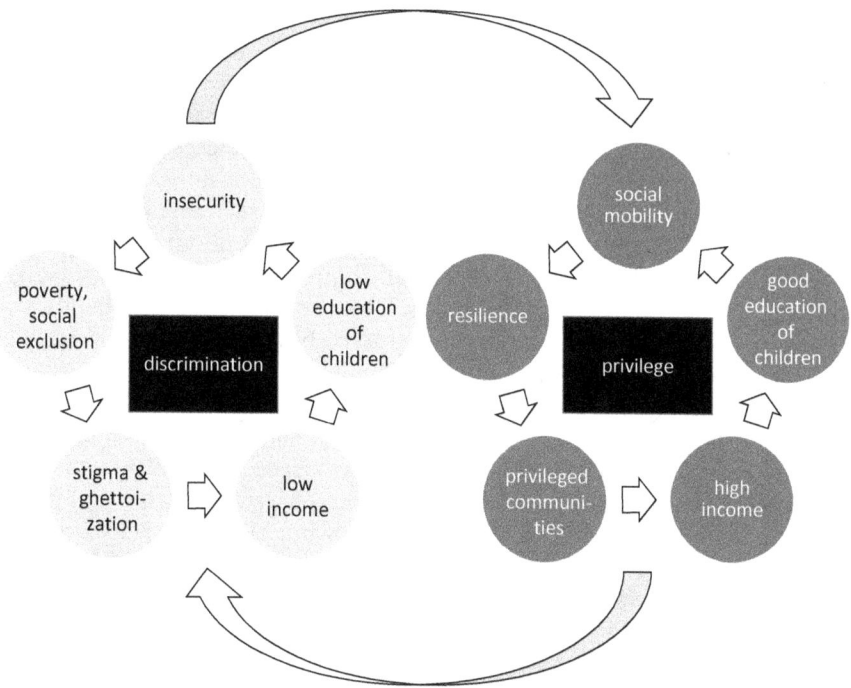

Fig. 1 Cumulative causation. (Source: author)

opposite of discrimination is not the absence of it, a neutral situation, but privilege.[14] Because the disadvantaged positioning of the one group, with exploitation, lack of access to resources, and social exclusion, is not separate from the advantaged positioning of the other group, which, in turn, enjoys social inclusion, access to resources including social welfare, and the benefit of cheap services delivered by a precariat, consisting of the disadvantaged group. Examples of this last intersecting dynamics abound, from Uber and Deliveroo in developed countries, to outsourced manufacturing and tourist services in developing countries.

Feedback effects occur through several mechanisms. For example, the observation by the privileged group of the low-end jobs and high unemployment of the discriminated group, may reinforce the negative attitude towards the discriminated group, and hence the stigma. This stigma, in turn, may induce those belonging to the privileged group to withdraw their children from schools with relatively many children from disadvantaged groups and move out to neighbourhoods with more privileged households. Hence, the tendency to ghettoization on the one hand and privileged communities on the other hand—a trend towards segregation. In this way, feedback effects between the two dynamics will reinforce prejudice, stigma and segregation.

The idea of dynamics and feedback effects in Myrdal's cumulative causation theory is very different from the idea of equilibrium in neoclassical economics. In the case of an outside shock, for example, a strong decline in tourism due to a pandemic, a new equilibrium will soon arise, according to neoclassical economics, due to price adjustments that will eliminate the excess supply. But in practice, markets do not always adjust very well and within a short period of time. Hence, excess supply may remain (think about structural unemployment) or excess demand may be around for a long time (think about hunger).

Myrdal observed that after a crisis, the adjustment of markets may be particularly slow. And because he looked beyond the idea of market equilibrium, relying on insights from sociology, he was asked by a policy institute in the US to analyse the situation in the 1930s in which many blacks lived in severe poverty despite the abolition of slavery many decades earlier and the formal equality before the law of African Americans. Myrdal employed a social economic approach and found out that blacks do not have an equal position with whites at all. Black people had less access to education, agricultural land, and decent housing. That is why the jobs at the bottom of the labour market were occupied largely by black workers. And this, Myrdal argues, meant a waste of the capabilities of blacks in the US economy. So, his analysis included another dynamic process interrelated with discrimination and privilege, namely the dynamics of production and productivity. The first feedback effect of the discrimination of blacks that he observed was a loss of productivity throughout the economy. By systematically excluding blacks from education, land and better jobs, they got stuck in unemployment and low productive jobs. The second feedback effect he discovered was that the white population saw its prejudice confirmed in the unemployment, poverty, apathy and petty crime that was the inevitable result of the deficient living conditions of the black population. That feedback mechanism prevented any positive change and support for social policies that would address the fundamental problem of discrimination. The whites held on to the status quo by defending segregation, holding on to their prejudice, while they benefitted from their own social mobility in those days and the ubiquity of cheap labour provided by black people.

Myrdal's theory of cumulative causation can be helpful in understanding many other social economic problems in which power works through a series of economic, psychological and social mechanisms that reinforce each other. The theory is therefore also helpful to explain the lack of resilience of certain groups in the economy. It is not difficult to explain the Korean care crisis with this theory, or the financial dependence on men or state benefits of so many women in the Netherlands. The care crisis is related to the quickly aging population and extremely low birth rate, which causes an increasing mismatch between demand for elderly care and supply of paid care through the public and private health care institutions of Korea. It is not surprising therefore, that migrants are hired to provide elderly care, or even more surprising, foreign brides are sought to care for elderly Korean men, according to an interesting study on the migrantization of care in the country.[15] The feedback effects of this ad hoc solution may include shortages in care provisioning in the countries of origin, as has been described with the term 'the global care chain', by sociologist Arlie Hochschield.[16] Another feedback effect of the Korean care crisis may be a stagnation of the move towards more gender equality because women in their reproductive years find it impossible to combine paid work with care for aging parents and parents-in-law, so that they may give up their jobs under the pressure of traditional gender norms in their families. But this will also halt the increase in female labour force participation, which was necessary for the tax revenue to finance long-term care policy. Negative feedback effects of the widespread part-time work by Dutch women also include a stagnation of gender equality. Not in labour force participation but in the distribution of housework and childcare in the household. While the role models of a breadwinner dad and a part-time earning mom may keep the aspirations of children limited to the same model—which is indeed observed in a survey among young people in the Netherlands.[17]

Perverse Effects

Some feedback effects are the unintended consequence of policies—that is why they are labelled *perverse effects*. Gunnar Myrdal discovered in his US research that indeed some well-meaning government policies had perverse effects for the black population. For his analysis of unintended policy consequences, he focused on Franklin D. Roosevelt's New Deal policy in response to the Great Depression. One of the policy measures was a reduction in cotton production in order to counter the low prices. This was meant to help the cotton farmers in the south of the country. The problem, however, Myrdal discovered, was that the policy affected tenants more than owners of land. Those who were growing cotton on leased land were no longer allowed to grow cotton. And since most tenants were black and most owners were white, the price-supporting policy turned out to particularly hit black cotton farmers and cotton pickers, whereas helping white farmers. This resulted in even more unemployment among blacks in rural areas in the south of the US. Another well-intended policy measure of the New Deal that Myrdal criticized was the minimum wage in the manufacturing sector. It turned out that the higher wages resulted in the displacement of black workers in favour of white workers, who had, on average, higher levels of schooling and skills. Even today, the best paid industrial jobs, protected by strong labour unions, are occupied by white workers.

Today, we see similar perverse effects of social policies. In home care, for example, there is a worldwide trend towards privatization based on the assumption that the market will deliver elderly care more efficiently than the state. In Europe, EU-regulation requires public procurement for local governments for a wide variety of policy areas, including home care. As a consequence, formerly public home care organizations are now forced to compete as private firms with each other for contracts with municipalities to deliver home care. The idea behind this was to enforce efficiency in service delivery. But the competition appeared to be too successful. Various home care organizations have cut their costs so radically, out of fear to lose their contract, that they have reduced personnel costs drastically, displacing experienced elderly care givers by inexperienced younger ones, and fixed labour contracts by flexible ones. In addition, some organizations have won the bid with such low hourly tariff offerings that they went bankrupt because the tariff appeared to be too low to survive, even with lower costs and reduced services.[18] In the US, the trend has led to similar perverse effects for workers and care receivers. In Florida, an accountability office report has concluded that non-profit home care provisioning in the state delivers the same quality of care and prevents institutionalization at the same rate as for-profit care but at lower cost.[19] This is because the nonprofit care providers reinvest surpluses back into care giving services. While commercial home care providers pay out a large share of the profit to shareholders. But there is a more fundamental side effect of the privatization in home care in the US: 'The loss of community-based long-term care services to outside corporate interests reduces communities' investment in the lives of their older residents and their families, and it weakens communities.'[20] In terms of Myrdal's perverse effects: the privatization of home care and the forced competition between private and public or semi-public home care providers results in both short term perverse effects for the care providers and in long term perverse effects for the care receivers and their communities.

We also see perverse effects of emancipation policies. As long as dominant social norms favour the breadwinner-and-housewife/part-time earner model and reinforce the idea that housework is women's work, policies that promote gender equality will continue to have negative side effects. For example, paternity leave, which many men either do not take up, even if it is paid, or do take up but don't spend on childcare. Research on paternal leave take-up in Spain suggests that male leaders who take up more leave days (two weeks up to three months) than the standard period (two days up to two weeks), receive more negative peer assessments than male leaders who do not take up more than the standard period.[21] Also, lower status was attributed to male leaders taking up parental leave as compared to female leaders taking up parental leave. So, even when the policy seems effective at first sight—men taking up parental leave—it does not seem to deliver on the expected change in gender norms, at least not at the company level due to stigmatization of male leaders taking up parental leave as being inadequate leaders. The wide variation of perverse effects of policies concerning vulnerable groups, point at the strength of discriminatory social norms, irrespective if they concern race, gender, or the elderly. When social policy does not take the widespread impact of discriminating social norms into account, well-meant policies may reinforce existing inequalities. And then, we are back to Myrdal's first key concept of cumulative causation, which results in a lock-in effect of the status quo of discrimination and marginalization.

Today, Myrdal's insights are applied more often outside than inside economics. For example, by sociologists and geographers, who speak of self-perpetuating cycles of deprivation and inequality.[22] In economics, we only see Myrdal's insights in institutional economics with terms such as lock-in effects and path-dependency, and in social economics, with analyses of stigmatization and social exclusion. The wider insight of the importance of economic resilience has been largely lost in economics. Until the COVID-19 crisis broke out. Resilience, and its trade-off with specialization, risk and uncertainty, is making a comeback in economics. And with it, hopefully, policy options that increase the resilience of disadvantaged groups in the economy as well as the resilience of the economy as a whole. Myrdal suggested two types of resilience policies. First general social policies that are inclusive and provide social security for all, irrespective of economic status, ethnic background or gender identity. In addition, policies that strengthen the voice of disadvantaged groups—in public debate, politics and local communities. Perhaps this second type of policies is even more urgent today, because these tend to address the very social norms that perpetuate privilege and inequality.[23] The Black Lives Matter movement and the spread of its activism across the western world strongly call for such policies.

THE ECONOMIST

Karl Gunnar Myrdal (Skattungbyn, 1898–Danderyd, 1987)

Gunnar Myrdal was the son of a Swedish landowner and building contractor. He studied law and economics at the University of Stockholm and received his PhD from the same university, in 1927. He had a busy professional career, in which he combined positions in the academic world, public sector and politics. He was a member of parliament for the social democrats and served as Minister of Trade right after the Second World War, between 1945 and 1947. After this, he accepted the position of Secretary General of the UN Economic Commission for Europe, in Geneva. He also participated in the board of the Swedish Central Bank—the same bank that awards the annual prizes in memory of Alfred Nobel for the field of economics. In 1974 he was awarded the prestigious prize himself but his attitude to this honour was uncomfortable. He was quite critical of the discipline of economics. Myrdal, like Veblen, Keynes and Sen, acknowledged that economics is a social science and therefore not entirely free from ethics. But he experienced that most of his colleagues ignored or denied that. For that reason, he had intended to refuse the prize. When asked why he had accepted it anyway, he replied that the committee had rang him very early in the morning while he was not completely awake yet.

Gunnar Myrdal was married to the sociologist Alva Myrdal, who also won a Nobel Prize (the 'real' one, awarded by the Swedish Academy of Sciences). It was the Nobel Price for Peace, which she received in 1982 for her role in the UN-negotiations about nuclear disarmament of the superpowers after the Second World War. She had a great influence on her husband. For example, it was Alva who suggested Gunnar to study economics, when he did not like law anymore. Together, they have played an important role in Swedish social policy and the construction of the welfare state.

Myrdal earned his fame with his study of race and the disadvantaged position of blacks in the US. He had visited the country for the first time in 1929 and studied the position of black farmworkers and black manufacturing labour against the background of the financial crisis. It was for that reason that he noted that the recovery measures did not automatically help the black population. He uncovered some key mechanisms that held them back and identified policies that had the opposite effect as compared to the effect on the white labour class. In 1944, he published his study with the title *An American Dilemma*.[24] He had a hand of picking catchy titles. His other much-cited study, which became a classic study in development economics, dealt with poverty in India. It was published in 1968 with the title *Asian Drama*.[25] He developed his theory of cumulative causation on the basis of the empirical insights on discrimination, exclusion and stigmatization that he gained from his two large country studies. His theory is a dynamic, contextual alternative to the neoclassical concept of market equilibrium. He found neoclassical theory rather absurd, given the fact that the 1929 crisis in the US and the persistence of deep poverty in India did not show any signs of excess labour supply being absorbed by the labour market, even though there were no minimum wages and the unemployed were willing to work for very low wages. Myrdal's theory of cumulative causation has contributed importantly to the field of social economics, which emerged in the 1940s with its own journal and association.[26]

Myrdal the economist was very much influenced by Myrdal the policy maker and administrator. His theory, of which feedback loops and perverse policy effects were the key dynamics, was therefore complemented with concrete policy recommendations. The first characteristic of these recommendations was that they do not concern local policies or sectoral policies (such as labour market policy), but national level policies. The second characteristic was that they are broad and cover the basic elements of people's livelihoods: housing, education and income security. The third characteristic was that he connected economic, social and political rights as the basis for policies: he insisted on equal voting rights for blacks, requiring simple and affordable voter registration procedures. This was the same problem for which Dr Martin Luther King led the great protest march from Selma to Montgomery in the southern state of Alabama, 20 years after the publication of Myrdal's seminal study.

His interest in poverty and developing countries was triggered when he accompanied Alva to India, where she was appointed as ambassador in Delhi. Although insightful on the poverty dynamics at the time, his prediction of continued misery in India turned out to be wrong. He had been too pessimistic about the rate of population growth and the capacity of the Indian economy to keep pace with it. Today, India is the most populous country of the world, the largest democracy, poverty has declined steadily and the country ranks among the fastest-growing economies. Myrdal retired from Stockholm University in 1967 after a second professorship, this time in international economics (in the 1930s and 1940s his chair was in political economy). The daughter of Gunnar and Alva, Sissela Bok, would become a well-known scholar in the field of practical ethics, and was affiliated with Brandeis University and Harvard University.

Reading Myrdal
Örjan Appelqvist and Stellan Andersson (eds), *The Essential Gunnar Myrdal. A Comprehensive Introduction to the World-Renowned Social Scientist's Political Thought* (New York: The New Press, 2005).

Reading About Myrdal
Thomas Etzemüller, *Alva and Gunnar Myrdal. Social Engineering in the Modern World* (Lanham: Lexington Books, 2014).

Practising Myrdal

Neighbourhood Nursing: Buurtzorg

The global trend towards privatization, private equity participation, internationalization, and de-professionalization in home care has triggered social entrepreneurship in home care. One of the best-known examples is Buurtzorg, a nonprofit in the Netherlands, with replications elsewhere, from Germany to China and the US to Japan. Buurtzorg means neighbourhood care in Dutch. It started in 2006 with just four district nurses in one town and has grown since to almost 900 teams with 9000 nurses and 25,000 patients per year across the country (which is 10% of all home care patients in the Netherlands). Buurtzorg is nurse-led and, paradoxically, its purpose is to make district nurses superfluous by empowering patients.[27] Teams operate independently and horizontally and receive coaching when necessary from a small group of specialized staff across the country. Each team cares for approximately 50 patients and manages its operational budget, largely funded through social insurance programmes. This works well with a team size of 10, which allows for self-management and complementarity, and, most importantly, shared responsibility both for patient care and for the team and its finances. Client surveys show that patients are happy with this approach and staff surveys point out that they appreciate their autonomy and prefer Buurtzorg over other home care employers.

An evaluation by the Dutch Ministry of Health found that the average cost per patient of Buurtzorg is well below that of the sector's average, despite a higher hourly tariff, to reward professional staff properly. The average number of hours spent per patient in the long run is lower than of other providers. And the overhead costs are very low: the headquarter is a modest office-building with a staff of only 30, and no fancy local offices but only small meeting units rented in low-cost neighbourhoods. The nurses spend most of their time on direct care thanks to a smart ict-system that helps to minimize administration time. The five guiding principles of the care model of Buurtzorg are trust, autonomy, creativity, simplicity and collaboration.[28] Buurtzorg was awarded the prize for best employer for several years onwards for companies of over 1000 employees.[29] In a review article of its development, researchers label the organization as a frontrunner of a transformative movement of long-term health care in the Netherlands.[30] The Buurzorg-model shows resilience in terms of flexibility, local embeddedness, cost efficiency, and commitment.

Financial Independence: The Swedish Case

Sweden ranks first on the EU Gender Equality Index and has maintained its top-position in Europe for 15 years in a row.[31] The fulltime employment equivalent rate of Swedish women is lower than that of men (59% against 66%), but the difference is much smaller than elsewhere, in particular the Netherlands (37% for women and 58% for men). In Sweden, women's incomes are on average 85% of men's incomes, again, the gap is smaller than in other EU countries (on average 80%). The most striking indicators concern time-use. In all categories of unpaid work and leisure, the gender difference in time spent is smallest in Sweden. For example, 30% of women and 27% of men spend time on childcare, elderly care or care for disabled persons on a daily basis. The EU-average rates are 38 and 25%, respectively. The gap with the EU-average in the share of people doing housework on a daily basis is large: in Sweden, 66% more men do daily housework as compared with the average EU man, while 6% fewer women do daily housework in Sweden as compared to the average EU woman.

What are the policies of Sweden that stimulate women's relatively high financial independence and men's relatively high participation in caring tasks? First, an early start with the promotion of women's employment: in Sweden already in the 1960s.[32] Hence, today, already the third generation of men and women are growing up with (almost) fulltime working mothers. Second, public and affordable childcare and a generous parental leave policy, irrespective of employment status. Parental leave is up to 480 days per child and 80% paid of one's earnings. And, importantly, part of the leave days (60 days) cannot be transferred between men and women, so that they are lost if fathers don't take them up. This has significantly increased the number of parental leave days taken up by fathers. Third, policies promoting fulltime work for men and women. The majority of those with a part-time job prefers a full-time job in Sweden. Local government bodies have taken the lead in providing those who do involuntary part-time work with full-time employment, by addressing issues of worktime, childcare and elderly care. An example is the municipality of Avesta in the county Dalarna (where Gunnar Myrdal's family is from), where the municipality and the local division of the labour union set-up a program in which all union members were guaranteed a fulltime job.[33] Today, 90% of the workers in Avesta have a fulltime job. Interestingly, this policy is the opposite of the one in the Netherlands, where since 2000, a national law entitles everyone to part-time employment.

Finally, the fertility rate of Sweden is slightly higher than elsewhere in Europe (1.75 versus 1.56 in the EU),[34] but the difference is small, and also the Swedish rate is well below the replacement rate of 2.1. Moreover, this is more attributable to the slightly higher—but declining—fertility rates among those with an immigrant background, who make up 25% of the Swedish population.[35] Hence, the gender-equality policies of Sweden are not effective to counter the trend of ageing, even though the Myrdal's had hoped for this.[36] But that is not the purpose of today's policies: they serve to enable people to make their own choices about work, income and division of labour. And in addition the benefit for small children to enjoy the two options of prolonged periods of full-time parental care and high-quality and accessible childcare services.

Notes

1. https://stats.oecd.org/. Accessed on July 15, 2020.
2. The OECD definition of social support is having friends or relatives to count on in times of trouble.
3. Eun Jeong Nam and Jong-Eun Lee, "Mediating Effects of Social Support on Depression and Suicidal Ideation in Older Korean Adults with Hypertension who Live Alone," *The Journal of Nursing Research* 27, 3 e20 (2019). https://doi.org/10.1097/jnr.0000000000000292. Accessed on July 15, 2020.
4. Hyungchul Park, Il-Young Jang, Hea yon Lee, Hee-Won Jung, Eunju Lee and Dae Hyun Kim, "Screening Value of Social Frailty and its Association with Physical Frailty and Disability in Community-Dwelling Older Koreans: Aging Study of PyeongChang Rural Area," *International Journal of Environmental Research and Public Health* 16, 2809 (2019). https://doi.org/10.3390/ijerph16162809. Accessed on July 15, 2020.
5. https://data.oecd.org/inequality/poverty-rate.htm. Accessed on July 15, 2020.
6. Boyoung Jeon, Haruko Noguchi, Soonman Kwon, Tomoko Ito, and Nanako Tamiya, "Disability, Poverty and Role of Basic Livelihood Security System on Health Services Utilization among the Elderly in South Korea," *Social Science & Medicine* 178 (2017): 175–183. https://doi.org/10.1016/j.socscimed.2017.02.013. Accessed on July 15, 2020.
7. Minsung Sohn, Patricia O"Campo, Carles Muntaner, Haejoo Chung and Mankyu Choi, "Has the Long-term Care Insurance Resolved Disparities in Mortality for Older Koreans? Examination of Service Type and Income Level," *Social Science & Medicine* 247, 112812 (2020).
8. Sujin Kim and S.V. Subramanian, "Income Volatility and Depressive Symptoms among Elderly Koreans," *International Journal of Environmental Research and Health* 16, 19 (2019). https://doi.org/10.3390/ijerph16193580. Accessed on June 26, 2020.
9. SCP, Armoede in kaart 2019 (Den Haag: Sociaal en Cultureel Planbureau, 2019). https://digitaal.scp.nl/armoedeinkaart2019/de-omvang-van-armoede/. Accessed on March 31, 2020.

10. Wil Portegijs and Marion van den Brakel, "Emancipatiemonitor 2018" (Den Haag: Sociaal en Cultureel Planbureau, 2018). https://digital.scp.nl/emancipatiemonitor2018/. Accessed on March 31, 2020.
11. Ans Merens and Freek Bucx, "Werken aan de start. Jonge vrouwen en mannen op de arbeidsmarkt" (Den Haag: Sociaal en Cultureel Planbureau, 2018).
12. Guy Standing, The Precariat—the New Dangerous Class (New York: Bloomsbury, 2011). See also a blog by Guy Standing, "Meet the Precariat, the New Social Class Fuelling the Rise of Populaism." November 9, 2016. https://www.weforum.org/agenda/2016/11/precariat-global-class-rise-of-populism/. Accessed on July 15, 2020. David Graeber has also written an interesting book about this phenomenon, to which he refers as bullshit jobs: David Graeber, *Bullshit Jobs – a Theory* (New York: Simon & Schuster, 2018).
13. For an introduction to this, see: Ping Chen, "Equilibrium Illusion, Economic Complexity and Evolutionary Foundation in Economic Analysis," *Evolutionary Institutional Economic Review* 5, 1 (2008): 81–127.
14. This is precisely what social movements such as #MeToo and Black Lives Matter emphasize: the privilege that is often taken for granted by the dominant group – men and the white population in the case of these movements.
15. Gyuchan Kim, "The Patterns of "Care Migrantization" in South Korea," *Journal of Ethnic and Migration Studies* 44, 13 (2018): 2286–2302.
16. Arlie Hochschild, "Global Care Chains and Emotional Surplus Value," in *On The Edge: Living with Global Capitalism*, edited by Will Hutton and Anthony Giddens (London: Jonathan Cape, 2000: 130–146).
17. Ans Merens and Freek Bucx, "Werken aan de Start – Jonge Vrouwen en Mannen op de Arbeidsmarkt" (Den Haag: Sociaal en Cultureel Planbureau, 2018). https://www.scp.nl/publicaties/publicaties/2018/01/22/werken-aan-de-start. Accessed on April 2, 2020.
18. In the Netherlands for example, several large home care organizations have gone bankrupt over the past decade: TSN, Diafaan, Solace, Thebe, and Thuiszorg Noord-Holland. It implies job losses and waiting lists and inadequate care for tens of thousands of patients, in majority frail elderly: https://www.zorgwelzijn.nl/thuiszorgorganisaties-failliet-door-bezuinigingen-gemeenten/. Accessed on April 28, 2020.
19. OPAGA, "Report No. 10-33" (Tallahassee: OPAGA, 2010). http://elderaffairs.state.fl.us/doea/Evaluation/The%20State%20Could%20Consider%20Several%20Options%20to%20Maximize%20%20Its%20Use%20of%20Funds%20for%20Medicaid%20Home%20and%20Community-Based%20Services.pdf. Accessed on April 28, 2020.
20. Larry Polivka and Baozhen Luo, "Neoliberal Long-Term Care: from Community to Corporate Control," *The Gerontologist* 59, 2 (2019): 222–229, p. 227.
21. Leire Gartzia, Maria Eugenis Sánchez-Vidal and David Cegarra-Leiva, "Male Leaders with Paternity Leaves: effects of work norms on effectiveness evaluations," *European Journal of Work and Organizational Psychology* 27, 6 (2018): 793–808.
22. See, for example, Richard Torraco, "Economic Inequality, Educational Inequity, and Reduced Career Opportunity: A Self-perpetuating Cycle?," *New Horizons in Adult Education & Human Resource Management* 30, 1 (2018): 19–29; D. Massey, *Categorically Unequal: The American Stratification System* (New York: Russel Sage, 2008).

Finally, the fertility rate of Sweden is slightly higher than elsewhere in Europe (1.75 versus 1.56 in the EU),[34] but the difference is small, and also the Swedish rate is well below the replacement rate of 2.1. Moreover, this is more attributable to the slightly higher—but declining—fertility rates among those with an immigrant background, who make up 25% of the Swedish population.[35] Hence, the gender-equality policies of Sweden are not effective to counter the trend of ageing, even though the Myrdal's had hoped for this.[36] But that is not the purpose of today's policies: they serve to enable people to make their own choices about work, income and division of labour. And in addition the benefit for small children to enjoy the two options of prolonged periods of full-time parental care and high-quality and accessible childcare services.

NOTES

1. https://stats.oecd.org/. Accessed on July 15, 2020.
2. The OECD definition of social support is having friends or relatives to count on in times of trouble.
3. Eun Jeong Nam and Jong-Eun Lee, "Mediating Effects of Social Support on Depression and Suicidal Ideation in Older Korean Adults with Hypertension who Live Alone," *The Journal of Nursing Research* 27, 3 e20 (2019). https://doi.org/10.1097/jnr.0000000000000292. Accessed on July 15, 2020.
4. Hyungchul Park, Il-Young Jang, Hea yon Lee, Hee-Won Jung, Eunju Lee and Dae Hyun Kim, "Screening Value of Social Frailty and its Association with Physical Frailty and Disability in Community-Dwelling Older Koreans: Aging Study of PyeongChang Rural Area," *International Journal of Environmental Research and Public Health* 16, 2809 (2019). https://doi.org/10.3390/ijerph16162809. Accessed on July 15, 2020.
5. https://data.oecd.org/inequality/poverty-rate.htm. Accessed on July 15, 2020.
6. Boyoung Jeon, Haruko Noguchi, Soonman Kwon, Tomoko Ito, and Nanako Tamiya, "Disability, Poverty and Role of Basic Livelihood Security System on Health Services Utilization among the Elderly in South Korea," *Social Science & Medicine* 178 (2017): 175–183. https://doi.org/10.1016/j.socscimed.2017.02.013. Accessed on July 15, 2020.
7. Minsung Sohn, Patricia O"Campo, Carles Muntaner, Haejoo Chung and Mankyu Choi, "Has the Long-term Care Insurance Resolved Disparities in Mortality for Older Koreans? Examination of Service Type and Income Level," *Social Science & Medicine* 247, 112812 (2020).
8. Sujin Kim and S.V. Subramanian, "Income Volatility and Depressive Symptoms among Elderly Koreans," *International Journal of Environmental Research and Health* 16, 19 (2019). https://doi.org/10.3390/ijerph16193580. Accessed on June 26, 2020.
9. SCP, Armoede in kaart 2019 (Den Haag: Sociaal en Cultureel Planbureau, 2019). https://digitaal.scp.nl/armoedeinkaart2019/de-omvang-van-armoede/. Accessed on March 31, 2020.

10. Wil Portegijs and Marion van den Brakel, "Emancipatiemonitor 2018" (Den Haag: Sociaal en Cultureel Planbureau, 2018). https://digital.scp.nl/emancipatiemonitor2018/. Accessed on March 31, 2020.
11. Ans Merens and Freek Bucx, "Werken aan de start. Jonge vrouwen en mannen op de arbeidsmarkt" (Den Haag: Sociaal en Cultureel Planbureau, 2018).
12. Guy Standing, The Precariat—the New Dangerous Class (New York: Bloomsbury, 2011). See also a blog by Guy Standing, "Meet the Precariat, the New Social Class Fuelling the Rise of Populaism." November 9, 2016. https://www.weforum.org/agenda/2016/11/precariat-global-class-rise-of-populism/. Accessed on July 15, 2020. David Graeber has also written an interesting book about this phenomenon, to which he refers as bullshit jobs: David Graeber, *Bullshit Jobs – a Theory* (New York: Simon & Schuster, 2018).
13. For an introduction to this, see: Ping Chen, "Equilibrium Illusion, Economic Complexity and Evolutionary Foundation in Economic Analysis," *Evolutionary Institutional Economic Review* 5, 1 (2008): 81–127.
14. This is precisely what social movements such as #MeToo and Black Lives Matter emphasize: the privilege that is often taken for granted by the dominant group – men and the white population in the case of these movements.
15. Gyuchan Kim, "The Patterns of "Care Migrantization" in South Korea," *Journal of Ethnic and Migration Studies* 44, 13 (2018): 2286–2302.
16. Arlie Hochschild, "Global Care Chains and Emotional Surplus Value," in *On The Edge: Living with Global Capitalism*, edited by Will Hutton and Anthony Giddens (London: Jonathan Cape, 2000: 130–146).
17. Ans Merens and Freek Bucx, "Werken aan de Start – Jonge Vrouwen en Mannen op de Arbeidsmarkt" (Den Haag: Sociaal en Cultureel Planbureau, 2018). https://www.scp.nl/publicaties/publicaties/2018/01/22/werken-aan-de-start. Accessed on April 2, 2020.
18. In the Netherlands for example, several large home care organizations have gone bankrupt over the past decade: TSN, Diafaan, Solace, Thebe, and Thuiszorg Noord-Holland. It implies job losses and waiting lists and inadequate care for tens of thousands of patients, in majority frail elderly: https://www.zorgwelzijn.nl/thuiszorgorganisaties-failliet-door-bezuinigingen-gemeenten/. Accessed on April 28, 2020.
19. OPAGA, "Report No. 10-33" (Tallahassee: OPAGA, 2010). http://elderaffairs.state.fl.us/doea/Evaluation/The%20State%20Could%20Consider%20Several%20Options%20to%20Maximize%20%20Its%20Use%20of%20Funds%20for%20Medicaid%20Home%20and%20Community-Based%20Services.pdf. Accessed on April 28, 2020.
20. Larry Polivka and Baozhen Luo, "Neoliberal Long-Term Care: from Community to Corporate Control," *The Gerontologist* 59, 2 (2019): 222–229, p. 227.
21. Leire Gartzia, Maria Eugenis Sánchez-Vidal and David Cegarra-Leiva, "Male Leaders with Paternity Leaves: effects of work norms on effectiveness evaluations," *European Journal of Work and Organizational Psychology* 27, 6 (2018): 793–808.
22. See, for example, Richard Torraco, "Economic Inequality, Educational Inequity, and Reduced Career Opportunity: A Self-perpetuating Cycle?," *New Horizons in Adult Education & Human Resource Management* 30, 1 (2018): 19–29; D. Massey, *Categorically Unequal: The American Stratification System* (New York: Russel Sage, 2008).

23. The civil movements of Black Lives Matter and #MeToo may be examples of such voices that help to change discriminatory norms. They are not immediately economic but have important economic impacts, on employment, wages, status, security and wellbeing.
24. Gunnar Myrdal, *An American Dilemma – the negro problem and modern democracy* (New York: Harper, 1944).
25. Gunnar Myrdal, *Asian Drama – an inquiry into the poverty of nations* (New York: Pantheon, 1968). In a column by the well-known Indian development economist on the occasion of the fiftieth anniversary of the book, Ravi Kanbur argued that although Myrdal's prediction of misery did not come true, the book contains important analytical insights for today's development economics: Ravi Kanbur, "Gunnar Myrdal and "Asian Drama" in context", *VOX*, 9 March (2018). https://voxeu.org/article/gunnar-myrdal-and-asian-drama-context. Accessed on June 26, 2020.
26. See the *Review of Social Economy* of by the Association for Social Economics, which was created in 1941: https://socialeconomics.org/about/history/. Accessed on May 10, 2020.
27. Tony Sheldon, "Buurtzorg: the district nurses who want to be superfluous," *British Medical Journal* 358, j3140 (2017). https://doi-org.eur.idm.oclc.org/10.1136/bmj.j3140. Accessed on May 11, 2020.
28. Karen Monsen and Jos de Blok, "Buurtzorg: Nurse-led Community Care," *Creative Nursing* 19, 3 (2013): 122–127.
29. https://www.hpbbnieuws.nl/?p=721. Accessed on May 11, 2020.
30. Françoise Johansen and Suzanne van den Bosch, "The Scaling-Up of Neighbourhood Care: from experiment towards a transformative movement in healthcare," *Futures* 89 (2017): 60–73.
31. https://eige.europa.eu/gender-equality-index/2019/SE. Accessed on May 12, 2020.
32. Åsa Lundqvist, "Activating Women in the Swedish Model," *Social Politics* 22, 1 (2015): 111–132.
33. https://eige.europa.eu/gender-mainstreaming/good-practices/sweden/promoting-full-time-employment. Accessed on May 12, 2020.
34. See for these data the website of Eurostat: https://appsso.eurostat.ec.europa.eu/nui/show.do?dataset=demo_frate&lang=en. Accessed on July 21, 2020.
35. For an analysis of the declining fertility rate among women with a nonwestern migration background, see: Marianne Tønnessen, "Declined Total Fertility Rate among Immigrants and the Role of Newly Arrived Women in Norway," *European Journal of Population* 36, 2020: 547–573. https://doi.org/10.1007/s10680-019-09541-0. Accessed on July 21, 2020.
36. Alva Myrdal, *Nation and the Family – The Swedish Experiment in Democratic Family band Population Policy* (New York: Harper and Brothers, 1941).

Bibliography

Chen, Ping. "Equilibrium Illusion, Economic Complexity and Evolutionary Foundation in Economic Analysis." *Evolutionary Institutional Economic Review* 5, 1 (2008): 81–127.

Gartzia, Leire, Maria Eugenis Sánchez-Vidal, and David Cegarra-Leiva. "Male Leaders with Paternity Leaves: effects of work norms on effectiveness evaluations." *European Journal of Work and Organizational Psychology* 27, 6 (2018): 793–808.

Graeber, David. *Bullshit Jobs – a Theory*. New York: Simon & Schuster, 2018.

Jeon, Boyoung, Haruko Noguchi, Soonman Kwon, Tomoko Ito, and Nanako Tamiya. "Disability, Poverty and Role of Basic Livelihood Security System on Health Services Utilization among the Elderly in South Korea." *Social Science & Medicine* 178 (2017): 175–183. https://doi.org/10.1016/j.socscimed.2017.02.013. Accessed on July 15, 2020.

Johansen, Françoise, and Suzanne van den Bosch. "The Scaling-Up of Neighbourhood Care: from experiment towards a transformative movement in healthcare." *Futures* 89 (2017): 60–73.

Kanbur, Ravi. "Gunnar Myrdal and 'Asian Drama' in context." *VOX*, 9 March 2018. https://voxeu.org/article/gunnar-myrdal-and-asian-drama-context. Accessed on June 26, 2020.

Kim, Gyuchan. "The Patterns of 'Care Migrantization' in South Korea." *Journal of Ethnic and Migration Studies* 44, 13 (2018): 2286–2302.

Kim, Sujin, and S.V. Subramanian. "Income Volatility and Depressive Symptoms among Elderly Koreans." *International Journal of Environmental Research and Health* 16, 19 (2019). https://doi.org/10.3390/ijerph16193580. Accessed on June 26, 2020.

Lundqvist, Åsa. "Activating Women in the Swedish Model." *Social Politics* 22, 1 (2015): 111–132.

Massey, Douglas. *Categorically Unequal: The American Stratification System*. New York: Russel Sage, 2008.

Merens, Ans, and Freek Bucx. "Werken aan de start. Jonge vrouwen en mannen op de arbeidsmarkt." Den Haag: Sociaal en Cultureel Planbureau, 2018.

——— "Werken aan de Start – Jonge Vrouwen en Mannen op de Arbeidsmarkt." Den Haag: Sociaal en Cultureel Planbureau, 2018. https://www.scp.nl/publicaties/publicaties/2018/01/22/werken-aan-de-start. Accessed on April 2, 2020.

Monsen, Karen, and Jos de Blok. "Buurtzorg: Nurse-led Community Care." *Creative Nursing* 19, 3 (2013): 122–127.

Myrdal, Alva. *Nation and the Family – The Swedish Experiment in Democratic Family band Population Policy*. New York: Harper and Brothers, 1941.

Myrdal, Gunnar. *An American Dilemma – the negro problem and modern democracy*. New York: Harper, 1944.

——— Asian Drama – an inquiry into *the poverty of nations*. New York: Pantheon, 1968.

Hochschild, Arlie. "Global Care Chains and Emotional Surplus Value," in *On the Edge: Living with Global Capitalism*, edited by Will Hutton and Anthony Giddens. London: Jonathan Cape, 2000: 130–146.

OPAGA. "Report No. 10-33." Tallahassee: OPAGA, 2010. http://elderaffairs.state.fl.us/doea/Evaluation/The%20State%20Could%20Consider%20Several%20Options%20to%20Maximize%20%20Its%20Use%20of%20Funds%20for%20Medicaid%20Home%20and%20Community-Based%20Services.pdf. Accessed on April 28, 2020.

Hyungchul Park, Il-Young Jang, Hea yon Lee, Hee-Won Jung, Eunju Lee, and Dae Hyun Kim. "Screening Value of Social Frailty and its Association with Physical Frailty and Disability in Community-Dwelling Older Koreans: Aging Study of Pyeong Chang Rural Area." *International Journal of Environmental Research and*

Public Health 16, 2809, (2019). https://doi.org/10.3390/ijerph16162809. Accessed on July 15, 2020.

Polivka, Larry, and Baozhen Luo. "Neoliberal Long-Term Care: from Community to Corporate Control." *The Gerontologist* 59, 2 (2019): 222–229.

Portegijs, Wil, and Marion van den Brakel. "Emancipatiemonitor 2018." Den Haag: Sociaal en Cultureel Planbureau, 2018. https://digital.scp.nl/emancipatiemonitor2018/. Accessed on March 31, 2020.

Jeong Nam, Eun, and Jong-Eun Lee. "Mediating Effects of Social Support on Depression and Suicidal Ideation in Older Korean Adults with Hypertension who Live Alone." *The Journal of Nursing Research* 27, 3 e20 (2019). https://doi.org/10/1097/jnr.0000000000000292. Accessed on July 15, 2020.

SCP. "Armoede in kaart 2019." Den Haag: Sociaal en Cultureel Planbureau, 2019. https://digitaal.scp.nl/armoedeinkaart2019/de-omvang-van-armoede/. Accessed on March 31, 2020.

Sheldon, Tony. "Buurtzorg: the district nurses who want to be superfluous." *British Medical Journal* 358, j3140 (2017). https://doi-org.eur.idm.oclc.org/10.1136/bmj.j3140. Accessed on May 11, 2020.

Sohn, Minsung, Patricia O'Campo, Carles Muntaner, Haejoo Chung, and Mankyu Choi. "Has the Long-term Care Insurance Resolved Disparities in Mortality for Older Koreans? Examination of Service Type and Income Level." *Social Science & Medicine* 247, 112812 (2020).

Standing, Guy. *The Precariat – the New Dangerous Class*. New York: Bloomsbury, 2011.

——— "Meet the Precariat, the New Social Class Feulling the Rise of Populism." November 9, 2016. https://www.weforum.org/agenda/2016/11/precariat-global-class-rise-of-populism/. Accessed on July 15, 2020.

Tønnessen, Marianne. "Declined Total Fertility Rate among Immigrants and the Role of Newly Arrived Women in Norway," *European Journal of Population* 36, 2020: 547–573. https://doi.org/10.1007/s10680-019-09541-0. Accessed on July 21, 2020.

Torraco, Richard. "Economic Inequality, Educational Inequity, and Reduced Career Opportunity: A Self-perpetuating Cycle?," *New Horizons in Adult Education & Human Resource Management* 30, 1 (2018): 19–29.

Chapter 9: Adam Smith on the Abuse of Markets

THE PROBLEM

Since the year 1900 we have been using eight times as much natural resources. These include biomass, oil and gas, as well as ore and building materials. The increase in material use is a consequence of population growth but even more so of an increase in consumption per head and of the use of fossil energy in the production of those consumer goods. Next to deforestation, poisoned rivers, smog and the rapid extinction of species, the human exploitation of earth's resources contributes to climate change. Moreover, all these impacts are interrelated. Therefore, the consequences for the capacity of our planet to provide inputs to our growing world economy are unknown. Nobody knows what will happen exactly when we would exceed the global warming threshold of 2 degrees Celsius as countries agreed to prevent in the Paris Agreement on Climate Action. That is why it is wise, also economically, to change our economies to remain below this threshold.

CO_2 emission is the major contributor to climate change as the IPCC, the UN International Panel on Climate Change, has calculated. And this is not the result of natural variation in CO_2 levels over time but due to human behaviour—in fact, our economic behaviour. The evidence is provided by a comparison of the level of CO_2 before and since the Industrial Revolution. Since 1880, the average temperature on earth has increased by 1 degree Celsius, while the sea level has risen by 25 cm.[1] Figure 1 shows the increase in the concentration of CO_2 in the atmosphere between 1990, the reference year of various climate agreements, and mid-2020. The line shows a steep increase. And given the combination of population growth and consumption growth, the line is not likely to flatten soon. Hence, we are seriously running the risk to pass the critical threshold for global warming.

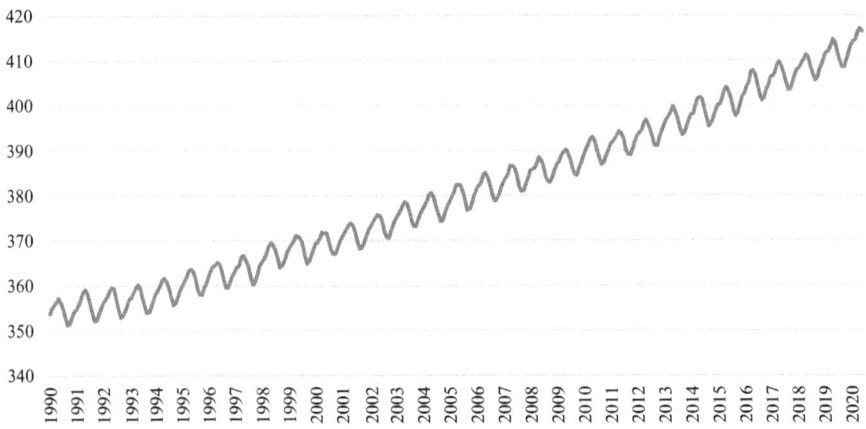

Fig. 1 CO_2 concentration 1990–2020 (parts per million). Note: CO_2 concentration is subject to seasonal variation, which explains the pattern along the trendline. (Source: author, based on publicly available data from NOAA: www.esrl.noaa.gov/gmd/ccgg/trends/, Accessed on 22 July 2020)

The Price of Global Warming

In order to remain well below the critical threshold of 2 degrees temperature increase, international agreements about carbon reduction are crucial. The first agreement was made in Kyoto in 1997. But the US never signed, and the fastest growing economies of the world, India and China, were exempted due to the fact that their historical contribution to greenhouse emissions was negligible compared to developed countries. The Kyoto Protocol held that between 2005 and 2012, emissions of greenhouse gases should decline by 5.2% as compared to the year 1990. But that goal was not achieved. Worse, the concentration of CO_2 has increased further, as Fig. 1 has shown. The Paris Agreement of 2015 was the next international agreement on climate change. But, again, the goal seems out of reach unless the Great Lockdown following the COVID-19 pandemic will have a lasting effect on greenhouse emissions and the post-COVID-19 economy is a structurally different one than the one up to the Spring of 2020.

Why have agreements and subsequent policies not been effective? This is clearly not just due to the lack of participation by the US and emerging markets. No, the main reason is that the agreements so far did not involve compulsory measures to force the producers of greenhouse gases—mainly industry but also other sectors such as transport and agriculture—to reduce their emissions. Instead, governments have relied on a theory by a Nobel Memorial Prize winning economist who argued that markets can solve externalities of markets. The economist, Ronald Coase, argued that these externalities would obtain a price as soon as a market would be created for the permits to generate such externalities. In other words, if one party desires to pollute, it needs to pay a price for the right to pollute. This will result in a market price for everyone. The higher the price, the stronger the incentive for the ones causing harm to end it, while the money paid could be used to invest in compensatory measures by those who receive the money. Let me give an example. If you like to play loud music and your neighbour is unhappy with it, the two of you can negotiate about a price for the noise she experiences. The higher the price you have to pay for every hour of loud music, the more likely you are willing to turn the volume lower. Until there is an equilibrium reflected by a market price, which satisfies both of you: you accept lower decibels of your favourite music, or decide to invest in a headset, and she will have much of her quietness back and money for sound-insulation of her walls. This market-based solution for externalities is based on freedom of choice, exchange and a market price. But, as Coase admitted himself, it will only work under three conditions: when the externality is limited to a small circle, the absence of transaction costs, and the possibility to measure the externality. Hence, the Coase Theorem provides an alternative for government regulation and employs the market to deal with externalities. It seems a smart solution. One does not get a Prize in Memory of Alfred Nobel just like that.

But does it work? Well, first the three conditions have to be fulfilled. And next, there should be a market price sufficiently high to provide an incentive to reduce the externality. But the more important question is: does it effectively reduce the externality? In the case of carbon emissions, we have no time to lose. The answer to the question is: it depends on the opportunity cost and state of the economy. If the economy is booming and your income is increasing, you may be willing to pay an increasing price to refrain from investment in noise reduction or green energy. Alternatively, if the economy is in a recession and you have to take a side job and have very little time left to listen to music, or your CO_2 emissions are much lower due to a drop in production, the externality will be automatically less and there will not be investments in structural measures. In short, a market for externalities is not immune to economic cycles. Worse, such markets may not achieve their social objective precisely because of economic cycles. The market is a wonderful transaction mechanism—but often mostly during boring economic times.

A Market for Carbon Emissions

Various countries and economic communities, such as the European Union, have decided to implement the Kyoto Protocol with the help of the idea by Ronald Coase rather than through mandatory caps for CO_2 emissions. In the EU this has resulted in the European Trading System (ETS) in which one ton of CO_2 equals one emission permit. The ETS is an artificially created market in which many (but not all—energy producers, e.g., have been exempted until recently) large European industrial firms have to buy permits to pollute. They have to do so based on their production plans and buy the number of emission permits that parallels their planned emissions. If they want to produce more, they have to purchase additional permits and pay a fine. If they produce less than planned they will have a surplus of emission permits which can be used later. The trading system covers almost 50% of all European carbon emissions. The assumption behind this artificial market is, in line with the Coase Theorem, that firms will reduce their CO_2 emissions in order to reduce production cost by using filters, recycling, green energy, or energy saving. In that way, the market would work for the benefit of greenhouse gas reduction.

In the meantime, the Kyoto Protocol has ended, and the EU has agreed to reduce carbon emissions by at least 40% in the year 2030 as compared to 1990.[2] The trading system not only requires the participating firms to buy emission permits at the beginning of their production year but also allows, and even stimulates, trading on a daily basis. This way, the most efficient allocation of emission permits will be achieved. Firms who reduce their emissions through cleaner production will have a surplus of permits which they can sell to firms that have not invested in clean technology. Each firm will make its own cost calculation comparing buying permits and investing in carbon reductions. The carbon market implies no caps or fines for firms who choose not to reduce their level of CO_2 emissions. No moral signal about a responsibility to reduce global warming. The ETS clearly favours free choice over considering a reduction in greenhouse gases as a common cause. Firms will make a comparison of marginal costs and benefits of investing in greener production technologies. The cost of buying an additional permit for CO_2 emissions will be compared with the returns of the additional products sold with that ton of CO_2. When the cost of an additional permit exceeds the returns from extra sales, as will be the case with a relatively high price of emission permits, a firm will have an incentive to reduce emissions. So, the ETS will only be effective when the market price for a ton CO_2 will be high enough to induce firms to invest in green technology and energy saving.

Has the ETS been effective? The answer is no. The problem is that scarcity on markets is always relative. The impact of the market on reducing emissions per unit of output produced by factories is weak or absent during recessions, such as the 2009–2014 recession and the lockdown during the COVID-19 crisis. And when the economy was booming, before the financial crisis and after recovery, between 2015 and 2020, industrial firms had no problem paying the going carbon price, even when it reached a level of 30 euro per ton, because their sales and profit margins were high. Hence, the carbon price does not provide an incentive for energy efficiency and renewable energy. Moreover, unsold permissions remained in the market, adding to the surplus that was created at the beginning. As a consequence, the market price for carbon emissions moved close to zero several times between 2009 and 2018, and it has remained below five euro per ton during most of these ten years. So, the carbon market in fact signalled that air pollution was costless. Free pollution—completely legitimate. Firms could generate as much emissions as they wanted—the limit was not a serious price, not a cap, not a tax, but simply their own marginal cost calculations. And worse, the signal of this policy instrument at level zero is that carbon emissions are not a threat and that there is no urgency to shift to greener production processes at all.

Figure 2 shows the price development of the carbon permits since the financial crisis. It shows that most of the time, the price has been less than ten euro per ton and often even less than five euro. A price of thirty euro is exceptional and occurred just before the financial and the COVID-19 crises. In both cases, it took only a few months before the price plummeted. Hence, the economic cycle largely explains the long-term movement of the carbon price, which will not contribute to a steady decline in line with the Paris Agreement and the EU's own targets of carbon reductions.

The problem of a surplus of permissions in the market is serious and has been there since the beginning of the system in 2005—courtesy of the industrial lobby in Brussels. The majority of the permits are provided freely by the EU on an annual basis, in order to protect energy-intensive industries from international competition by firms outside the EU that do not pay carbon taxes. Hence, there is an oversupply of permits in the market. If these would expire on an annual basis, the problem could be corrected quickly. But firms are allowed to purchase more permits than they need and keep them on their balance sheets as tradable financial assets. Indeed, the stock of permits has become so large that it equals a whole year of carbon emissions. Moreover, the possibility to trade in surplus permissions has resulted in speculation. Firms can

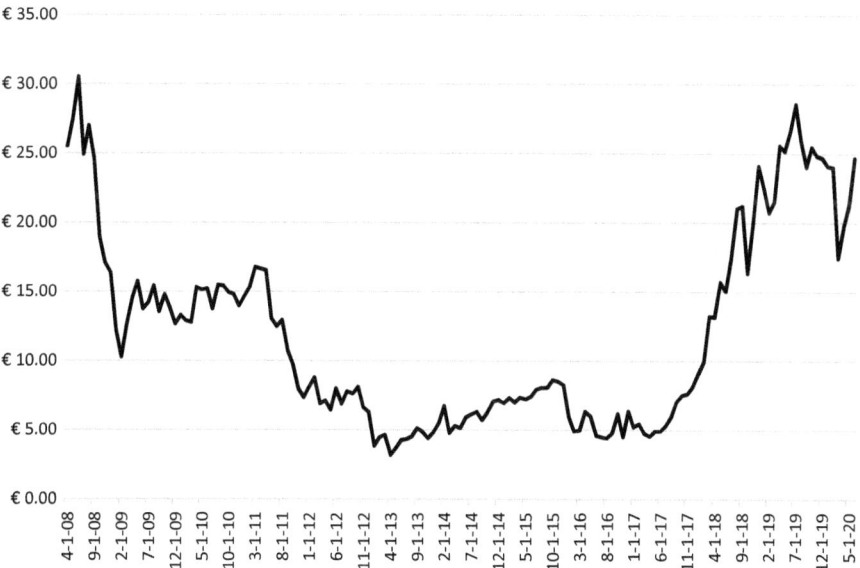

Fig. 2 Price per ton CO_2 in the ETS since the financial crisis (euro). (Source: Author, based on data from EMBER: https://ember-climate.org/carbon-price-viewer/, Accessed 29 June 2020)

make money by trading in permits as if they were any other type of financial asset. This explains much of the short-term volatility in the carbon price.

What to be done? In phase 4, which is starting up now, the EU will implement a set of policies that should help to reduce the surplus of permits.[3] First, a lower number of new annual permits has started in 2018. However, the surplus has not come down yet by mid-2020. Second, the EU has started a reserve for emission permits when the surplus exceeds a certain threshold. In May 2019, this resulted in a reserve holding worth 400 million permits. Third, from 2023 onwards, part of the holdings in the reserve will expire and hence lose their validity. The irony of these additional regulations of the ETS is that the carbon emissions market requires more and more regulation to make it work. But the whole idea of the market was that it would be a simpler and more efficient alternative to the state. Even from the beginning the artificial market required already a lot of bureaucracy. Every year, more than ten thousand European companies need to submit their production plans, and an estimate of the level of CO_2 emissions that go along with them, to the EU for verification. And at the end of the period, EU needs to monitor the actual production and emissions. In my view, this looks more like a USSR-type of central planning than a free market.

Another problem with the ETS is that some traders have abused the value-added tax rules of the EU (VAT) in order to profit from tax benefits in the trade of permits. And there is also a legal escape from investment in clean energy for participating firms. The system allows companies to use their permits to reduce carbon emissions not of their own operations in the EU but in developing countries by investing in programmes such as planting trees in Asia. Airlines often promote these programmes among their passengers, so that in fact the passengers pay for the emissions, weakening the incentive for the airlines to shift to cleaner energy sources and fuel-saving airplanes.[4] This example relates to a larger problem with the carbon market. That is that the (marginal) increase in production cost is often transferred to consumers through higher product prices—not only in the case of flights but in many other sectors as well. The result is that the incentive for firms to reduce their energy inputs is undermined. According to a UK study, between 75 and 100% of emission cost is transferred to consumers. Hence, in the end, it is the consumer who pays for the carbon emissions while profit rates remain the same and the climate does not benefit.[5]

Such transfer of cost is not possible in fully competitive markets, because consumers would quickly shift to suppliers who do not pass the environmental costs on to consumers. But many energy-intensive firms, such as coal power plants, don't operate in competitive markets but in oligopolistic markets or they are regional monopolists. Firms in such markets are not punished by consumers when they raise their prices due to a lack of choice for consumers (in case of a monopoly) or because the few firms forming an oligopoly follow each other with price increases. So, even though the market for carbon emissions may be competitive, if there is limited competition in the *sales markets* of energy firms, steel companies and chemical factories, the price incentive of the ETS has very limited effect on CO_2 emissions—even when the price is high.

Climate Change and Clean Energy

The International Energy Agency (IEA) keeps track of the various energy sources that countries have used over the past decades.[6] The data shows that for the world as a whole there has hardly been any reduction in the share of fossil fuels over the past 45 years. Coal, oil and gas made up 87% of the world's energy mix in 1973 and 81% in 2017. The difference is largely due to an increase in nuclear energy, not renewable energy sources. Europe's energy use has increased steadily over time and is flattening since the financial crisis, but not declining despite numerous energy-saving policies. The CO_2 emissions have started to decline somewhat in OECD countries since the financial crisis but have increased in all other regions of the world. Indeed, emerging economies are catching up, with China and India contributing increasingly to global carbon emissions. But at the same time, they invest heavily in renewable energy production capacity. For example, the majority of electricity in Brazil is from hydropower. When we look at the production of electricity in the world, coal is still the main source, with China and the US as the biggest producers of coal-based power. However, both countries also top the ranking of renewable sources of power, although the energy generated with renewables by these two countries is only 40% of the energy they produce with coal. China is world leader in solar power and quickly increasing its capacity—faster than most European countries.

The data collected by IEA also entails information about energy prices per source and end consumer, which gives an indication of fossil energy taxes and subsidies. The data shows large differences between countries. For example, the price per litre unleaded premium fuel varies between 0.72 dollar in the US and 1.80 in the Netherlands. Even more striking is the implicit subsidy for industry as compared to households. Everywhere, industry pays much less for fuel oil, gas and electricity than households. For example, in France, industry pays 60% of the fuel price of what households pay and in Italy even 36%. For electricity, the shares that industry pays are 58% in France and 62% in Italy. The EU has agreed to phase out fuel subsidies but without a clear target. A recent report by three environmental NGOs demonstrates the lack of transparency about fossil fuel subsidies across Europe.[7] The report reveals that France, for example, spends 6 billion euro annually to subsidize renewable energy but at the same time it has spent on average 7 billion euro per year on fossil fuel subsidies over the period 2014–2016. In Italy, about 20 billion euro is spent on fossil fuel subsidies compared to 12 billion euro on renewable energy. The report calls for more transparency and serious reductions in fossil fuel subsidies in line with EU's commitment to phase them out. Up to now, several countries spend more on subsidies for fossil fuels than on renewable energy, even though many citizens believe the reverse is the case. They believe that wind and solar energy are heavily subsidized in order to compete with fossil fuels. But implicit subsidies for fossil fuel industries cause a serious bias in energy prices.

Carbon emissions trends differ widely in Europe. In the UK and Spain, for example, large reductions have been realized over the past few years, whereas in France and the Netherlands, emissions have increased. The success of the UK is largely due to a carbon tax that is in place since 2013, which functions as a floor price to the ETS price, first of 9 pounds and since 2015 it was 18 pounds per ton CO_2. This comes down to a doubling of the market price for carbon emissions for industry in the UK. As a consequence, many old coal plants in the UK are no longer profitable—their marginal production costs are now higher than the marginal benefits from selling an additional KWh of electricity. So, in the UK many coal plants have closed down and since 2016, the UK generates more power though wind turbines than with coal plants.[8] In Spain, a significant shift towards renewable energy sources has been realized, so that today more than 40% of electricity is generated by various renewable sources. The French increase in emissions is largely due to the downsizing of nuclear energy plants for safety reasons. But the Netherlands has recently built two new coal plants (which use biomass from imported wood as complementary fuel). In countries with only the ETS price and no carbon tax, the low carbon price has functioned as an incentive for old coal plants to remain open and even for new coal plants to be built. That is in fact, as Gunnar Myrdal has labelled it, a perverse effect of the trade in carbon permits.

Looking at the share of renewable sources in the energy consumption of EU countries, we see great variation. The overall EU target for 2020 is 20% renewable energy, with different targets per country. In 2018, Sweden was in the lead with 55% and the Netherlands at the bottom with 7%.[9] The Netherlands and France are the two countries furthest removed from their individual targets for 2020. Other countries, including Sweden, Finland, Denmark, Estonia, Croatia and Bulgaria have reached their targets already before 2018. Interestingly, this group includes some of the poorest EU-members. Hence, the level of GDP per capita is not a constraint for investment in renewable energy. The Baltic states stand out with their growth of renewable energy production. In 2018, the shares were 24% in Lithuania, 30% in Estonia and 40% in Latvia. Latvia is strong in hydropower, Estonia is strong in biomass and Lithuania is the biggest solar energy producer of the region. Of course, these states have an additional motivation to shift away from fossil fuels, which is their desire to become independent from Russian oil and gas. For the realization of their green ambitions, the Baltic states receive financial support from the EU. The outperformance in renewables by various poorer EU-member states demonstrates that the old member countries can do much better. The policies that are necessary for better performance are obvious: a shift in subsidies away from fossils and a carbon tax. States with a serious carbon tax include California, UK, Norway, Sweden and Switzerland. In 2019, I signed a public letter with seventy other Dutch economists calling for a carbon tax of at least fifty euro per ton CO_2.[10] With effect: from January 2021 onwards, there will be a carbon tax for all Dutch firms participating in the ETS, although it starts at a very low rate. It is even more urgent considering the fact that energy-efficiency in Dutch industry is lower than elsewhere in the EU, according to a recent study by the Dutch national statistics office.[11] The report also signals that after a period of decline of carbon emissions, the emissions have increased again. The main contributors are the oil sector, the chemical industry and the steel industry. The emission-intensity of the Dutch industrial sector is 50% higher than the European average. So, the tax would need to be sufficiently high to reduce both the level of emissions and the inefficiency of energy-use.

In conclusion, the ETS-market appears to be an ineffective mechanism to reduce carbon emissions. State regulation could be more effective, through the removal of subsidies for fossil fuels and the introduction of effective carbon taxes. This implies both regulation at the EU-level and by individual countries, following the examples set by the UK, Norway and Sweden. However, regulation is resisted by a strong industry lobby in Europe.[12]

The Insight

Markets are an important and often very effective economic mechanism, as Adam Smith already claimed: it is thanks to the market that the baker makes our bread and not because the state is forcing him or out of charity for us. In his famous 1776 book *An Inquiry into the Nature and Causes of The Wealth of Nations*,[13] Smith acknowledges that people can provide each other with almost everything they need but not all of it through 'benevolence only' as he phrased it. Some of our needs can be fulfilled by making smart bargains: 'Give me that which I want, and you shall have this which you want,' he writes. And he continues: 'it is in this manner that we obtain from one another the far greater part of those good offices which we stand in need of.'[14] He explains that such exchanges happen by addressing each other's interests and advantages—precisely what ideally markets do as win-win mechanisms. Indeed, in his days, people could satisfy a large part of their needs through exchange, much more than in earlier times. Smith wrote during the Industrial Revolution when markets expanded enormously and the scale of production increased massively from workshops to factories, with an increase in the number of units produced per hour and a decrease in the cost per unit. This allowed for lower sales prices and more people being able to purchase consumer goods. And it enabled manufacturers to purchase capital goods, such as steam-power looms replacing handlooms in the textile sector. Moreover, buying such factory goods was cheaper than making them individually at home, so that both at the production side and the consumption side people benefitted from the expanded market—indeed a clear win-win situation in which the interests at both sides of the market were satisfied. This insight from Smith illustrates that the market, at a certain level of technology and with a sufficient market size, is potentially beneficial for both sides and in that sense requires a willingness to cooperate in trade, relying on mutual trust and the ability to understand each other's needs and wants. This was his key message. Not that markets reflect our selfishness, or even require selfishness, as some economists claim today. Smith sharply observed that the market challenges us to use our talents and allocate scarce resources in such a way that others are happy to pay us for the goods we produce. And this allows us to purchase those goods we want from others—exactly as Karl Marx described the working of pre-capitalist market, before capitalism ran away with it.

The general form of the market, as Smith saw it, is a mechanism that stimulates innovation, flexibility, investment, quality and cost reduction. Many markets operate perfectly well and greatly benefit society by delivering ever better (or more fancy) products at lower cost. It is the market mechanism which decides that the best person will be hired on a vacancy, and not the boss's cousin or the highest contributor to the political party of a state employer. The market is what we make of it and therefore also requires a legal framework referring to property rights and contracts, quality control and sometimes even fixing minimum or maximum prices (such as the UK floor price for carbon emissions or an upper limit to the increase of house rents in many countries).

Smith, however, also observed that the market requires a stable social system with shared values and social norms, routines and relationships. Sociologists today would refer to this as social cohesion. This, Smith recognized, is necessary for many ordinary markets to function well. The baker cannot plan the number of breads she should make if she cannot count on a large group of more or less loyal customers with stable preferences. If people would behave selfishly, as some economists believe to be the only market motive, and compare the bread price of every bakery in town every day and always buy from the cheapest store, this may lead to slightly lower bread prices but eventually such behaviour would be disadvantageous for both the bakers and the consumers. The baker will regularly experience large quantities of unsold bread, which lowers her earnings. The consumer will regularly experience that her favourite bread has been sold out. This, in turn, may induce the selfish baker to put the leftovers of Yesterday in the shop, because she faces different consumers every day anyway. But the selfish consumers, in turn, will become distrustful of the selfish bakers and some may decide to bake their own bread again, even though it costs them more time than buying bread. So, Smith realized that for markets to function well, they need to be embedded in a well-functioning society with social values of trust, honesty and loyalty, next to individual values of prudence, diligence and creativity. He in a way already foresaw Amartya Sen's rational fool as a very ineffective economic agent.

The Embeddedness of Markets

Markets don't exist in a legal and social vacuum and Adam Smith knew this. Smith is regularly labelled the father of economics but for the wrong reason. He wrote three impressive volumes. Next to the one about the role of the market in the economy, he wrote *Letters on Jurisprudence*[15] about the state 14 years before *The Wealth of Nations*, and a book about society, titled *The Theory of Moral Sentiments*,[16] which he published almost 20 years before *The Wealth of Nations*. Hence, his book about markets should be understood as founded upon his earlier ideas of the state and society and not in isolation or preceding those ideas. But most economists have not read any of these books. When I was a bachelor student, there was only a one semester course in the history of economic thought, and we used a textbook with small excerpts from Smith's *Wealth of Nations* only. During my master's education the name Smith was not mentioned anymore. It was thanks to my PhD thesis supervisor that I read the two-volume book and the *Theory of Moral Sentiments* as well—to be surprised by their connections and logical coherence.

Many economists only refer to Smith as the economist who claimed that markets are driven by an invisible hand (which appears only once in the book) and the sentence about the baker who would bake bread out of self-interest (which for Smith had a different meaning than in today's economic textbooks). When we consider his three books together, he is clearly not a cheering apologist for markets. The Scottish philosopher and political economist recognized that every economy consists of three domains: state, market and community, each with its own values: justice, liberty and benevolence, as he labelled them. The state as the economic domain of justice, with security, laws, regulation and redistribution through taxation and public goods. The market as the domain of freedom through exchange, based on prudence, through competitive markets (not oligopolies and monopolies). And communities consisting of groups of people, from households to members of commons, who cooperate and share on a voluntary basis for the benefit of its members, driven by what Smith termed 'moral sentiments'. Today, feminist economists use the term caring, social economists refer to social capital or social cohesion, and institutional economists refer to the management of common pool resources. The key insight from Smith is that every economy consists of three domains which are interrelated: the state, the market and the community economy, or care economy—each with their own values. That is precisely why we have a moral problem with the trade in human organs and in the appointment of incompetent family members on vacancies. The three domains are distinct and although some substitution is possible—think about childcare by parents at home on the one hand and state or private sector creches on the other hand—the substitution is limited. Not only by our morality, though, but also by economic standards such as efficiency, which has been demonstrated with the example of voluntary blood donations versus commercial donor blood.

The Market Can't Do It Alone

The lesson from Smith is that markets are unable to lead to socially desirable outcomes when operating out of balance with the state and communities. A well-functioning market must be embedded in a fair legal context that provides the necessary redistribution. And it must be embedded in society with the values and social norms of communities in which market relationships are additional to community relationships without undermining or exploiting these. If such embedding of market operations is not possible, economic interaction is better left to either public services provided by the state or to commons and caring behaviour. Ronald Coase seems to have forgotten this lesson from Smith, just like the EU did when it decided to create the market for carbon emissions rather than a binding legal framework or a carbon tax reflecting a commitment of the community of EU-citizens to prevent climate change.

Interestingly, well-functioning markets generally emerge by themselves. They do not need to be created artificially with a whole set of bureaucratic rules to make them work. A well-known example is given by the provisional little shops emerging in no time in refugee camps. There, barbershops, food stalls, bakers and phone card sellers emerge out of nothing. But where the market does not emerge by itself, there is either no legal framework available to shape it or social and public values don't support it. Such artificial markets need either brute power (drug gangs) or bureaucracy (as in the ETS) to function, but even then, they may not be very effective in allocating the scarce commodity in such a way that the outcome is socially desirable.

So, why not skip the market and achieve some goals through the state? The reason why policy makers tend to ignore the productive role of the state has been explained by Mariana Mazzucato in her book *The Value of Everything*.[17] She argues that economists since Smith have regarded the state (and communities) as unproductive. The state would merely redistribute money through taxes and subsidies. But this is a too narrow view of the economic role of the state, Mazzucato argues. First, the state also provides public goods and often in an efficient or even profitable way—think about national train and airline companies, hydropower plants and national development banks. Even services like land registry are profitable in various countries. Second, the state invests in research and development (R&D) which eventually results in key innovations that are picked up by firms without any payment for it, in order to make private profit—think about the US government investments in the internet, which have helped firms such as Facebook and Google to become the most profitable firms in the world. Third, it is simply an established accounting rule that only businesses provide value added to the economy and not the state. But statistics show that this rule is biased. Mazzucato illustrates this with a comparison of the value added by the US government and the finance industry: the value added of the government is about 11–15% of GDP, whereas the value added of the finance industry is around 4–8% of GDP. Hence, governments are not 'just spending' as the current accounting system and economic models portray, but they are investing without reaping the monetary returns on their investments because these are largely public: knowledge (innovation and even technology), health (e.g. decent sanitation) and infrastructure.

Parallel to the undervaluation of the economic role of the state, Mazzucato signals an overvaluation of the role of private business, and of financial firms in particular. The reason is that not all private firms create value in the sense of producing new goods and services (without negative externalities) that consumers need or want. Many large firms, she explains, engage more in value extraction, which she defines as 'activities focused on moving around existing resources and outputs, and gaining disproportionately from the ensuing trade'.[18] That is why Adam Smith, she writes, was in favour of free markets in the sense of markets free from rent-seeking by large landowners, urban landlords and monopolists. These rents, Smith observed, were choking the English economy, and the state should intervene to reduce such rent-seeking behaviour, he argued.

Contrary to the carbon emissions trading system, there is a highly successful scheme to protect the ozone layer. There is no market mechanism involved. That environmental problem was addressed in the 1990s by the Montreal Protocol, which simply prohibited the use of chlorofluorocarbons (CFCs—a powerful greenhouse gas) in a range of products such as refrigerators and air conditioners.[19] The protocol included phasing out with different time-paths for developing and developed countries and provided funds for developing countries to cooperate and eventually got the support from the chemical industry who benefitted from selling substitutes for CFCs. The agreement was adopted by every single member of the UN (197 countries at the time in 1987). Twenty years later, another family of powerful greenhouse gases was included in the protocol: hydrochlorofluorocarbons (HCFCs). Developed countries should phase them out by 2020 and developing countries ten years later. This will also help in the reduction of CO_2 emissions, because these substances are 2000 times more potent greenhouse gases than CO_2 in terms of their global warming potential. Moreover, the ban on CFCs has saved an estimated two million people each year from skin cancer, according to the UN organization responsible for its monitoring.[20]

The market is too important to be left to neoliberal policy makers who believe that the economic performance of markets is by definition better than that of states. Markets function well for many goods, but not for everything we find valuable as a society. Smith teaches us that this is precisely why the economy is more than only markets. It consists of a delicate balance of market, state and community and cannot function without the values created, supported and protected in communities. When markets expand into the values of the state and community, the economy gets out of balance.[21] It undermines the values of the other domains, the values that Smith referred to as justice and benevolence—values that the market needs for its own functioning. Markets will be seriously hampered without, for example, reliable contracts or mutual trust. But when the common good is made into a commodity—such as the environment or the climate—what does this say about our values as a society? And who are we, in Europe, to tell China and India to reduce their emissions if we are responsible for most of the global warming up to now? Or to talk about population growth in Africa when the ecological footprints of Europeans are much higher than for Africans? Or, closer to home, what is the legitimacy to ask our children to make their beds and help wash the dishes if we demonstrate to them that such virtues are for sale? What is our response if they answer that they will only do those chores in exchange for money? The market is not inherently corrupt but when applied outside its own value domain of freedom for mutual gains based on socially useful goods and services, we may turn it into a corrupt mechanism.

The EU ETS is a dangerous experiment with the future of the earth—a vulnerable planet that today not even allows seven billion people to make a decent living. We have a very small margin of rising temperatures left. Adam Smith would know what to do: strict regulation with help of a tax, an end to fossil subsidies, and new subsidies for the expansion of the capacity of renewable energy production in developing countries. When it is possible to regulate more than 10,000 companies in a European-wide carbon trading system, then it must be easier to fight climate change with a follow-up of the Montreal Protocol for carbon dioxide and related greenhouse gases.[22] Sometimes, regulation is more efficient than the market, with lower cost and with faster and more sustainable results.

THE ECONOMIST

Adam Smith (1723 Kirkcaldy–1790 Edinburg)

The father of economics held a Chair in Moral Philosophy because economics was not yet a recognized field of science. But his famous 1776 book *The Nature and Causes of the Wealth of Nations*—*The Wealth of Nations* for short—would later be named as the start of economics. Smith was Scottish and remained in Scotland for most of his life, teaching at the universities of Edinburg and Glasgow. He himself studied at Oxford but was not satisfied with his education there. He found his teachers lazy and therefore spent most of his days in self-study in the university library. After graduation he went to France as a private teacher and started writing there. But he moved back to his mother's house in Scotland three years later and never married—he lived with his mother until her death. He has been characterized by his contemporaries as a typical absent-minded professor, talking to himself and often oblivious of his surroundings. The story goes that one night he was sleepwalking on the streets and only woke up at the sound of the church bells in the next town.

The fundament under his economics has three pillars: public value provided by the state (on the basis of the value of 'justice'), exchange value generated in the market (on the basis of the values of 'prudence' and 'liberty') and social value in communities (on the basis of the value of 'benevolence'). He commented about the 'political economy' that it functions not only to help people to provide a living for themselves but also 'to supply the state or commonwealth with a revenue sufficient for the public services.'[23] For Smith, market and state were interrelated and not placed in a hierarchy: the market needs a legal system of laws and regulations. At the same time, the state needs revenue from taxing market activity in order to fulfil its public services for the common good. This insight also means that Smith acknowledged that some goods and services are better left to the market (such as food production), while other functions are better left to the state (such as education).

Smith was in favour of free markets as opposed to feudalism and monopolies. He saw how markets could easily become monopolies through mergers, acquisitions, corruption and rent-seeking, resulting in value extraction for a happy few at cost of workers, entrepreneurs and consumers. And he already noted the problem of negative externalities and stated that the state must address these. He did not simply argue for free markets and a small and passive state, but carefully made the argument in line with his previous two books on the state and society, that markets will only flourish when they are embedded in a just state and when people trade on the basis of shared values and social norms. This view resulted in statements in *The Wealth of Nations* that some would sooner ascribe to Marx. For example, Smith stated that day-labourers should be able to earn a wage sufficient enough to live in dignity according to the standards of their times. For Glasgow and Edinburgh, this meant in the second half of the eighteenth century that 'a creditable day-labourer would be ashamed to appear in public without a linen shirt' and that 'leather shoes' are 'a necessary of life in England' for men and women alike.[24] Fortunately, Smith was not a Dutchman because the custom to wear wooden shoes would not have made his argument very convincing.

The message from Smith's view of the economy as consisting of three interrelated value domains—with value referring both to ethics and economics, connecting the two—is that when markets do not support human dignity (or human rights as we would say today), justice (represented by the state) should correct the value of liberty of the market. And that requires taxation, which Smith preferred to be levied on luxury goods, profits and immoral behaviour. This view is reflected today in our relatively high taxation of vehicles and alcohol. But profit taxes have reduced substantially today. A carbon tax would fit Smith's view, based on the principle that those who harm the common good should be taxed for doing so.

If you would like to remember Smith, there is no need to travel to his grave in Edinburgh. Getting a twenty-pound note from the bank is sufficient. Since 2007, it carries Adam Smith's profile and thereby features the first Scot on an English bank note. But Smith would not have appreciated it—he disliked his appearance.

Reading Smith
Adam Smith, *An Inquiry into the Nature and Causes of the Wealth of Nations*, vol. I and II, Indianapolis: Liberty Fund, 1981 [1776].

Reading About Smith
Ian Simpson Ross, *The Life of Adam Smith* (Oxford: Oxford University Press, 2010).

Practising Smith

In line with Smith's three pillars of the economy, we find activities against climate change in all three value domains. The more effective ones can be found in the state and in communities, while the market generates innovations for the energy transition, but often not without support from the state in the initial phase. The state's role in preventing climate change is certainly not limited to taxation (such as a carbon tax) or pricing policy (such as the UK price floor for carbon emissions) or regulation of substances (as is the case for substances affecting the ozone layer). The state's role also extends to the public supply of green energy. For example, through the Akosombo Dam that was built in the 1960s in the Volta River in Ghana, which has resulted in the fact that Ghana has a higher rate of access to electricity for households and entrepreneurs than other sub-Sahara African countries. Moreover, the state may set up an investment fund to finance the energy transition. Through these diverse ways, the state can provide public value, contributing to the common good of preserving our climate and environment. Also, communities have shown to be innovative in preventing climate change, through collective investments in solar panels, for example, or by car-pooling or collecting plastic on the beach. Not all green innovation happens on markets: many ideas are developed in universities and non-profit organizations.

A Sovereign Wealth Fund for Sustainable Development

State investment funds—called sovereign wealth funds by economists—are a good example of the creation of public value. Norway, a country with five million inhabitants, has the world's largest sovereign wealth fund, established in 1990. It is a state investment fund worth over a trillion dollar, which means more than 200.000 euro per inhabitant. The total amount exceeds Norwegian GDP. The fund is built on oil revenues and the annual revenue of the investment fund is spent on pensions and education, but also on the transition towards an energy neutral economy. This may sound paradoxical—using revenue from Norway's oil industry to reduce its national consumption of oil, but in the long run this makes perfectly sense. That is also why the fund manager—the Norges Bank, which is the Central Bank of Norway—has recently decided to reduce the investments in the oil and gas industry to less than 6%. Another smart strategy of the state oil fund is that the government cannot use its value for government expenditures because the law only allows spending part of annual revenues, not of the fund itself.

The state oil fund of Norway is exceptional. Other countries have started much later, for example China and various OPEC-countries. But other oil and gas producing countries have spent their annual oil and gas revenues instead of building an investment fund, for example the Netherlands (that is where the economic concept of Dutch Disease comes from: it refers to windfall export gains which lead to a currency appreciation). Still others, in particular developing countries producing oil, see much of the oil revenues going to foreign private companies rather than to their own nation.

Thanks to the decision to invest oil revenues in the energy transition, Norway has a much higher share of renewable energy than other European countries. All its electricity is generated with hydropower (which the Norwegians have used since the nineteenth century already). Hydropower is a widely available energy source with Norway's many rivers and is used with small scale installations spread over the country rather than with a single big dam as in Ghana. The ambition of the Norwegian government is to have all means of transport—cars, boats, airplanes—run on hydropower. As a start, the country has the highest share of electric cars in the world.

Commons for Climate

The other non-market mechanism that is employed for renewable energy production is the common. Already in the 1970s, in reaction to the first oil crisis, citizens in various countries have set up cooperatives for the local production of wind and solar energy. Over the past decade, there has been an enormous increase in renewable energy commons across the world. Some refer to these as climate commons, but many are in fact not commons as such—citizen's owned and managed initiatives—but government agreements, with or without partnerships with businesses. But all initiatives, to be successful, require shared social norms to be effective on a larger scale.[25] Some commons are small scale, with local communities going off the grid with their own solar panels. Others are larger through collectives of owner-investors who invest in a joint wind turbine or solar park, or by collectives renting rooftops of farms and business parks to place solar panels. What they all have in common is that these are not individual projects or commercial projects but commonly owned and managed projects: commons. These are bottom-up citizen's initiatives, contributing increasingly to the transition to renewable energy. For example, in 2019, the Netherlands had over 582 energy cooperatives, generating more than 300 MW green energy.[26] These solar and wind energy coops provide electricity to a quarter million of Dutch households. Also, in the US, despite the federal government's withdrawal from the Paris Climate Agreement, some individual states promote renewable energy production by communities. An example is the People Power Solar Cooperative in Oakland, California.[27] It rents local rooftops and invests in solar panels with members' financial contribution, which varies between 100 and 1000 USD. In Denmark, a joint venture between the local state-owned energy company on the one hand and 10,000 community members as a collective on the other hand jointly owns a wind park at sea. This wind park, called Middelgrunden, delivers wind power to its members in the country's capital, Copenhagen.[28]

Notes

1. For the most recent data, see the website of NASA on climate change: https://climate.nasa.gov/, Accessed on May 18, 2020.
2. https://ec.europa.eu/clima/policies/strategies/2030_en, Accessed on May 18, 2020.
3. Information can be found on the website of the European Energy Agency, for example in their briefings: https://www.eea.europa.eu/publications/the-eu-emissions-trading-system, Accessed on May 19, 2020.
4. This is called the Clean Development Mechanism and is a policy instrument of the UN to help poorer countries to reduce their carbon emissions: https://cdm.unfccc.int/, Accessed on May 19, 2020.
5. J.P.M. Sijm, K. Neuhoff & Y. Chen. "CO_2 Cost Pass Through and Windfall Profits in the Power Sector." *Climate Policy* 6, 1 (2006): 49–72.
6. See www.iea.org. For an overview of energy use, see the report: IEA. "Key World Energy Statistics 2019." https://webstore.iea.org/key-world-energy-statistics-2019, Accessed on May 20, 2020.
7. ODI. "Fossil Fuel Subsidies in Draft EU National Energy and Climate Plans." ODI Working Paper 562 (London: ODI, 2019), https://www.odi.org/sites/odi.org.uk/files/resource-documents/12895.pdf, Accessed on May 20, 2020.
8. The data can be found on the independent monitoring website Carbon Brief: https://www.carbonbrief.org/analysis-uk-wind-generated-more-electricity-coal-2016 Accessed on May 22, 2020.
9. EUROSTAT: renewable energy statistics, https://ec.europa.eu/eurostat/statistics-explained/index.php?title=File:Share_of_energy_from_renewable_sources_2018_infograph.jpg, Accessed on May 20, 2020.
10. https://www.nrc.nl/nieuws/2019/01/25/die-co2-heffing-voor-de-industrie-moet-er-komen-a3651737, Accessed on May 20, 2020.
11. CBS. "Emissie-intensiteit broeikasgassen Nederlandse industrie" (Den Haag/Heerlen: CBS, 2018), https://www.cbs.nl/nl-nl/maatwerk/2018/51/emissie-intensiteit-broeikasgassen-industrie, Accessed on May 20, 2020.
12. Corporate Europe Observatory. "Captured States: When EU Governments are a Channel for Corporate Interests" (Brussels: CEO, 2019). https://corporateeurope.org/en/2019/02/captured-states, Accessed on May 16, 2020.
13. Adam Smith. *An Inquiry into the Nature and Causes of the Wealth of Nations*, vol. I and II (Indianapolis: Liberty Fund, 1981 [1776]). From here onwards, I will refer to this book as *TWN*.
14. *TWN*: Book I, Chapter ii, p. 26.
15. Adam Smith, *Lectures on Jurisprudence* (Oxford: Oxford University Press, 1987 [1763]).
16. Adam Smith, *The Theory of Moral Sentiments* (Indianapolis: Liberty Fund, 1981 [1759]).
17. Mariana Mazzucato, *The Value of Everything—Making and Taking in the Global Economy* (London: Allan Lane, 2018).
18. Mazzucato, *The Value of Everything*, p. 6.
19. https://www.unenvironment.org/ozonaction/who-we-are/about-montreal-protocol, Accessed on May 22, 2020.
20. See the previous note.

21. This was the key argument in my PhD thesis, which was published as Irene van Staveren, *The Values of Economics—An Aristotelian Perspective* (London: Routledge, 2001).
22. One type of greenhouse gas that is not having an effect on the ozone layer has been added to the Montreal Protocol recently in the Kigali Amendment (hydrofluorocarbons—HFCs). This illustrates that the protocol is flexible enough to add more substances. Time to add CO_2 to it!
23. *TWN*, Book IV, Introduction, p. 428.
24. *TWN*, Book V, Chapter II, p. 870.
25. Stefano Carratini, Simon Levin, and Alessandro Tavoni. "Cooperation in the Climate Commons." *Review of Environmental Economics and Policy* 13, 2 (2019): 227–247.
26. Hier Opgewekt—Lokale Energiemonitor 2019, www.hieropgewekt.nl, Accessed 29 May 2020.
27. https://www.peoplepowersolar.org/, Accessed 29 May 2020.
28. https://base.socioeco.org/docs/a118_doc1.pdf, Accessed 29 May 2020.

Bibliography

Carratini, Stefano, Simon Levin, and Alessandro Tavoni. "Cooperation in the Climate Commons." *Review of Environmental Economics and Policy* 13, 2 (2019): 227–247.
CBS. "Emissie-Intensiteit Broeikasgassen Nederlandse industrie." Den Haag/Heerlen: CBS, 2018. https://www.cbs.nl/nl-nl/maatwerk/2018/51/emissie-intensiteit-broeikasgassen-industrie, Accessed on May 20, 2020.
Corporate Europe Observatory. "Captured States: When EU Governments are a Channel for Corporate Interests." Brussels: CEO, 2019. https://corporateeurope.org/en/2019/02/captured-states, Accessed on May 16, 2020.
"Die CO_2-heffing voor de industrie moet er komen." NRC Handelsblad, January 25, 2019. https://www.nrc.nl/nieuws/2019/01/25/die-co2-heffing-voor-de-industrie-moet-er-komen-a3651737, Accessed on May 20, 2020.
IEA. "Key World Energy Statistics 2019." https://webstore.iea.org/key-world-energy-statistics-2019, Accessed on May 20, 2020.
Mazzucato, Mariana. *The Value of Everything—Making and Taking in the Global Economy*. London: Allan Lane, 2018.
ODI. "Fossil Fuel Subsidies in Draft EU National Energy and Climate Plans." ODI Working Paper 562. London: ODI, 2019. https://www.odi.org/sites/odi.org.uk/files/resource-documents/12895.pdf, Accessed on May 20, 2020.
Sijm, J.P.M., K. Neuhoff, and Y. Chen. "CO_2 Cost Pass Through and Windfall Profits in the Power Sector." *Climate Policy* 6, 1 (2006): 49–72.
Smith, Adam. *The Theory of Moral Sentiments*. Indianapolis: Liberty Fund, 1981a [1759].
———. *Lectures on Jurisprudence*. Oxford: Oxford University Press, 1987 [1763].
———. *An Inquiry into the Nature and Causes of the Wealth of Nations*, vol. I and II. Indianapolis: Liberty Fund, 1981b [1776].
Staveren, Irene van. *The Values of Economics—An Aristotelian Perspective*. London: Routledge, 2001.

Chapter 10: Joan Robinson on Economic Pluralism

THE PROBLEM

The image of the melting economics textbook on the cover of *The Economist* in 2009 was clearly too optimistic. More than ten years later, not much has changed in economics education. Students are being taught the same subjects with largely the same textbooks. Many BA and MA programmes in economics do not offer obligatory courses in the history of economic thought or economic history. Neither do they offer courses in ethics or economic sociology. But they do offer lots of mathematics and modelling techniques—in the disguise of theory. In fact, when an economist talks about theory, this often refers not to logical, analytical thinking about why-questions and internal consistency at the philosophical level, but is shorthand for mathematical modelling. I discovered this when, during my time as a PhD student, I had sent a paper without a model to an economic journal, discussing the theoretical relationships between Adam Smith, John Stuart Mill and Thorstein Veblen. It was sent back almost immediately with the comment that the paper did not contain any theory.

The economic theory that has become dominant since the 1980s is generally referred to as neoclassical theory, because it builds on the work of the classical economists like Ricardo, Smith and Mill. More often, the dominant theory is referred to as mainstream economics. It is basically what most economists do and therefore it is generally felt that it does not need any reflection on how it distinguishes itself from other theories and why that matters. The other theories are, as a consequence, often not regarded as serious competitors.

The most important characteristics of mainstream theory have been discussed in this book. The hedonistic human being who constantly weighs costs and benefits in order to maximize his utility. The market which is, without government interference, always in equilibrium in a context of risk but not uncertainty. Prices reflecting real values. Average risk levels of zero, precluding systemic risk. Government action disturbing market equilibrium and resulting in inefficiency. Negative externalities that should not be prohibited or taxed but traded on an artificially created market. Employees motivated by monetary reward or threat of dismissal. And, of course, income as the best measuring rod of wellbeing.

The 2008 crisis has certainly made some cracks in these dogmas. But the damage to neoclassical theory is largely limited to the Efficient Market Hypothesis theory (EMH-theory) of finance because it had predicted an end to financial crises. Even Alan Greenspan, Chair of the Fed in the years running up to the crisis, has admitted that he had put too much faith in this theory. In October 2008, he said in a hearing by Congress:[1] 'Yes, I found a flaw …. in the model that I perceived is the critical functioning structure that defines how the world works, so to speak.' And he continued his response to senator Waxman: 'I had been going for 40 years or more with very considerable evidence that it was working exceptionally well.' Queen Elizabeth will not be happy with this explanation. The very idea, that one of the key persons overseeing the stability of the world economy had believed in a theory that appeared to be wrong must not be reassuring. But economists like me, who had always wandered off on the more realistic side paths of economics, felt relieved. For a short while, we shared the optimism of *The Economist*. At last, we thought, there is a recognition that neoclassical theory is built on quicksand. The shaky grounds of its assumptions which are too narrow, logically inconsistent, and sometimes even absurd. In short, the kind of economics that demonstrates how economies may work perfectly well in the world of models. We were hoping that, like Greenspan, also other well-known economists would reflect on their theoretical beliefs, or, as Greenspan labelled it himself, their ideology, when he continued his explanations to Congress: 'And we have this extraordinarily complex global economy, which as everybody now realizes is very difficult to forecast in any considerable detail.'

Since then, very little was heard of Greenspan. Most economists went back to business as usual with the same ideology, whereas policy makers tried to prevent a next financial crisis against the odds of an enormous banking lobby in Washington, London, Brussels and Frankfurt. While many other policy makers, outside the world of finance, have shown to be immune for Greenspan's moment of enlightenment. For example, many health economists have continued to advise policy makers to privatize health care, to stimulate mergers for the sake of efficiency, and to measure human lives in money terms for the sake of cost benefit analyses. And university managers have developed a straightjacket for the performance management of academics, with publication targets and research funding targets, resulting in an increase of precious research time spent on reporting one's own performance and being a member of funding committees for the assessment of the expected performance of others. The bureaucracy has increased so much, and the job insecurity has risen to such heights, that the transformation of universities to globally competitive businesses with influential ranking systems, has resulted in the characterization of universities as 'anxiety machines' in an authoritative report on mental health in academia.² The opportunity to learn fundamental lessons from the crisis about economics as a discipline and its policy advice has largely gone wasted. The next two subsections will each elaborate on this problem. First, on the lack of realism in economics and then on the view that teaching economics consists of delivering a toolbox to students.

Lack of Realism

In the high days of neoclassical economics, the cream on the cake of neoclassical economics was prediction. Forecasts of economic indicators such as GDP growth, inflation or the stock market index—for next week, month or year. Many economists thought, and still think despite Greenspan's disillusion, that they are able to make meaningful predictions. And despite the fact that it has been shown so many times how mistaken they tend to be.³ In an attempt of penance, the IMF has reviewed its own growth projections before and since the financial crisis. The result? They were all too optimistic. The error margins are not small. In the fall of 2007, IMF economists thought that the combined GDP of developed countries would be 15% higher five years later.⁴ A year later, they adjusted their forecast downward to 12%. And in 2014, they made a further adjustment to 5%. The financial news website Bloomberg has analysed IMF's all same-year GDP country forecast figures between 1999 and 2019.⁵ The conclusion is sobering: only in 6% of the cases the forecasts were within a 0.1 percentage-point margin of error (e.g. the forecast was 2.3% and the actual growth was 2.4%). Overall, the IMF's forecasts were more often underestimations than overestimations of growth, with an average error margin of 2.0 percentage-points (e.g. 2.6 instead of 4.6 growth rate). This illustrates that even real-world oriented policy analysts of a large and prestigious international institution are subject to the pessimistic and optimistic feelings that Keynes ascribed to investors. Those tasked with the explanation of the behaviour of economic actors appear to suffer from the same animal spirits as these economic agents experience. It demonstrates that economic predictions are surrounded by so much uncertainty that one wonders why so much research effort and media attention is spent on them. Some investors prefer to listen instead to what Warren Buffett says about a possible stock market crash.⁶

Of course, one should not settle the relevance of a discipline based on its miserable predictions. Although they are not harmless. Too much pessimism may result in further declines of investor confidence and the willingness of consumers to spend their money. Too much optimism may reinforce overvalued asset markets. Economic forecasts are not unrelated to economic behaviour, so that to some extent they can function as self-fulfilling prophesies—not because they are accurate but because they trigger the behaviour that they predict. So, what do people think about economics apart from the obscure activity of prediction? Well, there is very little enthusiasm about the realism of much economic analysis. The books about the crisis written by journalists like Gillian Tett (*Fool's Gold*) and Joris Luyendijk (*Swimming with Sharks*) tend to be more widely read than those written by economists.[7] Not to speak of economic reports meant for policy makers, which are full of narrowly defined concepts such as efficiency, rationality and wellbeing. The policy advise in those reports flows often straightforwardly from introductory economics courses without recognition of the discrepancy between the world of economic theory on the one hand and the real world with its abundance of externalities, rent seeking, uncertainties and imperfect information on the other hand. That is precisely the reason why many economic reports on the same topic are contradictory. Take, for example, the studies on the basis of which the Dutch government approved the construction of three new coal power plants in 2007. Since decades, the country ranks at the bottom of the production of renewable energy in Europe. But this fact did not enter into the calculations. What was taken into account instead, was the low European market price of carbon emissions, which kept the unit cost of electricity production with coal plants low. Now, only a few years later, the threat of a court case by an environmental NGO called Urgenda, has forced the government to close one of the oldest coal plants earlier than was foreseen.[8] The problem with the studies was not bad calculations. But a narrow view on which indicators were relevant for such a long-term decision—the point Urgenda defended successfully in the court room.

A recent trend in policy advise is the development of scenarios rather than the forecast of single indicators. This is an enormous improvement in the policy advise by economic institutions. Scenarios sketch possible futures with different parameters and levels of uncertainty, making clear to politicians that it is their deliberation and decision making, on political grounds, that is vital—not the questionable forecasts by economists based on fancy theoretical models.[9] But more can be done to make policy advise more useful. In a democracy, not only majority views should be taken into account, but also minority perspectives count. This implies that for crucial economic decisions such as building coal plants, or regulation of banks, or privatization of health care, different economic perspectives should be taken into account. Economics is not engineering. This requires that policy analyses employ more than one theory and method. It implies that policy makers commission reports from a variety of economic schools of thought. Or that economic policy advisors take lessons into account from economic history and take into account social context, institutions, and uncertainty.

That is precisely what Thomas Piketty has done in his bestseller *Capital in the 21st Century*. The book is heavy with numbers from historical statistics, and full of tables and diagrams. And with those statistics, Piketty tells an economic story that people recognize from their own life and the stories told by their parents and grandparents. The story is rich with context and explanation and requires only very limited use of mathematical equations—in fact, the book revolves around two equations, not derived from a mathematical model but from logic and the empirical trends in the data. Moreover, the story can be verified because he has put all the data online.[10] Piketty ends his book with useful advice for economists: 'To be useful, economists must above all learn to be more pragmatic in their methodological choices, to make use of whatever tools are available, and thus to work more closely with other social science disciplines.'[11]

Economics as a Toolbox

But Piketty's advice has fallen on deaf ears. The large majority of economists finds nothing wrong with the discipline and economics education. They are in favour of teaching students a toolbox with more and more sophisticated models and modelling techniques in order to solve optimization problems. Indeed, an engineering approach. Students, hence, learn that economics comes down to solving sets of equations, as in physics or engineering, rather than learning that economics is a social science, in which understanding human behaviour and interaction is what needs to be done in a context of uncertainty. A survey of bachelor economics programmes of seven top British universities reveals that only 10% of the courses mentioned other theories than the mainstream and that 50% of all exams consist of operating a model.[12] A similar survey among all Dutch undergraduate economic programmes shows that 86% of the courses are neoclassical and that 97% of the methods taught are quantitative.[13]

Why does the discipline resist change? The answer can be illustrated with the reaction to a group of economists who proposed to broaden economics education. The reaction came from another French economist, Jean Tirole, winner of the Nobel Memorial Prize of 2014. Shortly after the awarding event in Stockholm, he wrote a letter to the Minister of Education of France when he learned that the National Council of Universities had planned to set up a new department for Institutions, Economy, Territory and Society.[14] He was furious about the initiative, which he perceived as competing with economic departments. He wrote that 'it would cause a disaster for the visibility and future of research in economics in our country.' He continued his defence of the monopoly of mainstream economics by stating that: 'It is inconceivable for me that France would recognize two communities within the same discipline.' He thereby ignored that pluralism is the standard in all sciences, from philosophy to literature and from astronomy to sociology. There, other theories than the mainstream, or simply a diversity of theories, are cheerfully tolerated within a single department. But this is not the case for economics. At the University of Notre Dame, in the US, for example, heterodox economists were forced out in 2003 to set up their own department. Today, the Political Science Department at Notre Dame offers a minor in Philosophy, Politics and Economics. Other universities around the world have followed, with similar broad and interdisciplinary economic programmes, and they are increasingly popular among students. But for Jean Tirole, even separate degree programmes, outside economics departments, are not acceptable. He seems to assume that the new department in France would not comply with the requirement across the National Council of Universities to be assessed with objective quality standards including the number of publications by staff members in quality journals of each respective field of science. In the case of the newly planned department, that would imply publications in interdisciplinary journals. Instead, Tirole warned Madam Minister that the economists who propose the new department would represent 'the antechamber of obscurantism'.

Of course, the economists who have proposed the new department have written a reply to the fresh laureate.[15] Their argument relies on an analysis of the monopoly power by the mainstream over the economic top journals: economics among increasingly like-minded people resulting in an economics which ignores the work by the ten economists discussed in this book and in a narrowing down of the academic debate with less and less counter-voices. Figure 1 provides evidence for their argument. It demonstrates how the unanimity among most economists has undermined scientific debate in the discipline.

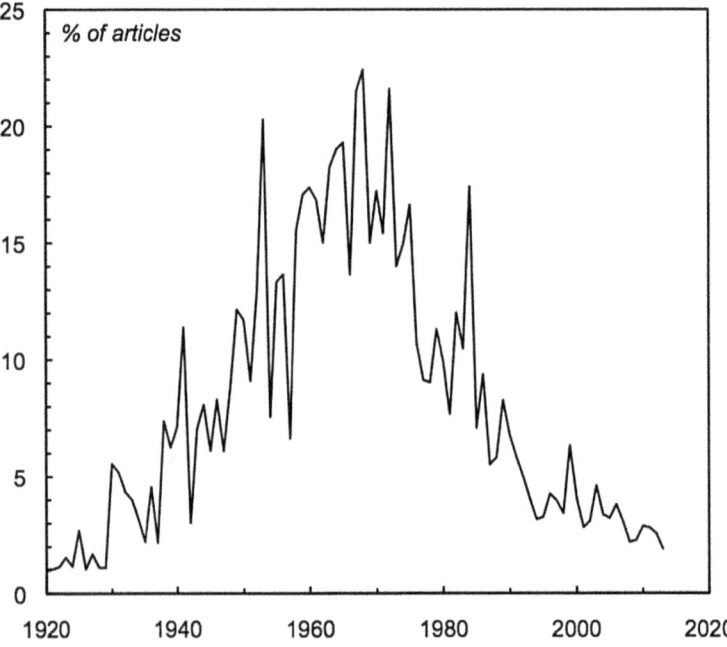

Fig. 1 Debate in the top-five economic journals 1920–2013. Note: The graph shows the number of articles in the big five economic journals that contain 'comment', 'reply' or 'rejoinder' in a title as percentage of all articles published in that year. The big five at the *American Economic Review, Econometrica,* the *Journal of Economic Literature,* the *Journal of Political Economy,* and the *Quarterly Journal of Economics.* (Source: Joe Francis, 'The Rise and Fall of Debate in Economics,' 2014. https://www.joefrancis.info/economics-debate/, Accessed on June 8, 2020)

As the diagram shows, until the end of the 1970s, the debate between economists increased steadily, resulting in a lively debating culture in the discipline. But after the 1970s, debate largely disappeared. Only in the early 1980s there was a short-lived peak again, but then, around the death of the star debater, Joan Robinson, the decline continued. Today, the debate is as low as it was at the start of the economic journals, with 1 or 2% of the articles per year engaging in debate, as compared to more than 20% in the 1960s and 1970s. The risk of this state of affairs is complacency. And that is a serious constraint to scientific progress.

The downward trend of scientific debate also illustrates the difficulty for non-mainstream economists to get their work published in the so-called top journals. We find it often easier to get published in top journals in other disciplines, such as sociology, political science or development studies, than in our own discipline. This suggests that there is nothing wrong with the quality of our work, but that there is very little interest by editors and peer reviewers of mainstream economic journals to engage with economic analyses that take, for example, a post-Keynesian, social-economic or institutional economic perspective. Or empirical papers that do not reduce theory to mathematical models and optimization problems but instead use descriptive statistics or qualitative methods, such as interviews or comparative case study analysis—methods that are, interestingly, widely accepted in business studies. Curiously, only some senior (often retired) economists seem to get away with alternative methods—think about Amartya Sen, Tony Atkinson and Joseph Stiglitz. Their papers are often the ones that stir debate in the discipline, for example, about inequality and economic growth. But younger economists, let alone PhD students, simply don't get their heterodox research published in the so-called top journals.

Scientific progress benefits from diversity—it even requires diversity and innovation in terms of perspectives and methods. That is precisely why the response of the French economists who favour the new, interdisciplinary department, states: 'Let us not confuse sectarianism with quality.' The response ends with the question asked by Queen Elizabeth and the reminder that those economists who had warned for a bubble building up in the US financial market and housing market had published their analyses in books, non-mainstream journals and blogs—which were all ignored by the mainstream.

The Insight

The answer to the problem of a single dominant theory is not another dominant theory but pluralism. The discipline will only be able to understand real-world economic problems when it draws on a variety of theoretical insights, philosophical groundings and empirical methods. Pluralism is a precondition for democracy, with the protection of minority views and adequate public space for the expression of alternative views. The same counts for science—without pluralism, we still would have believed that the sun turns around the earth. The dominance of a single theory is not common in science but is the reality in economics. And since economics informs many policy decisions, there is also a democracy-concern with the current state of the discipline. How democratic is it when policies are informed by a single theory and method, whereas there exist other valid perspectives? When generations of students learn only one theory, the other perspectives will gradually disappear—not only from academia but also from policy research and economic advice.

Joan Robinson, who was part of Keynes' circle of trusted colleagues, recognized the problem very well. She wrote in *Contributions to Modern Economics*: 'The purpose of studying economics is not to acquire a set of ready-made answers to economic questions, but to learn how to avoid being deceived by economists.'[16] She called neoclassical economists 'false prophets', who defend a theory based on wrong assumptions and 'bastard theorems'. She was not afraid to use strong wordings and defended legitimate space for the Keynesian tradition all her life. Her view of economics recognized that it is a social science, and even, as Keynes but also Smith, Veblen, Myrdal and Sen had noted, a science that inevitably has ethical dimensions. She argued that the idea that one could study problems such as poverty and unemployment in a purely positivistic way, assuming full objectivity, is simply nonsense and even harmful. She gave the example of the neoclassical assumption that labour generates negative utility and that this is only compensated by the positive utility derived from wages. Joan Robinson argued, backed with empirical evidence from sociology, that unemployment tends to make people feel useless or even a failure instead of joblessness being experienced as enjoyable leisure time.[17] Today, critical economists have added another important layer of criticism to neoclassical assumptions, namely from the perspective of the lives and experiences of people in the global south. Their realities are also not reflected in mainstream economic theory and policy advise, which expresses economic development in terms of modern European values and aspirations that are not necessarily shared by people living in Africa, Latin America and Asia.[18]

In her best-known book, *The Economics of Imperfect Competition*, Robinson developed the microeconomic side of Keynesian economics, complementary to Keynes' work at the macro level.[19] She argued that markets will never be fully competitive because competition does not only concern prices, but also quality, service, and marketing. And that is the reason, she argued, that market dynamics result in strategic segmentation, with some firms reaping additional profits. And that, in turn, will help them to grow bigger than the rest and obtain market power. Today, we see this happening in many consumer markets, from cola to sports brands. But it also happens in sectors related to public goods such as health care. An example can be found in some health insurance companies, which only accept students or people with higher education. Statistically, these groups have above average health status, and hence, firms focusing on that segment are more profitable even if they offer lower fees. But the other companies are then faced with clients whose average health is less. And the more clients move to firms that cater only for higher educated clients, attracted by a lower fee, the less the average health of the clients of the other insurance companies will be, with higher health care expenditures as a consequence. Over time, this will inevitably result in higher fees for these clients, further exacerbating the earnings gap between the two types of firms. But, more disturbingly in the case of health care insurance, the higher fees are to be paid by people who have lower disposable incomes.

Joan Robinson was the first economist studying strategic behaviour of firms and the effect of this on market dynamics in a systematic way. Her work led her to two unexpected conclusions, that are at odds with neoclassical theory. First, she demonstrated that the demand curve and the supply curve of firms are not independent of each other as soon as firms can reap benefits of scale. That is because demand influences production cost through economies of scale: the more one can sell, the lower the unit costs of production. That, in turn, results in concentration of firms through mergers, acquisitions, and entry barriers for start-ups. Think of mergers of car manufacturers, even if they keep the old brands (such as Peugeot, Citroen, Fiat, Alfa Romeo, Jeep and Dodge, which are united in FCA-PSA). Or think of the beer industry, with three firms controlling 50% of the world market.[20] We also see more concentration in the public sector, for example, with mergers of hospitals and schools, which does not necessarily result in efficiency gains because in services it is hard to reduce unit production costs. The second remarkable conclusion that Robinson arrived at was that monopolies are more efficient than oligopolistic markets, even though policy makers tend to reject the first and allow the emergence of the second type of market. Why would monopolies be more efficient? Because they do not need to spend much on branding and marketing. Moreover, they don't spend precious management time on strategies to beat competitors, they don't need to spend money (anymore) on costly mergers, and there is no need for unnecessary product differentiation in order to lure customers away from competitors. Fifteen years after the publication of her book, Robinson was appointed at the British consumer market authority.

And she continued her bold attacks on mainstream economics. She even turned to the centre piece of neoclassical theory: market equilibrium. She did this in her book on economic growth, published 30 years after the book on imperfect competition.[21] This time, she focused not on strategy and policy but on economics education. In the book as well as in her public lectures, she criticized the mechanistic metaphor used for explaining market equilibrium. This is the metaphor of balls in a rest-state in a bowl, which move briefly as soon as one ball is moved and then remain motionless gain. But, she argued 'In time, there is no motionless rest. Time marches on.'[22] She argues that the bowl filled with balls that do not move is an inadequate metaphor for market equilibrium because markets are always moving—adapting with quantities and prices to a wide variety of context variables. Even when it seems as if they are not moving: people have to invest in their education and that of their children, entrepreneurs have to replace capital goods, new firms access markets with new technologies or new products, and investors sometimes are too optimistic and other times too pessimistic, thereby reinforcing market movements. No standstill at all but continuous individual action and market dynamics. The whole idea of market equilibrium that is derived from physics, where an apple that falls from a tree indeed comes to a standstill, is just a 'famous fairy-tale' according to Robinson. For her, the important thing happens in the *dynamics* of markets and that is where economics should keep itself busy with. Her expression 'history versus equilibrium' became famous among her colleagues. What would be a better metaphor for markets? As soon as you think about coordinated forms of movement there are many candidates. One example is the traffic flow on highways. Just like in real-world markets, there are quantities added and subtracted, excess demand leading to traffic jams and peak hours as well as regulation in the shape of speed limits and seat belt obligations and there are general driving habits and errors.

Even though Robinson and many others have put in lots of energy to criticize neoclassical economics, the dominance of that theory remained a huge challenge for her. Until today, books are published about the problems with neoclassical economics—but they tend to be ignored even more than in Robinson's days, when there were still some post-Keynesian economists, institutional economists and Austrian economists around at top universities in the UK and elsewhere. Robinson argued that students should be able to learn different theoretical perspectives and that it would make them better economists. For that reason, she was equally critical of the textbooks in the Soviet Union, because these were just as one-sided as those in the West, she said. In her own teaching, she preferred small groups of students, often only two of them—in a typical Cambridge tradition—for tutoring and supervision. She liked to challenge them to be critical, also on her own work. And she could not stand it when students came to class unprepared or simply agreed with her to evade a debate. She despised the idea that teaching economics would be no more than delivering a toolbox. Again, this was an example of mechanical thinking, she said. What matters, in her view, is to teach students to think critically and provide them with a broad set of analytical skills which they can employ according to the character of an economic problem and its context—a question of learning by doing. She compared this to bicycling. When you have acquired that skill, it will be a second nature, she said.[23]

Her own attempt at writing an economic textbook failed. It became too philosophical. But she was a passionate teacher. With a cigarette in one hand and a pen in the other, she would draw diagrams on any piece of paper at hand, to answer her students' questions. After her death, a few economists have continued her battle for pluralism in economics. In 1992, 44 well-known and widely respected economists, among them the first Nobel Memorial Prize winner, Jan Tinbergen, published a manifesto for pluralism.[24] They stated that it is peculiar that economists are strong advocates for free markets but don't allow a free market for economic ideas. The economists called for critical debate and tolerant communication between different approaches. Their plea repeated what John Stuart Mill had argued a century earlier in his book *On Liberty*, 'the only way in which a human being can make some approach to knowing the whole of a subject, is by hearing what can be said about it by persons of every variety of opinion, and studying all modes in which it can be looked at by every character of mind.'[25] In my inaugural address, when I accepted the Chair in Pluralist Development Economics at the Institute of Social Studies, I described pluralism in line with Mill as an open attitude, open to other points of view. But that only works, of course, when these other views are being taught to students and published in economic journals that are read by economists belonging to different schools of thought. The financial crisis made the need for this clear again, with *The Economist* as its surprising messenger. But more than ten years later, not much has come from it. Why is that?

An interesting study titled *The Superiority of Economists*, commissioned by a well-known economics journal, has provided an answer to this question by comparing the culture in economics with that in other social sciences.[26] It starts with a figure from a survey among US graduate students of economics, indicating that 77% agreed with the statement that 'economics is the most scientific of the social sciences.' And it includes other facts familiar to economists but often raising eyebrows outside the discipline. One of these is that among all sciences—including the natural sciences—the share of women full professors is lowest in economics. This reality is paralleled with so much reported instances of sexism in economics departments, that the American Economic Association has recently developed a code of professional conduct, an ethics committee and even punitive measures for improper behaviour.[27] The code of conduct also includes respect for different points of view among economists—an implicit support for pluralism.[28] Another finding presented in *The Superiority of Economists* is that economists are not much interested in interdisciplinary work, as compared to the other social sciences. To the contrary, they tend to colonize other disciplines with their own, specific assumption of rationality and their econometrics. Finally, economics departments are characterized by a strong hierarchy, much more than elsewhere. In combination with strong norms of reciprocity and cohesion in recruitment, the authors of the study conclude that: 'these norms sustain a high stability of interdepartmental prestige hierarchies over time.'[29] In addition, the study finds that the economic journals market is much more concentrated than in other disciplines—a finding that would not have surprised Joan Robinson. This finding is reflected in the fact that the most-cited journals exhibit a heavier concentration of papers coming from elite departments in economics than in sociology but also by the numbers showing that 'several leading economics journals edited at particular universities have a demonstrable preference for in-house authors.'[30] The substance of most papers in the so-called top-journals shows a strong confidence of most economists in their judgment criteria: 'their predilection for efficiency over fairness, the eliciting of preferences from behaviour, and the design of experiments around a tight menu of choices'.[31]

The lesson of this chapter is that pluralism needs to be protected continuously. Not only against the domination of a single theory but more importantly against the idea that if a theory has become dominant that it has apparently won the battle for now and ever—as if progress in science by that time is more or less completed and new questions can all be addressed within a single framework based on the same old assumptions.

THE ECONOMIST

Joan Violet Robinson (1903 Surrey–1983 Cambridge)

Joan Robinson (family name Maurice), was born in a family of four daughters and one son. Her mother, Helen Margaret Marsh was the daughter of a surgeon who became professor of surgery at the University of Cambridge. Her grandfather was a well-known Christian socialist and her father, Sir Frederick Maurice, was Major General in the army. Joan studied economics at the University of Cambridge and never left—she has spent 50 years at the university, which was well known in her days for its Keynesian economics. She even married a Cambridge professor, also an economist—Austin Robinson—but had to wait for her own appointment as a professor until her husband, six years older, had retired. Despite this, she was the star economist at Cambridge while her husband featured as an old, friendly scholar. Joan was tireless. She took a leading role in the great debates in economics at those times and she was a great support for diligent students, but she was uncompromising towards people whom she considered lazy or dogmatic. She had long friendships with colleagues, such as Richard Kahn and Piero Sraffa.

Contrary to her colleagues, she came to college on a bicycle, showing her aversion of status. She had learned that no-nonsense attitude at home. Her father had been fired because he had publicly expressed criticism on the Defence Minister—which became the subject of heated debates in the House of Commons in 1918. He knew the consequences of being a whistleblower but that did not stop him. His daughter had a similar stubborn mind. Joan held strong views, loved debate, and always reacted bravely and sharply, according to those who have met her. Sometimes, she was considered arrogant, when she seemed to treat those who were not in agreement with her as being against her. But she could also be very friendly and concerned with people, although she was not good at small talk. The Robinsons spent a few years in India—before its independence—because Austin had accepted a job as tutor to the Maharadjah of Gwalior (who was not yet ten years old). There, as well as back in London, Joan helped Austin with his analysis of the economic relations between the British Crown and India. After those years in India, Joan kept coming back to the southern state of Kerala and visited China eight times. When the Robinson's had settled in Cambridge, where first Austin and five years later also Joan got an appointment, there were rumours about their marriage. Because Joan spent more and more time in the garden house until she practically lived there. But that too, was probably simply part of her way of life. Her biographers, most of them having known her personally, all claim that she had good friendships with her male colleagues but no affairs. Joan and Austin had two daughters and five grandchildren. The dominant gender norms in her days did not make it easy to combine motherhood with the life of an active academic, but her biographers note that, despite her own doubts, her family affirmed that she had been a good mother and grandmother.

Of course, Joan Robinson had many PhD students over the years. One of them was Amartya Sen, who had to endure her stubbornness in developing what was in her view the one and only real Cambridge approach to economics: Keynesian instead of neoclassical. Sen later described her as 'totally brilliant but vigorously intolerant'.[32] Another PhD student of hers and later Nobel Memorial Prize winner, Joseph Stiglitz, gave up the fight and found himself a new supervisor. Robinson had a sharp tongue but put it entirely at the service of her mission to elaborate and spread post-Keynesian theory as well as defending the space for other views, including those of Marxist economics. She contributed articles to a wide variety of international journals, newspapers and magazines. She considered herself as instrumental and was not concerned about her own status, supporting, with her articles, journals in various developing countries, including Brazil, Chile and Pakistan. For all her influence on economic theory and debate, others—both proponents and opponents—showed surprise about the fact that she was never awarded the Nobel Memorial Prize.

Her theoretical mission made her not only harsh on others but also hard on herself. For example, many years later she turned very critical on her book on imperfect competition, because she realized that it was too much embedded in a neoclassical framework.[33] Towards the end of her life, she even became disillusioned and found that economics, as a science, was completely derailed and that her own attempts to bring in more realism had failed. The last interview that she gave, a few weeks before she suffered a stroke, was very pessimistic. She said: 'I've spent my life in economic theory and it has come to pieces in my hands. I don't believe in it any longer.'[34]

Reading Robinson
Joan Robinson, *The Accumulation of Capital* (London: Palgrave Macmillan, 2013 [1956]).

Reading About Robinson
Geoffrey Harcourt and Prue Kerr, *Joan Robinson* (London: Palgrave Macmillan, 2009).

Reading About Economics from a Pluralist Perspective
Ha-Joon Chang, *Economics—The User's Guide* (London: Bloomsbury Press, 2014).

Practising Robinson

Due to the unwillingness of many economists to be open to other theoretical schools of thought, to learn from other disciplines and to include other methods, change is not likely to come soon from established economists, journals, and departments. But change is happening. The past decade has shown that it comes from disappointed students and from academic programs outside economics departments. Below, I will describe both types of alternatives and some of their achievements.

Rethinking Economics

Students of economics have begun to resist their curriculum, textbooks and classrooms that are detached from real-world economies. First came the graduate students, with protests and demands for change in Cambridge, Paris and Manchester. They demanded realism in their classrooms, instead of courses consisting entirely of model exercises. Next followed undergraduate students in more and more countries. They have set up an international network called Rethinking Economics a few years after the financial crisis. Their demand is to learn more about economics in terms of its history and applicability—they were surprised that they hardly learn about the causes and consequences of the 2008 financial crisis, as if it never happened. On their website, the students explain:

> Today's Rethinkers went to study economics hoping to understand why the financial crash happened; why was unemployment so high; why were public services being cut? The reality was a narrow, dispassionate exercise in some fairly basic calculus, coupled with a requirement to perform multiple-choice exams twice a year. Theory was not applied to the real-world, students worked with hypothetical apples and oranges rather than real case studies, past economic events were ignored and, perhaps most importantly, the theory that had led to the surrounding economic chaos was being imparted as if it was gospel, with no opportunity to evaluate its validity.[35]

The student movement has achieved quite a lot, despite the lukewarm or even harsh responses from their teachers. They have assembled at the University of Tübingen, Germany where they have drafted an open letter that was signed by nearly 100 student groups across the world. Their initiative has been picked up by major newspapers from the *Guardian* to the *New York Times*. They have published a book with a foreword written by Andy Haldane, the Chief Economist of the Bank of England,[36] and they have surveyed employers to find out that many of them are not entirely satisfied with the graduates of top economics departments.[37] Students at the University of Manchester have developed their own course material under the title of Post-Crash Economics, with contributions by economists from a variety of schools of thought. The university does not acknowledge it as an elective, so students in Manchester cannot earn any study points by attending that course. But the student movement responded with a whole textbook on pluralist economics.[38]

The Rethinking Economics movement is an active community of students, who passionately discuss different economic theories, methods and policy instruments. The network includes over 80 local groups—with some countries containing more groups. The countries include France, Bangladesh, Italy, Poland, Germany, Australia, the Netherlands, Russia, Colombia, Zimbabwe, the UK and the US, among others. The local groups include undergraduate and graduate students, and my interaction with them suggests that they are among the smartest students.[39] Like Joan Robinson, they question commonly accepted assumptions and methods and demand proper explanations for why so much of economics circles around highly abstract mathematical models. They do not complain about the mathematics because they would not be able to do it. As I said, they are probably among the best students. They can do the math. But they resist the idea that solving theoretical optimization problems is what economics is about and that the required skills come down to a narrow toolbox, to be applied to any economic problem regardless of context. They ask questions that most lecturers never ask themselves: Is economics a real science? If so, is it like the natural sciences or like the social and behavioural sciences? Should economists not be more modest and admit that often their predictions are no better than throwing a dice? Why do policy makers listen so often to economists, without any criticism and without comparing alternative economic analyses? Not accidentally, these are precisely the questions that many people outside economics have asked economists since the financial crisis.

The Tide Is Turning Outside Economics Departments

The anger of Jean Tirole at the initiative of an interdisciplinary economics programme in France suggests that mainstream economists consider such initiatives as a threat. Indeed, they should. There is a growing demand by students for such programmes. For example, programmes of political economy that teach economics as a pluralist science, starting with the classical economists such as Smith and Marx, and giving appropriate attention to Keynes and Veblen, Minsky or Robinson. Such programmes are generally not part of departments of economics but of departments of political science. But students don't care. They want to learn economics in all its diversity and connections to other social sciences for the sole reason of understanding the real-world economy better. Next to this, there is a recent increase in programmes in the philosophy of economics, focusing on the foundations of economic theories and methods. Courses on offer include critical analysis of assumptions and theorems underlying much of economic theory and analysis. And the third type of programme that is in demand among students is genuine interdisciplinary, with courses in economics and psychology, economic history, and social economics. All these programmes include neoclassical economics, because one cannot ignore the importance of that school of thought. But all of them discuss it critically and present alternative views. Some present one alternative view—for example, post-Keynesianism or behavioural economics. Others present more views and therefore come closer to pluralism. For new students, there is a website available with all heterodox programmes in economics, from undergraduate to MA and PhD level, in universities located all over the world.[40]

Genuine pluralist economics education is scarce and lecturers are still developing their skills and building their own knowledge base in economic pluralism.[41] But there are a few initiatives. For example, the University of Siegen (Germany) has an MA programme in Pluralist Economics.[42] And I developed an online introductory economics course with four theories on all standard topics in micro- and macroeconomics, called Introduction to Economic Theories, based on a pluralist textbook that I published in 2015.[43] Finally, business schools offer courses that are much more real-world oriented than the economic theory taught in economics departments. Many business schools today also offer courses, and sometimes complete programmes, in social impact and social change, often linked to the internationally agreed Sustainable Development Goals for the year 2030 or other important national and international commitments, such as the Paris Climate Agreement.

As long as economic departments show little interest in adapting their teaching supply to what employers and students need and want, change towards real-world economic teaching from different perspectives happens outside. Such teaching is what students of economics today deserve—in a world that seems to be more affected than ever by financial, health and environmental crises. They deserve and need the analytical skills for their future roles as policy makers, business leaders, administrators and researchers. Students are too important to be left to a narrow economics education.

Notes

1. The transcript is available from the US Public Broadcasting Service: https://www.pbs.org/newshour/show/greenspan-admits-flaw-to-congress-predicts-more-economic-problems, Accessed on June 4, 2020.
2. Liz Morrish, "Pressure Vessels: The Epidemic of Poor Mental Health among Higher Education Staff" HEPI Occasional Paper 20 (Oxford: HEPI, 2019). https://www.hepi.ac.uk/2019/05/23/pressure-vessels-the-epidemic-of-poor-mental-health-among-higher-education-staff/, Accessed on July 16, 2020. The good news is that academics worldwide have called for a change in the assessment of research: San Francisco Declaration on Research Assessment (DORA), https://sfdora.org/, Accessed on June 29, 2020.
3. See for example a report by IMF's Independent Evaluation Office (IEO), showing that IMF forecasts are generally incorrect and particularly optimistic after a crisis: Independent Evaluation Office of the IMF. "IMF Forecasts—Process, Quality, and Country Perspectives" (Washington, DC: IEO, 2014). https://www.elibrary.imf.org/doc/IMF017/20867-9781475599510/20867-9781475599510/Other_formats/Source_PDF/20867-9781484363836.pdf, Accessed on June 29, 2020.

4. IMF, World Economic Outlook—Uneven Growth, Short- and Long-Term Factors. Washington, DC: International Monetary Fund, April 2015. https://www.imf.org/en/Publications/WEO/Issues/2016/12/31/World-Economic-Outlook-April-2015-Uneven-Growth-42382, Accessed on June 29, 2020.
5. https://www.bloomberg.com/graphics/2019-imf-forecasts/, Accessed on June 8, 2020.
6. Here is a link to a website with a Buffet indicator: https://www.gurufocus.com/stock-market-valuations.php, Accessed on June 4, 2020. On 4th June 2020, his prediction was that the stock market was "significantly overvalued".
7. Gillian Tett. *Fool's Gold. The Inside Story of J.P. Morgan and How Wall St, Greed Corrupted its Bold Dream and Created a Financial Catastrophe* (New York: Simon & Schuster, 2010). Joris Luyendijk. *Swimming with Sharks. My Journey into the World of the Bankers* (London: Guardian Faber, 2015).
8. Urgenda is an NGO that demands the Dutch government to stick to its own commitments to reduce carbon emissions by 25% at the end of 2020 as compared to 1990. For information in English: https://www.urgenda.nl/en/home-en/, Accessed on June 4, 2020.
9. This is what two economists have argued for in a recent book: a much clearer separation of economic analysis and policy design based on the recognition that policy advise involves normative decisions that should be left to politicians and not to economists: David Colander and Craig Freedman. *Where Economics Went Wrong* (Princeton, Princeton University Press, 2019).
10. The data, tables and figures and spreadsheets can be found on the website of Thomas Piketty: http://piketty.pse.ens.fr/en/capital21c2, Accessed on June 4, 2020.
11. Thomas Piketty. *Capital in the 21st Century* (Cambridge, MA: Belknap Press of Harvard University Press, 2014, p. 575).
12. http://www.rethinkeconomics.org/wp-content/uploads/2016/09/CM-Curric-Review.pdf, Accessed on July 16, 2020.
13. J. Tieleman, S. de Muijnck, M. Kavelaars, and F. Ostermeijer. "Thinking like an Economist? A Quantitative Analysis of Economics Bachelor Curricula in the Netherlands." (Rethinking Economics NL, 2018). http://www.rethinkingeconomics.nl/uploads/5/3/2/2/53228883/thinking_like_an_economist.pdf, Accessed on June 16, 2020.
14. For the translation in English, see: https://assoeconomiepolitique.org/wp-content/uploads/TIROLE_Letter.pdf, Accessed on June 5, 2020.
15. The English version of the reply to Tirole can be found here: https://assoeconomiepolitique.org/wp-content/uploads/FAPE-Open-letter-to-Tirole-January-2015.pdf, Accessed on June 5, 2020.
16. Joan Robinson. *Contributions to Modern Economics* (New York: Academic Press of Harcourt Brace Jovanovich, 1978), p. 75.
17. Joan Robinson. *Economic Philosophy* (London: Watts, 1962).
18. See for example an important volume on postcolonialism and economics: Eiman Zein-Elabdin, and S. Charusheela, eds. *Postcolonialism meets Economics* (New York: Routledge, 2004).
19. Joan Robinson, *The Economics of Imperfect Competition*. Second Edition (London: Macmillan, 1962 [1933]).

20. In 2018, these were AB InBev, Heineken, and China Resources Snow Breweries: https://www.statista.com/statistics/257677/global-market-share-of-the-leading-beer-companies-based-on-sales/
21. Joan Robinson. *Essays in the Theory of Economic Growth* (London: Macmillan, 1962).
22. Robinson. *Theory of Economic Growth*, p. 76.
23. Zohreh Emami. "History versus Equilibrium: Joan Robinson on Teaching Economics." *International Journal of Social Economics* 19, 10/11/12 (1992): 83–94.
24. Interestingly, it was not published as an article or letter but as an advertisement in one of the top-five economic journals: 'A Plea for Pluralist and Rigorous Economics,' *American Economic Review* 82, 2 (1992).
25. John Stuart Mill. *On Liberty* (London: Walter Scott Publishing, 1859), p. 37.
26. Marion Fourcade, Etienne Ollion, and Yann Algan. "The Superiority of Economists." *Journal of Economic Perspectives* 29, 1 (2015): 89–114.
27. The AEA Code of Professional Conduct can be found here: https://www.aeaweb.org/about-aea/code-of-conduct, Accessed on June 29, 2020.
28. The code includes the following paragraph: "The AEA encourages the 'perfect freedom of economic discussion.' This goal requires an environment where all can freely participate and where each idea is considered on its own merits. Economists have a professional obligation to conduct civil and respectful discourse in all forums, including those that allow confidential or anonymous participation." https://www.aeaweb.org/about-aea/code-of-conduct, Accessed on June 29, 2020.
29. Fourcade et al. (2015), p. 97.
30. Fourcade et al. (2015), p. 99.
31. Fourcade et al. (2015), p. 108.
32. See Sen's autobiographical text for the Nobel Memorial Prize website: https://www.nobelprize.org/prizes/economic-sciences/1998/sen/biographical/, Accessed on June 15, 2020.
33. Geoffrey Harcourt. "Joan Robinson 1903–1983." *The Economic Journal* 105, September (1995): 1228–1243.
34. This quote can be found in Alex Millow. "Joan Robinson's Disillusion with Economics." *Review of Political Economy* 15, 4 (2003): 561–574 (p. 561).
35. http://www.rethinkeconomics.org/about/our-story/, Accessed on June 15, 2020.
36. Joe Earle, Cahal Moran, and Zach Ward Perkins. *The Econocracy. The Perils of Leaving Economics to the Experts* (Manchester: Manchester University Press, 2016).
37. Rethinking Economics UK. "Employer's Report 2018," http://www.rethinkeconomics.org/wp-content/uploads/2016/09/RE_Research_Report_2018_PROOF.pdf, Accessed on June 15, 2020.
38. Liliann Fischer, Joe Hasell, Christopher Proctor, David Uwakwe, Zach Ward Perkins, and Catriona Watson. *Rethinking Economics: An Introduction to Pluralist Economics* (London: Routledge, 2017).
39. The Rethinking Economics group in the Netherlands has asked me to be on their board in an advisory role—ah honourable position that I have gladly accepted.

40. http://www.heterodoxnews.com/hed/study-programs.html, Accessed on June 16, 2020.
41. See, for example, a recent book on how to teach pluralist economics: Samuel Decker, Wolfram Elsner, and Svenja Flechtner (eds.). *Advancing Pluralism in Teaching Economics: International Perspectives on a Textbook Science* (London: Routledge, 2018). There is also a journal about pluralism and economics education, called the *International Journal on Pluralism and Economics Education*: https://www.inderscience.com/jhome.php?jcode=ijpee#:~:text=Internatio nal%20Journal%20of%20Pluralism%20and,business%20and%20industry%20 through%20research, Accessed on June 16, 2020.
42. https://www.uni-siegen.de/zsb/studienangebot/master/pluraleoekonomik.html.en, Accessed on June 16, 2020.
43. The textbook: Irene van Staveren. *Introduction to Economics from a Pluralist and Global Perspective* (London: Routledge, 2015). The MOOC (Massive Open Online Course) can be found on platform Coursera and is free (unless one wants to obtain a certificate, which costs 50 US dollar). The course has had, at the moment of writing this chapter, over 35,000 learners. https://www.coursera.org/learn/intro-economic-theories, Accessed on June 16, 2020.

BIBLIOGRAPHY

"A Plea for Pluralist and Rigorous Economics." *American Economic Review* 82, 2 (1992).

Colander, David, and Craig Freedman. *Where Economics Went Wrong*. Princeton: Princeton University Press, 2019.

Decker, Samuel, Wolfram Elsner, and Svenja Flechtner (eds.). *Advancing Pluralism in Teaching Economics: International Perspectives on a Textbook Science*. London: Routledge, 2018.

Earle, Joe, Cahal Moran, and Zach Ward Perkins. *The Econocracy. The Perils of Leaving Economics to the Experts*. Manchester: Manchester University Press, 2016.

Emami, Zohreh. "History versus Equilibrium: Joan Robinson on Teaching Economics." *International Journal of Social Economics* 19, 10/11/12 (1992): 83–94.

Fischer, Liliann, Joe Hasell, Christopher Proctor, David Uwakwe, Zach Ward Perkins, and Catriona Watson. *Rethinking Economics: An Introduction to Pluralist Economics*. London: Routledge, 2017.

Fourcade, Marion, Etienne Ollion, and Yann Algan. "The Superiority of Economists." *Journal of Economic Perspectives* 29, 1 (2015): 89–114.

Harcourt, Geoffrey. "Joan Robinson 1903–1983." *The Economic Journal* 105, September (1995): 1228–1243.

IMF. "World Economic Outlook—Uneven Growth, Short- and Long-Term Factors." Washington, DC: International Monetary Fund, April 2015. https://www.imf.org/en/Publications/WEO/Issues/2016/12/31/World-Economic-Outlook-April-2015-Uneven-Growth-42382, Accessed on June 29, 2020.

Independent Evaluation Office of the IMF. "IMF Forecasts—Process, Quality, and Country Perspectives." Washington, DC: IEO, 2014. https://www.elibrary.imf.org/doc/IMF017/20867-9781475599510/20867-9781475599510/Other_formats/Source_PDF/20867-9781484363836.pdf, Accessed on June 29, 2020.

Luyendijk, Joris. *Swimming with Sharks. My Journey Into the World of the Bankers*. London: Guardian Faber, 2015.

Mill, John Stuart. *On Liberty*. London: Walter Scott Publishing, 1859.

Millow, Alex. "Joan Robinson's Disillusion with Economics." *Review of Political Economy* 15, 4 (2003): 561–574 (p. 561).

Morrish, Liz. "Pressure Vessels: the Epidemic of Poor Mental Health among Higher Education Staff." HEPI Occasional Paper 20. Oxford: HEPI, 2019. https://www.hepi.ac.uk/2019/05/23/pressure-vessels-the-epidemic-of-poor-mental-health-among-higher-education-staff/, Accessed on July 16, 2020.

Piketty, Thomas. *Capital in the 21st Century*. Cambridge, MA: Belknap Press of Harvard University Press, 2014, p. 575.

Rethinking Economics UK. "Employer's Report 2018." http://www.rethinkeconomics.org/wp-content/uploads/2016/09/RE_Research_Report_2018_PROOF.pdf, Accessed on June 15, 2020.

Robinson, Joan. *The Economics of Imperfect Competition*. Second Edition. London: Macmillan, 1962a [1933].

———. *Economic Philosophy*. London: Watts, 1962b.

———. *Essays in the Theory of Economic Growth*. London: Macmillan, 1962c.

———. *Contributions to Modern Economics*. New York: Academic Press of Harcourt Brace Jovanovich, 1978.

Staveren, Irene van. *Introduction to Economics from a Pluralist and Global Perspective*. London: Routledge, 2015.

Tett, Gillian. *Fool's Gold. The Inside Story of J.P. Morgan and How Wall St, Greed Corrupted its Bold Dream and Created a Financial Catastrophe*. New York: Simon & Schuster, 2010.

Tieleman, J., S. de Muijnck, M. Kavelaars, and F. Ostermeijer. "Thinking like an Economist? A Quantitative Analysis of Economics Bachelor Curricula in the Netherlands." Rethinking Economics NL, 2018. http://www.rethinkingeconomics.nl/uploads/5/3/2/2/53228883/thinking_like_an_economist.pdf, Accessed on June 16, 2020.

Zein-Elabdin, Eiman, and S. Charusheela (eds.). *Postcolonialism Meets Economics*. New York: Routledge, 2004.

Conclusion: Economics for a Postcapitalist Economy

WHERE TO GO FROM HERE?

In this book I have offered a selection of alternative economic views, which have become marginalized in teaching and research in economic departments since the 1980s. Here, in the conclusion, I would like to connect the alternative theoretical insights, to show how economics may be broadened and deepened, so that it may be better able to address the urgent challenges of today's world. I think that we cannot address climate change, increasing inequality, pandemics, geopolitical instability, political polarization, and the exhaustion of our planet's natural resources and biodiversity with the very same economics that has either regarded these as exogenous, or as problems to be solved with more markets rather than with a stronger role of the state and more space for community economies. To use the words from the article *The Superiority of Economists*, which I discussed in the last chapter: 'Economists do not simply depict a reality out there, they also make it happen by disseminating their advice and tools.'[1] We urgently need different tools, or better, analytical frameworks, concepts, assumptions, models and methods—diverse heterodox ideas instead of a single orthodox approach.

The ten economists discussed in this book each provide one or more alternative insights, which may be combined in endless variations. And when we add alternatives from other old but also from new heterodox economists, the discipline will be much more able to address the urgent real-world problems that we face today. But we should not make the mistake of replacing the old blueprint Chicago School policy advise with a new blueprint, as Colander and Freedman rightly warn in their book *Where Economics Went Wrong*.[2] The complexity of today's economic challenges requires diversity and modesty, and not a unitary perspective, as we learn from Ashby's *Law of Requisite Variety* in cybernetics.[3] That law states that complex problems must be faced with a level of diversity in approaches that matches the level of complexity.

In this conclusion, I would like to bring together the key elements of the various economic insights presented in this book. In the next section, I will summarize some basic contextual variables as well as insights about endogeneity of economic relationships, which will help us thinking about the economy in a much more real-world-oriented way. The next section will discuss key elements of the dynamics of an economics that takes context and endogeneity into account. And the final section will pull the elements together in terms of systems theory—a basic theory used in fields as diverse as mathematics and ecology for the understanding of endogenous dynamic processes under conditions of uncertainty. I would like to emphasize that these are elements than can be combined in different ways. What they have in common is that they recognize that (1) context matters, (2) variables are often endogenous where neoclassical economics often assumes exogeneity, and (3) markets reflect dynamics where neoclassical economics tends to assume statics or quick adjustments to a new static equilibrium.

Endogenous and Context Variables

The ubiquitous context variable for any science—from physics and biology to language studies and psychology—is uncertainty. It deserves also a central place in economics, following the seminal work by Frank Knight. In evolution theory, for example, uncertainty is the key explanatory variable for random variation in organisms at the level of genes, which allows natural selection to operate. Without random, unpredictable and unknown variation in the transmission of genes between generations, natural selection cannot happen, and organisms would not evolve. Uncertainty in the when and what of genetic variations, hence, is the key context variable for evolution. In economics, uncertainty helps to explain differences in access to resources, profitability, growth, accumulation and market power, for example, but also financial crises and poverty. It, therefore, requires much more space in economic analysis, at the micro and macro level, than is currently the case. Uncertainty is about the unknown unknowns and therefore must appear as a context variable in many economic analyses. For example, to remind us that the next crisis will come, even though prediction fails to tell us exactly when. But we are not completely empty-handed. Although uncertainty cannot be estimated because it has no probability distribution, its negative consequences can be reduced with the help of resilient institutions. The Glass-Steagall Act was such an institution—keeping the world from a serious financial crisis for 80 years. Economics therefore would benefit from a much wider study of existing and desirable resilient institutions in a wide variety of fields.

The next real-world context concepts describe the three domains of which every economy consists: market, state and community economy. What is so special about these, Adam Smith has taught us, is that they are embedded in the key shared social values of freedom, justice and care. And that is also the level at which they are related to each other: through their underlying values.

That explains why well-functioning markets are embedded in communities, which impose moral limits to markets. And it explains why markets are partially enabled and partially constrained by the state through regulation of prices, quality and the extent of trade. Market, state and community economy are interrelated, and together they form a balance, endogenously, from which a level of wellbeing results. I will elaborate on this in the next section, because there is also an important dynamic efficiency element to it.

When we look at resources, in particular capital and labour, these are endogenous. Not only are capital goods produced by labour, as Marx noted, but labour productivity largely depends on the technology embedded in capital. Labour is also an endogenous production factor in another way, both at the demand side and at the supply side. Labour demand is derived demand—derived from the demand for the goods that it produces, as Keynes already explained. Also, labour supply is derived: in the long run, new generations of labour supply are reproduced in communities, while in the short run, the daily regeneration of labour supply (its effort), stems from caring activities provided in households (with prepared food, adequate sleep, cleaned clothing, counselling, etc.). This also illustrates the previous point that a flourishing economy according to Smith consist of market, state and community.

Finally, rationality and people's aspirations and efforts to further their wellbeing tend to be endogenous too. Amartya Sen has therefore redefined rationality as consistent and meaningful choices. Consistent with one's individual and social identity, allowing for endogenous preferences. And meaningful in relation to one's values, allowing for intrinsic motivation to emerge in economic behaviour in the three value domains. Indeed, management researchers are very well aware of the connections between motivation and values and its positive externalities for performance, efficiency and trust. Rationality, therefore, has endogenous dimensions, through the combination of economic agent's various roles and their commitments and aspirations that are often interrelated, in households, firms and communities. This brings me to the final endogenous concept that I have discussed in this book: capability—also introduced by Sen. This concept connects rational decision making to wellbeing. Capabilities are the skills and capacities of economic agents that they have reason to value, so they are both ends and means at the same time. Instead, commodities, money and public goods are only means. That is why capabilities are the central concept for microeconomics, according to Sen, rather than utility or goods or needs. Capabilities are contextual in the sense that different people value different capabilities, or at least, value a different rank order. And they are endogenous because they are means (e.g. as skills) and ends (e.g. as aspirations) at the same time and go beyond the individual because their expansion is embedded in social relations, political debate, cultural traditions and emancipatory movements. Capability expansion would be a socially meaningful goal of economic policy, rather than the utility maximization of Pareto Optimality,[4] or GDP growth as it often comes down to. How the capability goals should be pursued in terms of priorities and distribution over groups of people is subject to democratic debate. This is a political issue, not an economic one, and may, for example, involve a maximin criterion, maximizing the capabilities of the least well off, or a threshold, such as implied by Smith's plea for decent wages. It is not up to economists to define the criteria for capability expansion. But it is up to economists to substitute the concept of utility and its ethics of utilitarianism and a preference for the status quo distribution, with the concept of capability.

There is also the endogeneity between supply and demand in product markets, as noted by Robinson, through economies of scale. I will, however, elaborate on this type of endogeneity in the next section because it also involves an important time dimension, which in turn affects markets more profoundly.

Economic Dynamics

In this section, I will focus on the dynamics of markets. As Robinson has noted, economies of scale allow for increased demand (in particular through mass production) to lower-income groups. The increased consumer demand enables further economies of scale, and so on. As a consequence, demand and supply are endogenous. This also involves concentration at the supply side of the market. The growth of firms through economies of scale eventually results in oligopolies or even monopolies. Once we acknowledge this market dynamic, it is a small step to recognize a related dynamic that was already noted by Marx: the speeding up of accumulation over time through the concentration of capital in larger firms, which have bargaining power over labour. In combination with technological change and globalization, this power increases the capital share of income and lowers the labour share of income. This is a key dynamic of capitalism (also analysed by Piketty) and is enabled by the asymmetry of capital and labour in capitalist firms, as Marx observed. But market dynamics are always embedded in the wider economy, which includes the state and communities, and therefore can also be held in check through these two other domains, as Smith already recognized. For example, the dynamics of capital over labour can be prevented or constrained through cooperative firms, international capital controls and labour protection in trade agreements.

Alternatively, some market dynamics are fed by social norms held in communities and by rules (or the lack thereof or a lack of enforcement) by the state. That is how discrimination and exclusion find their ways in supply and demand, as Bergmann noted for the case of gender discrimination and Myrdal observed for the case of racial discrimination. Moreover, such biases may be institutionalized in market behaviour, as Veblen observed. All three authors noted that such biases result in lower efficiency. Bergmann noted that exclusion of a group implies underutilization of their human resources; Myrdal argued that discrimination of a group, but also perverse effects of government policy, results in productivity losses and lower investment in human resources; while Veblen noted that status-types of institutions enable rentier-capitalism, which lowers investment in the real economy.

Another market dynamic was analysed by Keynes with the concept of effective demand. He noted that market equilibrium is only a real equilibrium, that is, without excess demand and excess supply, when effective demand is at the level of full capacity utilization. At that level of production there will be no unemployment (apart from friction unemployment). This implies that during a recession, government expenditures need to increase to stimulate effective demand. In this way, the economic cycle can be stimulated to pick up again after a crisis. Which brings us to the greatest market dynamic of all: the economic cycle.

It was Minsky who observed that the financial cycle is inevitable in a capitalist economy and that it is driven by credit. With commercial banks supplying credit and investors and homeowners taking on more debt, the economy becomes more fragile over time. The concept of fragility is very different from the neoclassical idea of low risk when derivatives are spread throughout the financial system. With rising debt levels in the economy, the increasing fragility will inevitably end at the Minsky Moment in a crash. But, again, this analysis also points at policy measures to prevent a shorter and more volatile boom-bust cycle and to institutional changes making the FIRE-sector more resilient. These include higher buffers, a separation between investment banking and retail banking, limits to market shares in credit markets and Central Bank Digital Currency.

The final market dynamic that I like to discuss goes partially beyond markets: efficiency. As Marx observed, capitalist firms have to be cost-efficient in their production, otherwise they will lose out in competition. They do so through specialization and economies of scale. Government policy today stimulates this efficiency by creating and enabling competitive markets through public procurement procedures, privatization and market authorities trying to keep market power by individual firms in check. But this only results in linear efficiency at the firm level, with low consumer prices as one result and maximum profit for shareholders, who are the residual claimants of capitalist firms, as the other result. But the cost of these benefits at two ends of the firm is high: pollution, climate change, exhaustion of natural resources, waste of material resources, rising inequality between capital and labour income, rising inequality between high and low skilled labour income and unequal gains from trade for developing countries, to mention a few key problems. In other words, many of the wicked problems that we face today are directly or indirectly related to the linear efficiency drive of capitalist firms, facilitated by governments. Moreover, as the COVID-19 crisis has shown, the focus on linear efficiency in long, highly specialized global value chains shows the lack of resilience of such an economy during a pandemic: for example, small and large firms need billions of state support to survive, while health care providers suffer from serious shortages in face masks. An economist whom I have not mentioned in this book, Margaret Reid, has suggested an alternative notion of efficiency in the 1940s: minimization of waste. Indeed, this is the normal language notion of efficiency that we tend to use in our roles in the community economy—for example, in households. Herein lies an alternative driving force for a postcapitalist economy. We could label it dynamic efficiency because it works through the connections in historical time between the three economic value domains.

Dynamic efficiency implies the internalization of externalities. Hence, it combines various forms of minimization of waste. First, material efficiency, which means production and consumption without material waste—which is precisely the whole idea behind a circular economy. So, if we want to achieve a circular economy, we need to shift our notion of efficiency away from linear to material, and do so with appropriate regulation, nudges and incentives. Second, inclusive efficiency, which means no waste of human resources in either of the three economic value domains. This implies that labour is hired on equal terms in the market, and not in an asymmetrical relationship with globally mobile capital. Where this is not possible due to low productivity (e.g. for those without diplomas or with health problems), the community economy is able to generate appropriate jobs with full dignity through social entrepreneurship, commons or community currency networks, provided that it is awarded the space for taking such initiatives. If that is insufficient to address widespread unemployment during recessions, the state could complement this with the creation of public employment for the production of public goods. These are all more efficient than unemployment and welfare support. The third type of efficiency as the minimization of waste is energy efficiency. This implies a transition toward full reliance on renewable resources with appropriate incentives against fossil energy.

In conclusion an economics that analyses economic dynamics is able to address the negative externalities of markets but also the volatility, low resilience, short time horizons and growing inequality inherent in capitalist markets. But it can only do so by shifting to a dynamic notion of efficiency, applied to markets but also to the economic role of the state and the community economy.

Systems Theory for Economics

Over the past decade, I have spoken with dozens of students of economics, in various countries in the global north and global south. What struck me is that many are both critical of their studies and at the same time dedicated to continue their studies after obtaining their BA degree. They are increasingly interested in interdisciplinarity and in systems theory. They look for graduate studies in complexity economics or broader, complexity studies in general. And I support their demand for this. When I was a PhD student, I did a one semester course in nonlinear dynamics. I was fascinated by the understanding of dynamics with concepts such as chaos, critical thresholds, phase transitions, lock-in effect and feedbacks. The math was very different from the one I was familiar with from my undergraduate economic studies and I was extremely relieved that I managed to pass the exam. At that time, I did not see clearly how I could use what I had learned in my research. Today, I see the connections much better, also because the theory behind it—systems theory—has entered other fields where it has made an impact. This is particularly the case in ecology, where uncertainty, context, endogeneity and feedback effects are all of crucial importance for the understanding of ecological processes.

In microeconomic models, systems theory has been translated into agent-based modelling, with heterogeneous economic agents. An interest in systems theory can be found among a small number of Post Keynesian economists, evolutionary economists, experimental economists and behavioural financial economists.[5] They often refer to it as open systems theory, as compared to the closed systems thinking of neoclassical economics.

Most of the economists that I have discussed in this book have used elements of systems theory—knowingly or unknowingly. Myrdal's cumulative causation cycles with positive feedback effects is clearly a heuristic derived from systems theory. The acknowledgment of uncertainty next to risk by Knight is what underlies the dynamics of chaotic systems when a systems' resilience is decreasing. Minsky's three phases from stability to fragility to crash reflect the phase transitions in an open, complex system with decreasing resilience—for Minsky characterized by increasing debt. And Veblen's understanding of path-dependency of certain institutions, long after their initial rationale has expired (e.g. the QWERTY-keyboard which prevented often-used letters of mechanical typing machines to collide), reflects the idea of lock-in effects in open systems. This allows for the persistence of inefficient institutions.

Systems theory is flexible, and it allows for applications at micro and macro level, as a heuristic or as a mathematical method, and it can be applied to policy analysis focusing on critical thresholds of key variables. Due to this flexibility it does not force a single theory upon economics, but it provides an open theoretical framework in which uncertainty, context, endogeneity and complex dynamics with positive and negative feedbacks can be analysed. I would welcome serious attention to complexity economics in undergraduate economics programmes. Students, as well as the wicked problems of our times, demand such an open theoretical framework for economic analyses from a plurality of perspectives.

Notes

1. Marion Fourcade, Etienne Ollion, and Yann Algan. "The Superiority of Economists." *Journal of Economic Perspectives* 29, 1 (2015): 89–114.
2. David Colander and Craig Freedman, *Where Economics Went Wrong* (Princeton, Princeton University Press, 2019).
3. https://www.edge.org/response-detail/27150, Accessed on July 16, 2020.
4. Pareto Optimality refers to the state of the economy in which nobody can be made better off without making anyone worse off, even if such redistribution would increase total utility.
5. See, for example: Victoria Chick, and Sheila Dow. "The Meaning of Open Systems." *Journal of Economic Methodology* 12, 3 (2005): 363–381. William

Brock and Cars Hommes. "A Rational Route to Randomness." *Econometrica* 65, 5 (1997): 1059–1095. Stephen Durlauf. "Complexity and Empirical Economics." *The Economic Journal* 115, 504 (2005): F225–F243. Stefano Battiston, J. Doyne Farmer, Andreas Flache, Diego Garlaschelli, Andrew G. Haldane, Hans Heesterbeek, Cars Hommes, Carlo Jaeger, Robert May, and Marten Scheffer. "Complexity Theory and Financial Regulation." *Science* 351, 6275 (2016): 818–819.

Bibliography

Battiston, Stefano, J. Doyne Farmer, Andreas Flache, Diego Garlaschelli, Andrew G. Haldane, Hans Heesterbeek, Cars Hommes, Carlo Jaeger, Robert May, and Marten Scheffer. "Complexity Theory and Financial Regulation." *Science* 351, 6275 (2016): 818–819.

Brock, William, and Cars Hommes. "A Rational Route to Randomness." *Econometrica* 65, 5 (1997): 1059–1095.

Chick, Victoria, and Sheila Dow. "The Meaning of Open Systems." *Journal of Economic Methodology* 12, 3 (2005): 363–381.

Colander, David, and Craig Freedman. *Where Economics Went Wrong*. Princeton, Princeton University Press, 2019.

Durlauf, Stephen. "Complexity and Empirical Economics." *The Economic Journal* 115, 504 (2005): F225–F243.

Fourcade, Marion, Etienne Ollion, and Yann Algan. "The Superiority of Economists." *Journal of Economic Perspectives* 29, 1 (2015): 89–114.

Index[1]

A
ABN AMRO, 11, 13, 20, 24, 31, 37, 38, 66, 117, 118
Agentic, 84–86, 88
Alienation, 15
American Economic Association, 75, 187
Amsterdam, 6n15, 12, 18, 28n21, 29n31, 119
Animal spirits, 55, 59, 73, 82, 179
Antoncic, Madelyn, 66
Anxiety, 132, 178
Apple, 21, 107
Aramco, 20
Arbitrage, 67
Argentina, 82, 133, 135n18
Asian financial crisis, 11, 138
Austerity, 9, 10, 14, 27n1, 55
Autonomy, 15, 120, 121, 128, 132, 149, 150

B
Bailouts, 16, 38
Bair, Sheila, 66, 72
Bankocracy, 15, 28n17, 41
Bank of England, 53
Bankruns, 31, 34
Bankruptcies, 15, 31, 34, 38, 46, 61, 62, 66, 72, 76, 83, 91, 127, 137
bankruptcy laws, 61, 62
Banks, 2, 9–12, 14–16, 24, 31–38, 44, 45, 50, 51, 53–55, 57, 58, 65, 66, 72, 74, 76, 77, 77n1, 79, 81, 83, 102, 111, 117–121, 123, 126, 133, 137, 168, 180, 201
Bargaining position, 19, 140
See also Power, bargaining power
Basel III, 76
Becker, Gary, 74, 90
Behavioural finance, 55, 71
Bergmann, Barbara, 4, 87, 89–92, 94n19, 119, 127, 142, 200
Bernanke, Ben, 44
Bonds, 10, 17, 40, 41, 49, 50, 52–54, 58, 81, 82, 91
Bonuses, 24, 72, 76, 77, 91, 102, 108
Born, Brooksley, 66, 72, 79
Bubble, 9, 12, 14, 33, 42–44, 49, 51, 52, 55–57, 66, 70, 71, 73, 102, 141, 183
Buchanan, James, 75
Buffers, 18, 35, 38, 46, 74, 76, 77, 91, 117, 201
Buffett, Warren, 91, 112, 179
Business cycle, *see* Cycle, economic cycle

[1] Note: Page numbers followed by 'n' refer to notes.

C

Cambridge, 59–60, 129, 186, 188–190
Capital, 3, 15, 16, 20–22, 28n16,
    28n17, 28n20, 28n23, 77n7, 91,
    94n25, 112, 114n20, 180,
    189, 193n11
  capital accumulation, 14, 16–18,
    20, 23, 25
  See also Das Kapital
Capitalism, 1, 5n5, 9, 11–16, 18, 20–22,
    36, 41, 72, 103, 104, 128, 142,
    166, 200
  capitalist, 2–4, 13–27, 28n16, 36, 61,
    62, 102, 125, 140, 166, 200–202
Capitalist economy, 3, 4, 14, 24, 62, 201
Carney, Marc, 66
CBDC, *see* Central Bank Digital
    Currency
Central Bank, 12, 19, 27n1, 27n9, 32,
    35, 36, 38, 40, 45, 52, 54, 60, 147,
    172, 201
Central Bank Digital Currency (CBDC),
    45–46, 201
Chicago, 5n5, 43–44, 74–75, 82, 93n7,
    108, 109, 197
Children, 15, 21, 33, 72, 74, 85,
    138–140, 143, 145, 169, 185
Circular, 26, 142, 202
Client interest, 83, 119, 120
Club of Rome, 3
Collective action, 2
Commons, 2, 6n12, 15, 167, 168,
    173, 202
Communal, 84–86, 88
Communist Manifesto, 14, 16, 22
Community, 2, 5n6, 20, 25–27,
    133, 134, 135n19, 146,
    167–169, 173, 191, 197–199,
    201, 202
Community economy, 2, 5n6, 20,
    25–27, 167, 198, 199, 201, 202
Computer models, 79–80
Cooperatives, 21, 28n25, 173
  cooperative firm, 24
  coops, 24, 25, 173
Cortisol, 81, 85
Countercyclical, 58
Covid-19, 10, 11, 13, 14, 50, 139, 141,
    147, 201
Credit, 2, 9, 24, 31, 35, 36, 41, 45, 51,
    54, 56, 57, 72, 102, 106, 107, 117,
    122, 123, 126, 127, 137, 201
Crowding theory, 87, 89
Cycles, 11, 14, 39, 147, 159, 203
  economic cycle, 13, 19, 20, 161, 201

D

Das Kapital, 14
Debt, 10–12, 27n11, 33, 42, 44, 46,
    49–59, 61, 62, 70, 103, 108, 127,
    137, 201, 203
  debt cancellation, 61, 62
  debt forgiveness, 61, 62
  extreme problem debt, 54
  household debt, 51, 52
  indebtedness, 10
  jubilee, 61, 62
  private debt, 10, 44, 51
  public debt, 10, 54, 55, 58, 62, 137
Deposit guarantee system, 37, 45
Derivatives, 12, 34, 36, 41, 51, 56, 66,
    67, 69, 70, 74, 76, 201
Derived demand, 57, 199
Developing countries, 42, 62, 98, 99,
    143, 148, 162, 169, 170, 173,
    189, 201
Dijsselbloem, Jeroen, 9
Discrimination, 88, 89, 91, 141, 142,
    144, 146, 148, 200
Diversity, 4, 83, 84, 86, 93n10, 94n14,
    94n15, 181, 183, 191, 197
Dodd-Frank-Act, 38
Draghi, Mario, 40
Dugan, John, 66

E

Eagly, Alice, 84
East India Company, 18
ECB, *see* European Central Bank
Economic cycle, *see* Business cycle
Effective demand, 57–59, 201
Efficient Market Hypothesis
    (EMH), 67, 178
EIB, *see* European Investment Bank
Elizabeth, Queen, 11
EMH, *see* Efficient Market Hypothesis

Endogenous, 69, 130, 198–200
Energy transition, 59, 172, 173
Engels, Friedrich, 14, 16, 22
England, 15, 36, 53, 59, 62n6, 66, 171, 190
Equality, 21, 24, 87, 92, 100, 107, 138, 144–146
  gender equality, 145
Equity, 34, 35, 38, 74, 77, 97, 102, 149
Ethics, 75, 124, 125, 130, 147, 149, 171, 177, 187, 200
Ethics of Competition, 75
EU, *see* European Union
Euro-crisis, 40
European Central Bank (ECB), 27n1, 32, 36, 38, 53, 54, 58
European Investment Bank (EIB), 58
European Monetary Union, 53
European Union (EU), 10, 11, 35, 38, 53, 79, 111, 145, 150, 159–165, 168, 170
Eurozone, 10, 27n1, 27n3, 38, 40, 53, 54
Exogenous, 1, 69, 70, 141, 197
Expectations, 40, 55, 57, 70, 87–89
Exploitation, 15, 19–21, 106, 143, 157
Externalities, 26, 142, 158, 159, 169, 171, 178, 180, 199, 202

F
Fama, Eugene, 12, 70, 74
Fannie Mae, 33, 46
FDIC, *see* Federal Deposit Insurance Corporation
Fed, *see* Federal Reserve Bank
Federal Deposit Insurance Corporation (FDIC), 66
Federal Reserve Bank, 32, 36, 44, 51, 52, 60, 68, 102, 178
Female, 79, 80, 82–85, 87–89, 91, 92, 109, 139, 140, 145, 146
Feminine, 84, 86, 87, 91
Feminist economics, 6n12, 80, 86–90
Financial behaviour, 80, 123
Financial instability, 39
Financialization, 34–37, 45, 62n2
Financial sector, *see* FIRE-sector

FIRE-sector, 1, 9, 12, 31, 35, 36, 40–45, 49, 50, 57, 74, 81, 111, 118, 128, 201
Fiscal policy, 33, 52, 58
  fiscal stimulation policy, 52, 54
Fisher, Irving, 70
Fragility, 40, 43, 44, 70, 117, 201, 203
France, 16, 21, 24, 27n15, 43, 54, 83, 103, 104, 163, 164, 170, 181, 191
Fraud, 66, 79, 120
Freddie Mac, 33, 46, 102
Friedman, Milton, 74
Fund managers, 41, 79, 80

G
Gender, 79–81, 83–89, 91, 92, 92n3, 122, 138, 140, 141, 145–147, 150, 189, 200
  gender differences, 80, 81, 83–86, 93n3
  gender norms, 86, 88, 91, 141, 145, 146, 189
  gender stereotypes, 85, 88
Germany, 21, 24, 27n15, 34, 43, 46, 54, 61, 62, 92, 104, 110, 149, 190–192
German, 28n15, 34, 61, 81, 84, 110
Glass-Steagall-Act, 35, 38, 45
Government expenditures, 54, 57, 172, 201
Greece, 9, 10, 40, 53, 54, 62
Greenspan, Alan, 68, 178

H
Hansen, Lars Peter, 12
Haute finance, 15, 28n17
Hegel, G. W. F., 21
Herd behaviour, 56, 59–60, 70, 71, 73, 80, 82
Heterodox, 4, 6n12, 12–14, 181, 183, 192, 197
Heterodox economics, 4, 6n12, 12
Hobbes, Thomas, 2
Homeowners, 11, 33, 102, 103, 201
Hormone, 81, 82
Housing market, 11, 12, 33, 51, 70, 183
Housing prices, 42

I

Icesave, 37, 123
Ideology, 16, 67, 91, 178
IMF, *see* International Monetary Fund
Industrialization, 15, 21
Industrial Revolution, 17, 157, 165
Inequality, 1, 3, 9, 15, 19, 20, 27, 33, 75, 87, 91, 97–108, 111, 112, 140, 142, 147, 183, 197, 201, 202
Inheritance, 75, 112
Instability, 12, 15, 22, 39, 40, 42, 43, 45, 49, 56, 61, 69, 72–74, 82, 197
Institutions
  institutional framework, 1, 45
Interest rate, 20, 31–35, 37, 40, 42, 44, 50–52, 54, 56, 57, 59, 81, 102, 123, 126
International Monetary Fund (IMF), 10, 27n1, 51, 52, 59, 62n1, 62n3, 79, 107, 113n12, 179, 192n3, 193n4
Ireland, 9, 10, 51
Italy, 10, 54, 60, 103, 163, 191

J

Jackson, Tim, 3, 6n8
Jones, Dow, 13, 14

K

Keen, Steve, 12, 42
Kenya, 92
Keynes, John Maynard, 4, 13, 14, 39, 43, 44, 49, 55–62, 63n13, 66, 69, 70, 73, 74, 82, 105, 108, 126, 130, 147, 179, 184, 191, 199, 201
Knight, Frank, 4, 41, 73–77, 77n4, 77n5, 105, 198, 203
Kroes, Nelie, 79

L

Labour, 2, 14–25, 27, 27n15, 28n18, 40, 57, 58, 67, 75, 86–89, 97, 98, 105, 106, 112, 118, 126, 129, 133, 138–142, 144–146, 148, 150, 184, 199–202
  labour income, 15, 20, 58, 98, 112, 201
  labour unions, 19, 118, 145

Lafargue, Paul, 16, 21
Lagarde, Christine, 79
Lange, Oskar, 43
Latin America, 11, 184
Leadership, 80, 83, 84, 86, 103, 120, 128
Lehman Brothers, 9, 15, 31, 34, 66
Lehman Sisters Hypothesis, 79, 80, 92n1
Loan-to-value ratios (ltv), 11, 46
Lobby, 35, 36, 38, 45, 59, 66, 76, 161, 165, 178
London, 11, 21–22, 35, 51, 53, 59, 67, 81, 82, 108, 178, 188
Lopokova, Lydia, 59
Loss averse, 80
Ltv, *see* Loan-to-value ratios

M

Maastricht, 10, 54, 58, 62
Maastricht criteria, 10, 54, 55, 58, 62
Madelyn, 79
Male, 39, 79–85, 87, 89–92, 140, 146, 188
Manchester, 5n1, 22, 190, 194n36
Market equilibrium, 3, 12, 43, 144, 148, 177, 185, 201
Marx, Karl, 4, 13, 14, 17–19, 21–23, 28n16, 28n19, 43, 166
Masculine, 81, 84, 86–88, 91, 119
MBS, *see* Mortgage-backed securities
Men, 15, 19, 57, 72, 79–89, 108, 109, 112, 138–140, 142, 144, 146, 150, 152n14, 171
Minsky, Hyman, 4, 12–14, 39–45, 49, 50, 56, 65, 70, 108, 191, 201, 203
Minsky Moment, 44, 57, 65, 201
Mishkin, Frederic, 12, 27n13
Mondragon, 24, 112
Monetary policy, 33, 50, 51
Money, 9, 17–19, 23, 25, 26, 34–38, 41, 43–45, 50, 52, 56, 62, 66, 67, 70, 72, 74, 80, 82, 89, 91, 97, 111, 112, 121, 123, 126–129, 131, 133, 159, 162, 168, 170, 178, 179, 185, 199

digital cash, 45
digital money, 45
Monopolies, 18, 167, 171, 185, 200
Moral, 37, 59, 75, 80, 82, 83, 119–121, 123, 124, 128, 130, 133, 160, 167, 199
  moral compass, 80, 82, 83, 120–123, 128, 133
  morality, 62, 167
  morally neutral, 59, 75, 125
Mortgage, 11, 27n11, 32–34, 40, 45, 46, 51, 62, 66, 77, 102, 103, 118, 122
  underwater mortgages, 11
Mortgage-backed securities (MBS), 34, 36, 49, 52, 72
Multinational, 21, 25
Multiplier, 56, 58–59
Myrdal, Gunnar, 4, 141, 145, 147–150, 153n24, 153n25, 164

N
Nationalization, 13, 15, 20, 66, 117
Nature, 18, 20, 23, 86, 142, 186
Neoclassical economics, 3, 124, 125, 130, 131, 144, 179, 186, 191, 198, 203
Neoclassical economists, 108
Neoliberalism, 1
The Netherlands, 10–11, 19, 21, 31, 34, 37, 38, 46, 51, 54, 55, 66, 83, 92, 103, 110, 111, 117, 123, 132, 138, 139, 144, 149, 150, 152n18, 163, 164, 172, 173, 191, 193n13, 194n39
New Deal, 60, 145
New York, 5n1, 5n6, 6n7, 6n8, 13, 28n24, 43, 44, 49, 63n13, 67, 70, 74, 77n3, 89–90, 93n6, 94n24, 113n10, 113n14, 134n4, 149, 152n12, 152n22, 153n24, 153n25, 190, 193n7, 193n16, 193n18
Nobel Memorial Prize, 3, 12, 69, 75, 89, 90, 112, 124, 129, 130, 158, 181, 186, 189, 194n32
Nobel, Alfred, 12, 147, 159

O
OECD, 79, 99, 101, 103, 104, 111, 112, 113n2, 113n4, 113n5, 113n6, 113n7, 114n17, 134n11, 138, 151n2, 163
Orthodox, 14
Oxytocin, 82, 85

P
Paradigm, 1, 3, 5n1, 5n3, 108
Paris, 3, 21, 79, 113n2, 113n4, 113n5, 113n6, 157, 158, 161, 173, 190, 192
Paris Climate Agreement, 3, 173, 192
Paulson, Henry, 66
Pension, 14, 18, 26, 41, 53, 122, 123, 134, 139
Pessimism, 34, 73, 80, 179
Philips, 21
Piketty, Thomas, 3, 6n8, 20, 28n23, 112, 114n20, 180, 181, 193n10, 193n11
Pluralism, 3, 4, 181, 183, 186, 187, 192, 195n41
Polanyi, Karl, 2, 5n6
Poor, 22, 32, 42, 57, 101, 102, 108, 122, 124, 128, 129, 138, 139, 142, 192n2
  poorer, 32, 142, 164
  poorest, 33, 55, 99, 101, 102, 164
Portfolio investment, 65
Portugal, 9, 10, 51
Postcapitalism
  postcapitalist economy, 2–4, 20, 197–203
Postcapitalist economy, 2–4, 20, 197–203
Power, 13, 15–21, 24–26, 33, 36, 39, 56–58, 74, 90, 106, 108, 109, 126, 129, 130, 133, 140, 142, 144, 162–165, 168, 173, 180, 182, 184, 198, 200, 201
  bargaining power, 19

Power (*cont.*)
  economic power, 1–4, 5n1, 5n3, 5n6, 9, 11–13, 15, 18–21, 23, 32, 33, 39, 41–43, 51–53, 55–60, 62, 73, 75, 80, 82, 84, 86–91, 92n3, 97, 100, 102, 104–107, 109, 123–126, 128–133, 137, 140–142, 144, 147, 148, 153n23, 157, 159, 161, 165–169, 172, 177, 179–192, 192n1, 193n9, 194n24, 194n28, 194n32, 195n43, 197–203
  market power, 18
Profit rate, 76, 132

Q
QE, *see* Quantitative easing
Quantitative easing (QE), 52, 53, 58, 62n6, 62n7
Queen Elizabeth, 178, 183

R
Rabobank, 24, 28n29, 37, 118
Raworth, Kate, 2, 6n7, 98, 113n1
Real estate, 11, 17, 31, 35, 41, 65, 102, 103
Recession, 9–11, 57, 58, 61, 103, 133, 137, 140, 159, 160, 201
Regulation, 16, 18, 20, 35, 38, 45, 66, 67, 69, 72, 74, 76, 109, 121, 145, 159, 162, 165, 167, 170, 172, 180, 186, 199, 202
Regulatory capture, 66, 67
Reykjavik, 79, 92
Ricardo, David, 21
Rich, 20, 33, 57, 74, 80, 97, 101, 104–106, 108, 111, 112, 113n9, 124, 180
Risk, 1, 10, 12, 17–19, 22, 25, 26, 34, 35, 37, 38, 40–43, 45, 49, 51, 54, 56, 58, 61, 65–76, 80–83, 86, 91, 93n6, 104, 117, 122, 127, 137, 140, 147, 157, 177, 183, 201, 203
  risk management, 65, 66, 73
  risk-taking, 17, 81

Robinson, Joan, 4, 59, 129, 183–185, 187–189, 191, 193n16, 193n17, 193n19, 194n21, 194n23, 194n33, 194n34
Roosevelt, President, 60

S
Schiller, Robert, 50, 71, 77n3
Securities, 35, 37, 41, 42, 52, 54, 72
Securities and Exchange Committee, 34, 66
Sen, Amartya, 4, 124, 128–131, 135n14, 166, 183, 189, 199
Sex, 27n7, 79, 80, 92, 92n3, 119
Shareholders, 14, 22–24, 37, 76, 146, 201
Shares, 41
Sheila, 79, 203n5
Shell, 21
Shiller, Robert, 12, 42
Short-term, 16, 51, 81, 86, 123, 128, 162
Skidelsky, Lord, 60
Smith, Adam, 4, 5n6, 21, 130, 165, 166, 169–171, 177, 198
Spain, 9, 10, 24, 54, 103, 112, 146, 164
Speculation, 31, 42, 55, 66, 73, 105, 161
Stakeholder, 24
State support, 11, 34, 37, 38, 44, 55, 108, 201
Stereotype, 84, 86–88, 91
Stress, 38, 77, 81, 82, 86, 122
Subprime, 9, 11, 32–34, 44, 66, 102, 113n3
Subprime crisis, 9, 11, 33, 113n3
Supervisors, 12, 42, 66, 69
Sustainability, 2, 25, 26, 126
Sustainable Development Goals, 3, 192
Sustainable Finance Lab (SFL), 12, 118
Sweden, 45, 83, 99, 134n5, 150, 164, 165
Systemic risk, 1, 41, 72, 73, 117, 177

T

Tax, 2, 10, 11, 20, 44, 58, 89, 97, 101, 103, 107, 111, 112, 121, 130, 131, 145, 160, 162, 164, 168, 170–172
  taxation, 33
  taxes, 2, 20, 21, 91, 100, 103, 111, 127, 161, 163, 165, 168, 171
  tax income, 2
  taxpayers, 10, 18, 37, 38, 123
Tax income, 2
Teaser rates, 33, 122
Testosterone, 81, 85
Thorstein, Veblen, 177
Too big to fail, 16, 37, 76
Troika, 9, 10, 27n1

U

UK, 34, 35, 38, 43, 51, 53, 54, 58, 62n2, 83, 91, 93n9, 98, 99, 103, 110, 127, 133, 134n5, 162, 164–166, 172, 186, 191, 194n37
Uncertainty, 1, 59, 69, 72–77, 80–83, 102, 105, 117, 122, 124, 127, 142, 147, 177, 179–181, 198, 203
Unemployment, 9–11, 14, 19, 20, 27n7, 31, 39, 51, 54, 57, 59, 67, 127, 130, 137, 140–145, 184, 190, 201, 202
  unemployed, 19
United States (US), 9, 62
Utility maximization, 3, 125, 130, 131, 199

V

Veblen, Thorstein, 4, 5n1, 105, 108–110, 113n10, 113n11, 113n14
Verry, Ethel, 74
Vestia, 66
Volatility, 40, 56, 67, 73, 74, 81, 82, 162, 202

W

Wage, 14, 15, 19, 20, 22, 32, 55, 57, 81, 86–89, 104–106, 126, 137, 140, 142, 145, 148, 153n23, 171, 184, 200
  minimum wages, 19, 111, 148
Wall Street, 9, 82, 93n8, 103
Whistleblowers, 12, 65, 69, 79
Women, 15, 19, 59, 79–92, 94n19, 105, 106, 109, 119, 128, 129, 133, 138–142, 144, 146, 150, 171, 187
  women on boards, 83, 84, 92
Workers, 14, 15, 18, 19, 21, 23, 24, 41, 57, 81, 87, 104–106, 108, 111, 128, 132, 141, 144–146, 150, 171
Working conditions, 15, 19, 21
World Bank, 41, 59

Y

Yellow vests, 54, 103, 104

Z

Zalm, Gerrit, 66, 108

GPSR Compliance

The European Union's (EU) General Product Safety Regulation (GPSR) is a set of rules that requires consumer products to be safe and our obligations to ensure this.

If you have any concerns about our products, you can contact us on

ProductSafety@springernature.com

In case Publisher is established outside the EU, the EU authorized representative is:

Springer Nature Customer Service Center GmbH
Europaplatz 3
69115 Heidelberg, Germany

www.ingramcontent.com/pod-product-compliance
Lightning Source LLC
LaVergne TN
LVHW010340260326
834688LV00036B/809